Beyond Left and Right

LIBRARY.

DEVELOPMENT STUDIES

KIMMAGE MANOR

Beyond Left and Right

The Future of Radical Politics

Anthony Giddens

Polity Press

110253

Beyond Left and Right

The Future of Radical Politics

Anthony Giddens

Polity Press

Beyond Left and Right -- The

Libermann Library Kimmage

110974

320/GID

Copyright © Anthony Giddens 1994

The right of Anthony Giddens to be identified as author of this work has been asserted in accordance with the Copyright, Designs and Patents Act 1988.

First published in 1994 by Polity Press
in association with Blackwell Publishers Ltd.

Reprinted 1995, 1996

Editorial office:
Polity Press
65 Bridge Street
Cambridge CB2 1UR, UK

Marketing and production:
Blackwell Publishers Ltd
108 Cowley Road
Oxford OX4 1JF, UK

All rights reserved. Except for the quotation of short passages for the purposes of criticism and review, no part of this publication may be reproduced, stored in a retrieval system, or transmitted, in any form or by any means, electronic, mechanical, photocopying, recording or otherwise, without the prior permission of the publisher.

Except in the United States of America, this book is sold subject to the condition that it shall not, by way of trade or otherwise, be lent, re-sold, hired out, or otherwise circulated without the publisher's prior consent in any form of binding or cover other than that in which it is published and without a similar condition including this condition being imposed on the subsequent purchaser.

ISBN 0 7456 1438 8
ISBN 0 7456 1439 6 (pbk)

A CIP catalogue record for this book is available from the British Library.

Typeset in 11 on 12½ pt Times
by CentraCet Limited, Cambridge
Printed in Great Britain by T.J. Press Ltd, Padstow, Cornwall.

This book is printed on acid-free paper.

Contents

Preface

This book began life some fifteen years ago, as the planned third volume of what I then termed a 'contemporary critique of historical materialism'. That third volume was never written, as my interests moved away in somewhat different directions. The present work is based on the ideas I sketched for the third volume, but also draws extensively on concepts I developed in subsequent published writings.

I should like to thank those colleagues and friends who have read and commented on initial drafts of the book, or have otherwise assisted in its preparation. Thanks, therefore, to Ulrich Beck, Ann Bone, Montserrat Guibernau, Rebecca Harkin, David Held, David Miliband, Veronique Mottier, Debbie Seymour, Avril Symonds and Dennis Wrong.

Introduction

What can it mean to be politically radical today? For the spectre which disturbed the slumbers of bourgeois Europe, and which for more than seventy years took on solid flesh, has been returned to its nether world. The hopes of radicals for a society in which, as Marx said, human beings could be 'truly free' seem to have turned out to be empty reveries.

The idea of political radicalism has long been bound up primarily with socialist thought. To be a 'radical' was to have a certain view of the possibilities inherent in history – radicalism meant breaking away from the hold of the past. Some radicals were revolutionaries: according to them revolution, and perhaps only revolution, could produce that sharp separation which they sought from what went before. Yet the notion of revolution was never the defining feature of political radicalism; this feature consisted in its progressivism. History was there to be seized hold of, to be moulded to human purposes, such that the advantages which in previous eras seemed given by God, and the prerogative of the few, could be developed and organized for the benefit of all.

Radicalism, taking things by the roots, meant not just bringing about change but controlling such change so as to drive history onwards. And it is that project which now seems to have lapsed. How should one react to such a situation? Some say that the possibilities of radical change have been foreclosed. History, as it were, has come to an end and socialism was a bridge too far.

Yet couldn't it be claimed that, far from the possibilities of change having been closed off, we are suffering from a surfeit of them? For surely there comes a point at which endless change is not only unsettling but positively destructive – and in many areas of social life, it could be argued, this point has certainly been reached.

Such a train of thought appears to lead well away from what are usually thought of as radical political philosophies, towards, in fact, conservatism. The main thrust of conservative thought from the days of Edmund Burke has been a suspicion of radical change in most or all of its forms. Yet here we find something very surprising, which demands explanation. Conservatism, in certain of its currently most influential guises in Europe, and to some extent elsewhere in the world, has come to embrace more or less exactly what it once set out to repudiate: competitive capitalism and the processes of dramatic and far-reaching change that capitalism tends to provoke. Many conservatives are now active radicals in respect of that very phenomenon which previously they held most dear – tradition. 'Away with the fossils we have inherited from the past': where is such a sentiment most commonly to be heard? Not on the left, but on the right.

Conservatism become radical here confronts socialism become conservative. With the fall of the Soviet Union, many socialists have come to concentrate their energies on protecting the welfare state in the face of the strains to which it has become subject. Some socialists, it is true, continue to say that authentic socialism has never been tried, arguing that the disappearance of Communism is a windfall rather than a disaster. Communism, in this view, was a form of authoritarian dogmatism, deriving from a revolution betrayed, while reformist socialism of the sort found in Western Europe was dragged down by trying to accommodate to capitalism rather than surpassing it. However, this thesis is threadbare indeed and socialists have mostly been thrown back on to the defensive, their position in the 'vanguard of history' reduced to the more modest task of protecting welfare institutions.

Of course, radicals on the left do have another direction towards which to turn their eyes: to the new social movements, such as those concerned with feminism, ecology, peace or human rights. The 'universal proletarian' cannot bear the weight of the left's historical aspirations; perhaps these other agencies will take over? For not only do such groups seem 'progressive', their chosen mode of political organization, the social movement, is the same as that which was supposed to convey the proletariat to its ultimate victory.

But it is plain enough that the new social movements cannot readily be claimed for socialism. While the aspirations of some such movements stand close to socialist ideals, their objectives are disparate and sometimes actively opposed to one another. With the possible exception of some sections of the green movement, the new social movements are not 'totalizing' in the way socialism is (or was), promising a new 'stage' of social development beyond the existing order. Some versions of feminist thought, for example, are as radical as anything that went under the name of socialism. Yet they don't envisage seizing control of the future in the way the more ambitious versions of socialism have done.

The world of the late twentieth century, one must conclude, has not turned out as the founders of socialism anticipated when they sought to give direction to history by overcoming tradition and dogma. They believed, reasonably enough, that the more we, as collective humanity, get to know about social and material reality, the more we shall be able to control them in our own interests. In the case of social life in particular, human beings can become not just the authors but the masters of their own destiny.

Events have not borne out these ideas. The world we live in today is not one subject to tight human mastery – the stuff of the ambitions of the left and, one could say, the nightmares of the right. Almost to the contrary, it is one of dislocation and uncertainty, a 'runaway world'. And, disturbingly, what was supposed to create greater and greater certainty – the advance of human knowledge and 'controlled intervention' into society and nature – is actually deeply involved with this unpredictability. Examples abound. Consider, for instance, the debate about global warming, which concerns the possible effects of human activities on climatic change. Is global warming happening, or is it not? Probably the majority of scientists agree that it is; but there are others who question either the very existence of the phenomenon or the theory advanced to account for it. If global warming is indeed taking place, its consequences are difficult to assess and problematic – for it is something which has no real precedents.

The uncertainties thus created I shall refer to generically as *manufactured uncertainty*. Life has always been a risky business. The intrusion of manufactured uncertainty into our lives doesn't mean that our existence, on an individual or collective level, is more risky than it used to be. Rather, the sources, and the scope, of risk have altered. Manufactured risk is a result *of* human intervention into the conditions of social life and into nature. The uncertainties (and opportunities) it creates are largely new. They cannot be dealt with by age-old remedies; but neither do they respond to the Enlightenment prescription of more knowledge, more control. Put more accurately, the sorts of reactions they might evoke today are often as much about *damage control* and *repair* as about an endless process of increasing mastery.

The advance of manufactured uncertainty is the outcome of the long-term maturation of modern institutions; but it has also accelerated as the result of a series of developments that have transformed society (and nature) over no more than the past four or five decades. Pinpointing these is essential if we are to grasp the altered context of political life. Three sets of developments are particularly important; they affect especially the industrialized countries, but are also to an increasing degree worldwide in their impact.

Globalization, tradition, uncertainty

First, there is the influence of intensifying *globalization* – a notion much bandied about but as yet only poorly understood. Globalization is not only, or even primarily, an economic phenomenon; and it should not be equated with the emergence of a 'world system'. Globalization is really about the transformation of space and time. I define it as *action at distance*, and relate its intensifying over recent years to the emergence of means of instantaneous global communication and mass transportation.

Globalization does not only concern the creation of large-scale systems, but also the transformation of local, and even personal, contexts of social experience. Our day-to-day activities are increasingly influenced by events happening on the other side of the world. Conversely, local lifestyle habits have become globally consequential. Thus my decision to buy a certain item of clothing has implications not only for the international division of labour but for the earth's ecosystems.

Globalization is not a single process but a complex mixture of processes, which often act in contradictory ways, producing conflicts, disjunctures and new forms of stratification. Thus, for instance, the revival of local nationalisms, and an accentuating of local identities, are directly bound up with globalizing influences, to which they stand in opposition.

Second, and partly as a direct result of globalization, we can speak today of the emergence of a *post-traditional social order*. A post-traditional order is not one in which tradition disappears – far from it. It is one in which tradition changes its status. Traditions have to explain themselves, to become open to interrogation or discourse. At first sight, such a statement might seem odd. For haven't modernity and traditions always been in collision? Wasn't overcoming tradition the main impetus of Enlightenment thought in the first place?

As expressed in the expansion of modernity, Enlightenment thought did destabilize traditions of all sorts. Yet the influence of tradition remained strong: more than this, in earlier phases of the development of modern societies a refocusing of tradition played a major part in consolidating the social order. Grand traditions were invented or reinvented, such as those of nationalism or of religion. No less important were reconstructed traditions of a more down-to-earth kind, to do with, among other areas of social life, the family, gender and sexuality. Rather than being dissolved, these became reformed in such a way as to plant women firmly in the home, reinforce divisions between the sexes and stabilize certain 'normal' canons of sexual behaviour. Even science itself, seemingly so wholly opposed to traditional modes of thought, became a sort of tradition. Science, that is, became an 'authority' which could be turned to in a relatively unquestioning way to confront dilemmas or cope with problems. In a globalizing, culturally cosmopolitan society, however, traditions are forced into open view: reasons or justifications have to be offered for them.

The rise of *fundamentalism* has to be seen against the backdrop of the emergence of the post-traditional society. The term 'fundamentalism' has only come into wide currency quite recently – as late as 1950 there was no entry for the word in the *Oxford English Dictionary*. In this case, as elsewhere, the appearance of a new concept signals the emergence of new social forces. What is fundamentalism? It is, so I shall argue, nothing other than tradition defended in the traditional way – but where that mode of defence has become widely called into question. The point about traditions is that you don't really have to justify them: they contain their own truth, a ritual truth, asserted as correct by the believer. In a globally cosmopolitan order, however, such a stance becomes dangerous, because essentially it is a refusal of dialogue. Fundamentalism tends to accentuate the purity of a given set of doctrines, not only because it wishes to set them off from other traditions, but because it is a rejection of a model of truth linked to the dialogic engagement of ideas in a public space. It is dangerous because edged with a potential for violence. Fundamentalisms can arise in all domains of social life where tradition becomes something which has to be *decided about* rather than just taken for granted. There arise not only fundamentalisms of religion but of ethnicity, the family and gender, among other forms.

The transformation of tradition in the present day is closely linked to the transformation of nature. Tradition and nature used to be relatively fixed 'landscapes', as it were, structuring social activity. The dissolution of tradition (understood in the traditional way) interlaces with the disappearance of nature, where 'nature' refers to environments and events given independently of human action. Manufactured uncertainty intrudes into all the arenas of life thus opened up to decision-making.

The third basic change affecting contemporary societies is the expansion of *social reflexivity*. In a detraditionalizing society individuals must become used to filtering all sorts of information relevant to their life situations and routinely act on the basis of that filtering process. Take the decision to get married. Such a decision has to be made in relation to an awareness that marriage has changed in basic ways over the past few decades, that sexual habits and identities have altered too, and that people demand more autonomy in their lives than ever before. Moreover, this is not just knowledge about an independent social reality; as applied in action it influences what that reality actually *is*. The growth of social reflexivity is a major factor introducing a dislocation between knowledge and control – a prime source of manufactured uncertainty.

A world of intensified reflexivity is a world of *clever people*. I don't mean by this that people are more intelligent than they used to be. In a post-traditional order, individuals more or less have to engage with the wider world if they are to survive in it. Information produced by specialists (including scientific knowledge) can no longer be wholly confined to specific groups, but becomes routinely interpreted and acted on by lay individuals in the course of their everyday actions.

The development of social reflexivity is the key influence on a diversity of changes that otherwise seem to have little in common. Thus the emergence of 'post-Fordism' in industrial enterprises is usually analysed in terms of technological change – particularly the influence of information technology. But the underlying reason for the growth of 'flexible production' and 'bottom-up decision-making' is that a universe of high reflexivity leads to greater autonomy of action, which the enterprise must recognize and draw on.

The same applies to bureaucracy and to the sphere of politics. Bureaucratic authority, as Max Weber made clear, used to be a condition for organizational effectiveness. In a more reflexively ordered society, operating in the context of manufactured uncertainty, this is no longer the case. The old bureaucratic systems start to disappear, the dinosaurs of the post-traditional age. In the domain of politics, states can no longer so readily treat their citizens as 'subjects'. Demands for political reconstruction, for the eliminating of corruption, as well as widespread disaffection with orthodox political mechanisms, are all in some part expressions of increased social reflexivity.

Socialism, conservatism and neoliberalism

It is in terms of these changes that we should look to explain the troubles of socialism. In the shape of Soviet Communism (in the East) and the Keynesian 'welfare compromise' (in the West), socialism worked tolerably well when most risk was external (rather than manufactured) and where the level of globalization and social reflexivity was relatively low. When these circumstances no longer apply, socialism either collapses or is turned on to the defensive – it is certainly not any more in the vanguard of 'history'.

Socialism was based on what might be called a 'cybernetic model' of social life, one which strongly reflects the Enlightenment outlook mentioned at the beginning. According to the cybernetic model, a system (in the case of socialism, the economy) can best be organized by being subordinated to a directive intelligence (the state, understood in one form or another). But while this set-up might work reasonably effectively for more coherent systems – in this case a society of low reflexivity, with fairly fixed lifestyle habits – it doesn't do so for highly complex ones.

Such systems depend on a large amount of low-level input for their coherence (provided in market situations by a multiplicity of local pricing, production and consumption decisions). The human brain probably also works in such a manner. It was once thought that the brain was a cybernetic system, in which the cortex was responsible for integrating the central nervous system as a whole. Current theories, however, emphasize much more the significance of low-level inputs in producing effective neural integration.

The proposition that socialism is moribund is much less controversial now than it was even a few short years ago. More heterodox, I think, is a second assertion I want to make: that conservative political thought has become largely dissolved just at the point at which it has become particularly relevant to our current condition. How can this be, for hasn't conservatism triumphed worldwide in the wake of the disintegrating project of socialism? Here, however, we must distinguish conservatism from the right. 'The right' means many different things in differing contexts and countries. But one main way in which the term is used today is to refer to neoliberalism, whose links with conservatism are at best tenuous. For if conservatism means anything, it means the desire to conserve – and specifically the conserving of tradition, as the 'inherited wisdom of the past'. Neoliberalism is not conservative in this (quite elemental) sense. On the contrary, it sets in play radical processes of change, stimulated by the incessant expansion of markets. As noted earlier, the right here has turned radical, while the left seeks mainly to conserve – trying to protect, for example, what remains of the welfare state.

In a post-traditional society, the conserving of tradition cannot sustain the sense it once had, as the relatively unreflective preservation of the past. For tradition defended in the traditional way becomes fundamentalism, too dogmatic an outlook on which to base a conservatism which looks to the achievement of social harmony (or 'one nation') as one of its main *raisons d'être*.

Neoliberalism, on the other hand, becomes internally *contradictory* and this contradiction is increasingly plain to see. On the one hand neoliberalism is hostile to tradition – and is indeed one of the main forces sweeping away tradition everywhere, as a result of the promotion of market forces and an aggressive individualism. On the other, it *depends upon* the persistence of tradition for its legitimacy and its attachment to conservatism – in the areas of the nation, religion, gender and the family. Having no proper theoretical rationale, its defence of tradition in these areas normally takes the form of fundamentalism. The debate about 'family values' provides a good example. Liberal individualism is supposed to reign in the marketplace, and the purview of markets becomes greatly extended. The wholesale expansion of a market society, however, is a prime force promoting those very disintegrative forces affecting family life which neoliberalism, wearing its fundamentalist hat, diagnoses and so vigorously opposes. This is an unstable mix indeed.

If socialism and conservatism have disintegrated, and neoliberalism is paradoxical, might one turn to liberalism *per se* (capitalism plus liberal democracy, but shorn of New Right fundamentalisms) in the manner, say, of Francis Fukuyama? Although I don't deal in the book with liberal political theory in any detail, I don't think so, and for reasons documented at greater length later. An ever-expanding capitalism runs up not only against environmental limits in terms of the earth's resources, but against the limits of modernity in the shape of manufactured uncertainty; liberal democracy, based on an electoral party system, operating at the level of the nation-state, is not well equipped to meet the demands of a reflexive citizenry in a globalizing world; and the combination of capitalism and liberal democracy provides few means of generating social solidarity.

All this reveals plainly enough the exhaustion of received political ideologies. Should we therefore perhaps accept, as some of the postmodernists say, that the Enlightenment has exhausted itself and that we have to more or less take the world as it is, with all its barbarities and limitations? Surely not. Almost the last thing we need now is a sort of new medievalism, a confession of impotence in the face of forces larger than ourselves. We live in a radically damaged world, for which radical remedies are needed.

There is a very real and difficult issue to be faced, however: the problematic relation between knowledge and control, exemplified by the spread of manufactured risk. Political radicalism can no longer insert itself, as socialism did, in the space between a discarded past and a humanly made future. But it certainly cannot rest content with neoliberal radicalism – an abandonment of the past led by the erratic play of market forces. The possibility of, even the necessity for, a radical politics has not died along with all else that has fallen away – but such a politics can only be loosely identified with the classic orientations of the left.

What might be called 'philosophic conservatism' – a philosophy of protection, conservation and solidarity – acquires a new relevance for political radicalism today. The idea of living with imperfection, long an emphasis of philosophic conservatism, here might be turned to radical account. A radical political programme must recognize that confronting manufactured risk cannot take the form of 'more of the same', an endless exploration of the future at the cost of the protection of the present or past.

It is surely not accidental that these are exactly the themes of that political force which can lay greatest claim to inherit the mantle of left radicalism: the green movement. This very claim has helped to obscure the otherwise rather obvious affinities between ecological thinking, including particularly 'deep ecology', and philosophic conservatism. In each case there is an emphasis on conservation, restoration and repair. Green political theory, however, falls prey to the 'naturalistic fallacy' and is dogged by its own fundamentalisms. In other words, it depends for its proposals on calling for a reversion to 'nature'. Yet nature no longer exists! We cannot defend nature in the natural way any more than we can defend tradition in the traditional way – yet each quite often *needs* defending.

The ecological crisis is at the core of this book, but understood in a quite unorthodox manner. That crisis, and the various philosophies and movements which have arisen in response to it, are expressions of a modernity which, as it becomes globalized and 'turned back against itself', comes up against its own limits. The practical and ethical considerations thus disclosed, for the most part, are not new, although novel strategies and proposals are undoubtedly required to resolve them. They express moral and existential dilemmas which modern institutions, with their driving expansionism and their impetus to control, have effectively repressed or 'sequestered'.

A framework for radical politics

Our relation to nature – or what is no longer nature – is one among other major institutional dimensions of modernity, connected particularly to the impact of industry, science and technology in the modern world. While this dimension forms a focus for ecological concerns and debates, the others are equally significant as contexts for the reforming of radical politics. One such dimension is that of capitalism, defined as a competitive market system in which goods and labour power are commodities. If the oppositional force of socialism has been blunted, must a capitalistic system reign unchallenged? I don't think so. Unchecked capitalistic markets still have many of the damaging consequences to which Marx pointed, including the dominance of a growth ethic, universal commodification and economic polarization.

The critique of these tendencies surely remains as important as it ever was, but today it cannot be derived from a cybernetic model of socialism. On the 'other side' of capitalism we see the possible emergence of a *post-scarcity order*, defined in a very particular way. Analysing the contours of a post-scarcity order means looking as much to the combined influence of philosophic conservatism and ecological thought as to socialism. The critique of capitalism, as I develop it here at any rate, continues to be focused on economic oppression and poverty, but from a different perspective from those characteristic of socialist thought.

Political and administrative power, a further dimension of modernity, does not derive directly from control of the means of production, whatever Marx may have said on the matter. Depending on surveillance capabilities, such power may be the source of authoritarian rule. Standing opposed to political authoritarianism is the influence of *democracy* – the favourite term of the moment, for who is not a democrat now? But what kind of democracy is at issue here? For at the very time when liberal democratic systems seem to be spreading everywhere, we find those systems under strain in their very societies of origin.

The problem of democracy, or so I shall argue, is closely bound up with a further dimension of modernity: control of the means of violence. The management of violence is not these days part of conventional forms of political theory, whether left, right or liberal. Yet where many cultures are thrust into contact with one another, as in current social conditions, the violent clash of fundamentalisms becomes a matter of serious concern.

On the basis of the foregoing comments I propose in the book what might be summed up as a six-point framework for a reconstituted radical politics, one which draws on philosophic conservatism but preserves some of the core values hitherto associated with socialist thought.

(1) There must be a concern to repair *damaged solidarities*, which may sometimes imply the selective preservation, or even perhaps reinvention, of tradition. This theorem applies at all the levels which link individual actions not just to groups or even to states, but to more globalized systems. It is important *not* to understand by it the idea of the revival of civil society, now so

popular among some sections of the left. The concept of a 'civil society' lying between the individual and state is a suspect one, for reasons I explain later in the text, when applied to current social conditions. Today we should speak more of reordered conditions of individual and collective life, producing forms of social disintegration to be sure, but also offering new bases for generating solidarities.

A starting point here is a proper assessment of the nature of individualism in present-day society. Neoliberalism places great stress on the importance of individualism, contrasting this with the discredited 'collectivism' of socialist theory. By 'individualism', however, neoliberals understand the self-seeking, profit-maximizing behaviour of the marketplace. This is a mistaken way, in my view, of interpreting what should more appropriately be conceived of as the expansion of social reflexivity. In a world of high reflexivity, an individual must achieve a certain degree of autonomy of action as a condition of being able to survive and forge a life; but autonomy is not the same as egoism and moreover implies reciprocity and interdependence. The issue of reconstructing social solidarities should therefore not be seen as one of protecting social cohesion around the edges of an egoistic marketplace. It should be understood as one of *reconciling autonomy and interdependence* in the various spheres of social life, including the economic domain.

Consider as an illustration the sphere of the family – one of the main arenas in which detraditionalization has proceeded apace. Neoliberals have quite properly expressed concern about disintegrative tendencies affecting the family, but the notion that there can be a straightforward reversion to 'traditional family values' is a non-starter. For one thing, in the light of recent research we know that family life in earlier times often had a quite pronounced dark side, including the physical and sexual abuse of children, and violence by husbands against wives. For another, neither women nor children are likely to renounce the rights they have gained, rights which in the case of women also go along with widespread involvement in the paid labour force.

Since once again there are no real historical precedents, we don't know how far family life can effectively be reconstructed in such a way as to balance autonomy and solidarity. Yet some of the means whereby such an aim might be achieved have become fairly clear. Enhanced solidarity in a detraditionalizing society depends on what might be termed *active trust*, coupled with a renewal of personal and social responsibility for others. Active trust is trust which has to be won, rather than coming from the tenure of pre-established social positions or gender roles. Active trust presumes autonomy rather than standing counter to it and it is a powerful source of social solidarity, since compliance is freely given rather than enforced by traditional constraints.

In the context of family life, active trust involves commitment to another or others, that commitment implying also the recognition of obligations to them stretching across time. Strengthening family commitments and obligations, so long as these are based on active trust, doesn't seem incompatible with the diversity of family forms now being pioneered in all the industrialized societies. High rates of separation and divorce are probably here to stay, but one can see many ways in which these could enrich, rather than destroy, social solidarity. Recognition of the prime importance of rights of children, together with responsibilities towards them, for instance, could provide the very means of consolidating the new kinship ties we see around us – between, say, two sets of parents who are also step-parents and the children they share in common.

(2) We should recognize the increasing centrality of what I call *life politics* to both formal and less orthodox domains of the political order. The political outlook of the left has always been closely bound up with the idea of emancipation. Emancipation means freedom, or rather freedoms of various kinds: freedom from the arbitrary hold of tradition, from arbitrary power and from the constraints of material deprivation. Emancipatory politics is a politics of life chances and hence is central to the creation of autonomy of action. As such it obviously remains vital to a radical political programme. It is joined today, however, by a series of concerns coming from the changes analysed earlier – the transformation of tradition and nature, in the context of a globalizing, cosmopolitan order. Life politics is a politics, not of *life chances*, but of *life style*. It concerns disputes and struggles

about how (as individuals and as collective humanity) we should live in a world where what used to be fixed either by nature or tradition is now subject to human decisions.

(3) In conjunction with the generalizing of social reflexivity, active trust implies a conception of *generative politics*. Generative politics exists in the space that links the state to reflexive mobilization in the society at large. For reasons already discussed, the state can only function as a cybernetic intelligence to a limited degree. Yet the limitations of neoliberalism, with its idea of the minimal state, have become very apparent. Generative politics is a politics which seeks to allow individuals and groups to *make things happen*, rather than have things happen to them, in the context of overall social concerns and goals.

Generative politics is a defence of the politics of the *public domain*, but does not situate itself in the old opposition between state and market. It works through providing material conditions, and organizational frameworks, for the life-political decisions taken by individuals and groups in the wider social order. Such a politics depends on the building of active trust, whether in the institutions of government or in connected agencies. A key argument of this book is that generative politics is the main means of effectively approaching problems of poverty and social exclusion in the present day.

Generative politics is not a panacea. The shifting character of the state, and the fact that more or less the whole population lives in the same 'discursive space' as state and government agencies, produce major new political dilemmas and contradictions. For example, where the national polity has become only one among other points of reference for an individual's life, many people might often not 'listen' to what is going on in the political domain, even though they may keep mentally 'in touch' on a more consistent basis than before. 'Tuning out' may express a distaste for the antics of politicians, but may also go along with a specific alertness to questions the person deems consequential. Trust here might mingle with cynicism in an uneasy combination.

(4) The shortcomings of liberal democracy in a globalizing, reflexive social order suggest the need to further more radical forms of democratization. Here I stress the importance of *dialogic*

democracy. Among the many forms and aspects of democracy debated in the literature today, two main dimensions of a democratic order can be distinguished. On the one hand, democracy is a vehicle for the representation of interests. On the other, it is a way of creating a public arena in which controversial issues – in principle – can be resolved, or at least handled, through dialogue rather than through pre-established forms of power. While the first aspect has probably received most attention, the second is at least equally significant.

The extension of dialogic democracy would form one part (although not the only one) of a process of what might be referred to as the *democratizing of democracy*. Where the level of social reflexivity remains quite low, political legitimacy continues to depend in some substantial part on traditional symbolism and pre-existing ways of doing things. In a more reflexive order however – where people are also free to more or less ignore the formal political arena if they so wish – such practices are liable to become called into question.

Greater transparency of government would help the democratizing of democracy, but this is also a phenomenon which extends into areas other than that of the formal political sphere. Outside the arena of the state, it may be suggested, dialogic democracy can become promoted in several main contexts. In the area of personal life – parent–child relations, sexual relations, friendship relations – dialogic democracy advances to the degree to which such relationships are ordered through dialogue rather than through embedded power. What I call a 'democracy of the emotions' depends on the integrating of autonomy and solidarity mentioned earlier. It presumes the development of personal relationships in which active trust is mobilized and sustained through discussion and the interchange of views, rather than by arbitrary power of one sort or another.

To the extent to which it comes into being, a democracy of the emotions would have major implications for the furtherance of formal, public democracy. Individuals who have a good understanding of their own emotional makeup, and who are able to communicate effectively with others on a personal basis, are likely to be well prepared for the wider tasks and responsibilities of citizenship.

Dialogic democracy can also be mobilized through the activities of self-help groups and social movements. Such movements and groups express, but also contribute to, the heightened reflexivity of local and global social activity. In contemporary societies, far more people belong to self-help groups than are members of political parties. The democratic qualities of social movements and self-help groups come in large part from the fact that they open up spaces for public dialogue in respect of the issues with which they are concerned. They can force into the discursive domain aspects of social conduct that previously went undiscussed, or were 'settled' by traditional practices. They may help contest 'official' definitions of things; feminist, ecological and peace movements have all achieved this outcome, as have a multiplicity of self-help groups.

Some such movements and groups are intrinsically global in scope, and thus might contribute to the wider spread of forms of democracy. Given that the idea of a world government is implausible, mechanisms of dialogic democracy working not just through states and international agencies, but through a diversity of other groupings, become of central importance.

(5) We should be prepared to *rethink the welfare state* in a fundamental way – and in relation to wider issues of global poverty. In many countries what remains of socialist ideology has become concentrated on protecting the welfare state against the attacks of the neoliberals. And indeed there may very well be basic features of the welfare state which should be preserved against the potential ravages of cutbacks or of privatization. In terms of trust and solidarity, for example, welfare provisions or services quite often embody commitments that would simply be eroded if a more market-led, 'business' orientation were introduced.

Yet the welfare state was formed as a 'class compromise' or 'settlement' in social conditions that have now altered very markedly; and its systems of security were designed to cope more with external than with manufactured risk. Some of the major problematic aspects of the welfare state have by now been identified clearly enough, partly as the result of neoliberal critiques. The welfare state has been less than wholly effective either in countering poverty or in producing large-scale income or wealth redistribution. It was tied to an implicit model of traditional gender roles, presuming male participation in the paid labour force, with a 'second tier' of programmes directed towards families without a male breadwinner. Welfare state bureaucracies, like bureaucracies everywhere, have tended to become inflexible and impersonal; and welfare dependency is probably in some part a real phenomenon, not just an invention of neoliberalism. Finally, the welfare state was consolidated in the postwar period at a point where chronically high levels of unemployment seemed unlikely to return.

A new 'settlement' is urgently required today; but this can no longer take the form of a top down dispensation of benefits. Rather, welfare measures aimed at countering the polarizing effects of what, after all, remains a class society must be empowering rather than merely 'dispensed'. They must be concerned with just that reconstruction of social solidarity mentioned earlier, on the level of the family and that of the wider civic culture. And such a settlement has to be one that gives due attention to gender, not only to class.

Coping with manufactured uncertainty creates a whole new spectrum of problems – and, as always, opportunities – for the reform of welfare. Here one should think of reconstruction along the lines of models of *positive welfare*. The welfare state grew up as a mode of protecting against misfortunes that 'happen' to people – certainly so far as social security is concerned it essentially picks up the pieces after mishaps have occurred. Positive welfare, by contrast, places much greater emphasis on the mobilizing of life-political measures, aimed once more at connecting autonomy with personal and collective responsibilities.

(6) A programme of radical politics must be prepared to confront the role of *violence* in human affairs. The fact that I leave this question until last in the book doesn't mean at all that it is the least important. It is, however, one of the most difficult of issues to deal with in terms of received political theory. Neither socialist thought nor liberalism have established perspectives or concepts relevant to producing a normative political theory of violence, while rightist thought has tended to think of violence as a necessary and endemic feature of human life.

The topic is a big one. The influence of violence, after all, stretches all the way from male violence against women through casual street violence to large-scale war. Are there any threads which connect these various situations and which therefore might be relevant to a theory of pacification? I think there are, and they bring us back to the themes of fundamentalism and dialogic democracy.

In any social circumstances, there are only a limited number of ways in which a clash of values can be dealt with. One is through geographical segregation; individuals of conflicting dispositions, or cultures hostile to one another, can of course coexist if they have little or no direct contact. Another, more active, way is through exit. An individual or group which does not get along with another can simply disengage or move away, as might happen in a divorce. A third way of coping with individual or cultural difference is through dialogue. Here a clash of values can in principle operate under a positive sign – it can be a means of increased communication and self-understanding. Understanding the other better leads to greater understanding of oneself, or one's own culture, leading to further understanding and mutuality. Finally, a clash of values can be resolved through the use of force or violence.

In the globalizing society in which we now live the first two of these four options become drastically reduced. No culture, state or large group can with much success isolate itself from the global cosmopolitan order; and while exit may be possible in some situations for individuals, it is usually not available to larger social entities.

The relation between dialogue and violence, strung out along the edge of possible fundamentalisms, thus becomes particularly acute and tensionful for us. This reduction of options is dangerous, but it also offers sources of hope. For we know that dialogue can sometimes replace violence, and we know that this can happen both in situations of personal life and in much larger social settings. The 'gender fundamentalism' that violent men sustain towards their partners, and perhaps towards women in general, can at least in individual cases be transformed through greater self-understanding and communication. Dialogue between cultural groups and states is both a force acting directly against fundamentalist doctrines and a means of substituting talk for the use of violence.

The dark side of all this is obvious. Violence plainly often stems from clashes of interest and joustings for power; hence there are many quite strictly material conditions which would have to be altered to contest and reduce it. Moreover, the centrifugal forces of dispersal within and between societies in the present day might prove too great to manage without explosions of violence, on the small and larger scale. Yet the connections I have explored between autonomy, solidarity and dialogue are real; and they correspond to observable changes in local settings of interaction as well as in the global order.

Coda: the question of agency

Finally, what of the question of agency? If it be agreed that there is still an agenda for radical politics, who is to implement it? Seemingly even more difficult: what values might provide guidance for such an agenda? For it appears to many that we must now deal with an irremediably pluralistic universe of values, and indeed that the suspension of all value judgements, save for contextual or local ones, is the condition of cosmopolitanism. Critics of value relativism, on the other hand, regard the very term 'cosmopolitan' with some despair: if all ways of life are condoned as equally authentic, how can any positive values remain at all?

As against both such views, however, one could say that this is probably the first time in history that we can speak of the emergence of universal values – values shared by almost everyone, and which are in no sense the enemy of cosmopolitanism. Such values are perhaps first of all driven by what Hans Jonas calls the 'heuristics of fear' – we discover them under a negative sign, the collective threats which humanity has created for itself.[1]

Values of the sanctity of human life, universal human rights, the preservation of species and care for future as well as present generations of children may perhaps be arrived at defensively, but they are certainly not negative values. They imply ethics of individual and collective responsibility, which (as value claims) are able to override divisions of interest. Responsibility is not duty and some have suggested that it therefore lacks that imperative power which the call to duty draws out in the 'true believer'.[2] As compared to duty, however, responsibility implies the spelling out of reasons, not blind allegiance. It runs counter to fanaticism, but has its own compelling power, for commitments freely undertaken often have greater binding force than those which are simply traditionally given.

Responsibility is also the clue to agency. Today we must disavow providentialism – the idea that 'human beings only set themselves such problems as they can resolve.' With it, we have to discard the idea that there are agents sent to fulfil history's purposes, including the metaphysical notion that history is 'made' by the dispossessed. Recognizing the irreducible character of risk means having a critical theory without guarantees. Yet this recognition is also a source of liberation. There is no single agent, group or movement that, as Marx's proletariat was supposed to do, can carry the hopes of humanity; but there are many points of political engagement which offer good cause for optimism.

1
Conservatism: Radicalism Embraced

The word 'conservatism' today conjures up an odd, but interesting, diversity of associations. To be a conservative is, in some sense or another, to want to conserve. Yet in current circumstances it is not only, or even mainly, those who term themselves conservatives who wish so to do. Socialists more often than not find themselves trying to conserve existing institutions – most notably the welfare state – rather than to undermine them. And who are the attackers, the radicals who wish to dismantle existing structures? Why, quite often they are none other than the conservatives – who, it seems, wish to conserve no longer.

How did such a situation come about? How can it be that conservative thought, which, one might think, is by definition opposed to radicalism, should have ended up by embracing it? Does the so-called New Right, the progenitor of such radicalism, share anything in common with the old?

In this chapter, I shall not attempt to offer anything like a comprehensive account of the development or present status of conservative thought. Although perhaps not as complex and diverse as socialism, conservatism varies widely between different countries and includes various contrasting strands. In many continental European countries, for example, 'conservatism' suggests the political influence of Catholicism. Christian democratic parties and the intellectual influences which have nourished them have sometimes favoured outlooks and policies generally associated only with left parties in the English-speaking countries.

Special mention, right at the outset of this analysis, must be made of the distinctive position of conservatism in the United States. American 'exceptionalism' has usually been discussed in relation to the non-existence of a major socialist party in the US. But, of course, as most interpreters from at least the days of Louis Hartz have recognized, the absence of socialism has been accompanied by the relative absence also of a certain style of conservatism – that style which I shall call below Old Conservatism.

American conservatism, in some of its major forms at least, has almost from its beginnings been aggressively procapitalist in ways that its European counterparts have not. Conversely, the struggle to establish certain sorts of welfare systems long found in most other industrial societies, most notably universal state provision for health care, is still happening in the US.

Since I want to situate my discussion in this chapter and the next in the context of changing relations between conservatism and socialism, I do not analyse the position of conservative thought and practice in the US at any length. I don't discuss the history of European christian democracy either. In this chapter and the succeeding one I have concentrated mainly, although not wholly, on British perspectives on conservatism and socialism. I hope, nevertheless, that American and Continental European readers will read on. For while there might be important divergences between the political histories of different industrial countries, the basic dilemmas now faced by conservative and socialist thought are everywhere similar.

An important terminological note has to be made. In speaking of those conservatives who favour the indefinite expansion of market forces, I have used the generic terms New Right or, more often, 'neoliberalism'. Neither of these terms means the same thing in an American as in a European context. The New Right in the US tends to be associated with the Protestant religious right. 'Liberals' in the United States have not been the Manchester liberals, but instead those who during the New Deal and subsequently favoured the expansion of the welfare state. In the book I don't follow these usages, but rather the ones that are more or less universal outside the US.

Old Conservatism

Conservatism, it is often said, opposes rationalism, with its advocacy of clear and definite principles; hence conservative thought resists exposition. It is bound up with feelings and with practices, not with the imposition of logic on a refractory and complex social world. As one author puts it, 'Conservatism may rarely announce itself in maxims, formulae, or aims. Its essence is inarticulate, and its expression, when compelled, sceptical . . . It is capable of expression . . . [but] not always with any confidence that the words it finds will match the instinct that required them.'[1]

Given that this is not just a call to obscurantism, or anti-intellectualism, there are two senses in which such an observation might be taken. One is somewhat technical, and I shall come to it later. The other sense is to suggest that conservatism cannot be developed as a systematic philosophy – and in this guise the comment is surely mistaken, at least when we enquire into the history of conservative doctrines.

Conservatism in Britain and the United States has rarely been overly 'theoretical', it is true, but then much the same applies to other political views in an Anglo-Saxon context. The aversion to theorizing in matters political was an expression of that love of empiricism that was, until fairly recently at any rate, something of a mark of English-speaking culture as a whole. Elsewhere, in France or Germany for example, conservatives have been no more loath than anyone else to theorize. What did conservatism mean in these countries, if one goes back to its point of origin?

It was, of course, in some large part a defence of the *ancien régime*, and especially of Catholicism, against the aggrandizing forces of the French Revolution. But conservatism was more than just a reaffirmation of how things used to be before progressivism took a hold. In its more elaborated forms, conservatism both took issue with the Enlightenment and developed theories of society that challenged those of emerging liberalism. The more sophisticated forms of conservative thought did not simply dismiss the new in favour of the old; they countered progressivism with contrasting theories of history, tradition and moral community.

Louis de Bonald and Joseph de Maistre, for example, provided an interpretation of the revealed truth of tradition in counterposing the lost harmony of medieval times with the disorder of the revolutionary society. The human individual is intrinsically social, deriving that social being from sedimented history and from the larger cultural community. There is no state of nature, such as posited by Rousseau. Society, including the individual's social being, is of divine origin and reflects God's authority; thus obligations always take precedence over rights.[2] Moral truth is intrinsic to the social order and transmitted to the individual through language, which is a creation not of humans but of God. Continuity of the social order is guaranteed by the moral communities of the family, church and state. Bonald rejected the ideas of a social contract, popular sovereignty and representative government. He was scathing about the expansion of commerce and industry and developed a hard-hitting critique of bourgeois society. Industrial production leads to social disintegration and to the breakup of the organic wholeness characteristic of an agrarian order.

The more capitalism and democracy spread, the more Old Conservatism did in fact breed radicalism – but this was always above all a radicalism of re-establishment, looking back towards the past. There are clear links here between French and German conservatism: as the German maxim put it, 'too conservative not to be radical'. It is not surprising that progressive liberals such as Émile Durkheim drew on Bonald and de Maistre just as Marx did on Hegel, or that for a period of more than a century left and right made use of many common sources.

What did Old Conservatism stand for? Briefly put, it stood for hierarchy, aristocracy, the primacy of the collectivity, or state, over the individual, and the overreaching importance of the sacred. All of these traits are present in Burke, even if he did retain misgivings about closed philosophical systems. In Burke's writings we find much the same disparagement of the individual as appears in the works of his continental counterparts. Burke's writings are complex and, like those of the more challenging of Continental authors, are by no means wholly backward-looking.

Tradition is never static, and needs to be balanced by correction, or reform: 'A state without the means of some change is without the means of its conservation.'[3]

However, looking forward must always be based on looking back: 'people will not look forward to posterity, who never look backward to their ancestors.' Innovation, as opposed to reform, is dangerous because it flouts the 'stupendous wisdom' contained within institutions that have stood the test of time. 'Rage and phrensy will pull down more in half an hour, than prudence, deliberation and foresight can build up in a hundred years.' The idea of society as an organic community is strongly developed in Burke, as in Bonald and de Maistre. The idea that the individual and individual rights should be prime values is for them a nonsense. The state cannot be founded on a contract and the individual has no abstract rights; rights and their accompanying duties come from the collectivity, which represents an endless chain of generations. Society is 'a partnership not only between those who are living, but between those who are dead and those who are to be born.' Democracy betrays that partnership. The idea that 'a majority of men, told by the head' should determine political decisions would be nothing short of disastrous.

What has happened to Old Conservatism? Not to put too fine a point on things, it is dead. In the nature of the case, conservative thinkers like to trace their ideas back to an established heritage – in other words, to Burke and his contemporaries. This can be done plausibly enough with some of Burke's themes, such as organicism, the 'test of time' and the emphasis on reform; but in several basic respects such a procedure makes little sense. Old Conservatism, at least in its more principled forms, is, as has been aptly said, the 'other God that failed' alongside Communism and radical socialism.[4] Old Conservatism was destroyed because the social forms it sought to defend came to be more or less completely swept away; and, in Continental Europe, because of its ties to fascism.

The beliefs that have effectively disappeared with the disintegration of Old Conservatism are quite easy to list. No one any longer sees in feudalism a social order that is politically instructive for the modern world. Correspondingly, no one seriously puts up a defence of aristocracy, of the primacy of landed property, or of the forms of hierarchy linked to aristocratic rule. Perhaps more relevant to current debates, few if any conservative authors persist with the idea of the overweening state or with Romantic conceptions of the *Volksgeist*. Among conservatives now, if states are still supposed to be 'strong', they are envisaged as (in principle) 'minimal' rather than overarching. Conservatives have become either reconciled to democracy (in some form or another) or are even in some instances fervent advocates of it. Hierarchy is justified in terms of functional inequality rather than inherited fitness to rule, even though some conservatives might continue to support the notion of a 'political class' having distinctive qualities of statecraft.

Old Conservatism – by and large – was hostile not just to commerce, but to capitalism more generally. The more processes of commodification advance, the more organic solidarities are destroyed; bourgeois society, in which 'all that is solid melts into air', to quote Marx's famous metaphor, undermines those very continuities through which the past is brought into contact with the present. This includes the domain of the sacred. Economic individualism, according to Old Conservatism, is the enemy of that permeating sense of the religious so important to premodern social life – it is a secularizing force. Many present-day conservatives continue to see religion as basic to their world-view; but most no longer propose that the social order itself is divinely ordained.

Conservatism, conservatisms

Philosophic conservatism

In the absence of Old Conservatism, how should conservative thought be characterized? Conservatism in the postwar period has had to reinvent itself and, with some necessary oversimplification, three variant perspectives may be recognized. In the first place, there are those who attempt something of a philosophic defence of conservatism, even if they are against rounded philosophical systems. A second group consists of those who may be called, and who sometimes call themselves, neoconservatives.

Although not everyone follows this usage, I shall distinguish the neoconservatives from the New Right or neoliberalism. Each of these perspectives has influenced the others, but the differences between them are fairly clear.

Philosophic conservatism claims affinities with Old Conservative thought, but in fact introduces a variety of innovations. In England the leading inspiration of such conservatism is to be found in the writings of Michael Oakeshott, although subsequent authors have picked up differing parts of his arguments in developing their own views.

According to Roger Scruton, who gives due obeisance to Oakeshott's work, conservatism depends on three main organizing concepts: *authority*, *allegiance* and *tradition*. 'The conservative', he says, 'places his faith in arrangements that are known and tried, and wishes to imbue them with all the authority necessary to constitute an accepted and objective public realm.'[5] Authority is opposed by Scruton to contract and to all social arrangements based on 'conscious choice'; authority comes from the 'transcendent' qualities of established institutions.

Allegiance is what the member of a collectivity – be it a family, other corporate body, or state – owes to authority. Allegiance expresses the organic character of society; human beings are only able to act as 'individuals' because they can identify with collectivities greater than themselves. Such collectivities are specific ones, having a particular historical nature: 'It is a *particular* country, a *particular* history, a *particular* form of life that commands the conservative's respect and energy, and while he may have an imaginative grasp of other real or ideal arrangements, he is not immersed in them as he is immersed in the society that is his own.'

Allegiance is not a matter of individual decisions, but arises from, and gives expression to, the socially and morally transcendent; transcendence is also at the core of tradition. Tradition refers to customs and ceremonials by means of which the past speaks to the present. It supplies reasons for the individual's actions: those reasons come from what has been rather than what will be. Traditions relate allegiance to authority, storing up as they do the sedimented wisdom of earlier generations. In the political sphere, the state brings authority, allegiance and tradition together, 'in order to define the citizen as *subject*'. Scruton accepts the importance of democracy, but only with some reluctance and hedging around. For democracy implies independent decision-making and the existence of some sort of contractual agreements. Democracy, he says, is 'certainly not possessed by some *a priori* legitimacy which its rivals lack'.[6]

A critical attitude towards ideals of human perfectibility for Scruton, as for other current authors, is a key part of conservatism.[7] Oakeshott provides a good deal of grist for this particular mill in his celebrated critique of rationalism. In objecting to liberal or leftist ideas of 'sovereign reason', Oakeshott makes a distinction between knowledge of technique – expressed in terms of abstract rules or principles – and 'particular' knowledge, which is also 'traditional'. In politics as elsewhere, rationalism presumes the superiority of 'universal' solutions to problems over answers coming from tradition or embedded practice. Oakeshott's critique of rationalism, which has affinities with the later Wittgenstein and with Hans-Georg Gadamer, is not directed against 'reason' as such, but against the identifying of reason with technique. All forms of knowledge, no matter how general they appear to be, are saturated by practice, by what cannot be put into words because it is the condition of linguistic communication.

Here we have a much more sophisticated account of the 'resistance to exposition' of conservative thought than the version noted earlier, for Oakeshott's ideas on this point are in accord with some of the main themes of modern philosophy. Rationalism is more than self-defeating: it undermines the very conditions which (unbeknown to itself) make it possible in the first place. 'The peculiar viciousness of rationalism is that it destroys the only knowledge which could possibly save it from itself, namely, concrete or traditional knowledge. Rationalism only serves to deepen the inexperience out of which it was originally generated.'[8]

The theme that 'one always works from within tradition' is here more elaborated than it was in its original statement by Burke. Oakeshott's 'traditionalism' has little to do with glorifying the past or providing vague assertions about things that have stood the test of time. The rationalist needs the discipline of conservatism because otherwise that individual is like someone in a foreign country, bewildered by customs seen only from the surface; 'a butler or an observant housemaid has the advantage of him.'[9] Ideals torn from the context of tradition become incapable of guiding a person's actions.

Traditions of behaviour, Oakeshott says, are never fixed or complete and they do not have a changeless essence in which understanding can be anchored. 'Everything', he remarks, 'is temporary,' a comment which locates him some way from the attitudes of Old Conservatism. There are always, and must be, continuities in tradition, but these should be pictured more like a moving river than as a set of fixed reference points. It is just because tradition does not offer unambiguous norms or principles that politics – even revolutionary politics – is said by Oakeshott to be the pursuit of 'intimations', 'a conversation, not an argument.'

The image of politics as a conversation has been much commented on, and has some affinities with views developed by Richard Rorty and others (most notably again, Gadamer). Oakeshott says:

> Civilisation (and particularly ours) may be regarded as a conversation being carried on between a variety of human activities, each speaking with a voice, or in a language, of its own . . . And I call the manifold which these different manners of thinking and speaking compose, a conversation, because the relations between them are not those of assertion and denial but the conversational relationships of acknowledgement and accommodation.[10]

Neoconservatism

Neoconservatism, such as I define it here at any rate, is more sociological than philosophical. Its major protagonists are to be found not in England, but in Germany and the United States. The neoconservatives accept the pervasive influence that capitalism, and liberal democracy, have come to have over our lives today; but they see the bourgeois order as destroying the traditional symbols and practices on which a meaningful social existence depends.

In Germany the most important neoconservative authors were those writing during the first two decades or so after the Second World War – authors such as Hans Freyer and Arnold Gehlen. Several such writers, including both of these, were tainted by associations with National Socialism, but recovered their reputations through their postwar writings. According to the German neoconservatives, modernity tends to dissolve institutions of historical continuity which provide a moral framework for life. In contrast to Old Conservatism, Freyer and Gehlen do not believe that the 'demoralizing' effects of capitalist society can be overcome through the state or large-scale collective action. The task of conservatism is to preserve institutions outside the spheres of politics and the economy (such as the family or the church) where moral meaning can still be forthcoming.

According to Freyer, in premodern societies the individual had a single status which specified most domains of her or his activity; that status was associated with a bundle of rights and duties. Premodern social orders were *auf gewachsenen Gründen* – close to the organic rhythms of historical experience.[11] Such orders, much as Oakeshott says, were tied to specific aspects of collective history and even landscape, and thus could not easily be transferred to other peoples or places. This is why there was so much cultural diversity. Modern institutions, however, have a homogenizing effect, erasing the particularities of place. For Freyer, capitalism, including the welfare state, is here to stay, but it actually depends for its stability on moral meanings that it cannot itself reproduce. The conservative must therefore seek to bolster the 'resistances' or 'forces of support' which provide sources of meaning.

Neoconservatism in the US has to be interpreted against the backdrop of the remarks made earlier about American exceptionalism. The American neoconservatives mostly come not from a background of old rightism but, on the contrary, from one of old leftism – with which they early on became disillusioned. American neoconservatism, as developed, for example, in the writings of Irving Kristol, is less cautious about the attractions of capitalism and democracy than are the German authors. The American neoconservatives sustain, however, the idea of a cultural and moral critique of modern institutions. Although neoconservatism wishes to protect or even revive traditions, it is, in Kristol's words, 'resolutely free of nostalgia'. Neoconservatism does not seek to contest progressivist thought, but wants instead to create a more subtle mixture of present and future. As Kristol somewhat laconically puts it, 'It, too, claims the future.'[12]

In Kristol's version, neoconservatism has a range of distinct characteristics. It is opposed to most forms of socialism, but is also driven by a disaffection from liberalism (in the American sense of the term). Unlike Old Conservatism, it is specifically anti-Romantic. It traces its ancestry, not to the *ancien régime*, but much further back to classical times. Classical political philosophy distinguished between *praxis* and *techne*, and concerned itself with the ethical dilemmas posed when the two get too far out of kilter – as has happened in contemporary capitalism.

Neoconservatism, Kristol says, has a 'modest enthusiasm' for liberal democratic capitalism and sees a 'predominantly' market economy as a necessary, but not a sufficient, condition for the good society. Neoconservatives believe in the desirability of economic growth, but not as an end in itself; growth is necessary for social and political stability in modern social conditions. Kristol 'is not in opposition to energetic government', but sees such energy as flowing in fact from the limited state. Neoconservatives, according to Kristol, are in favour of modest government intervention in the economy. They are opposed to (American) liberalism not just because the liberals want – in the eyes of the neoconservatives – massive government intrusion in the marketplace, but because liberals combine such programmes of intervention with a laissez-faire attitude towards manners and morals.

This last view is a point of connection between American and German neoconservatism. It is one of the main arguments from which flows a stress on the importance of social and moral renewal. Thus, according to Kristol, the neoconservatives are not just patriotic, but nationalist; for patriotism comes from attachment to a country's past, while nationalism springs from hope for its future. They emphasize the essential role of the family and of religion as 'indispensable pillars of a decent society'.[13] Much the same point is made by Allan Bloom, who contests what he calls 'moral relativism' – the acceptance of different value standards as equally authentic. The 'education of openness' is untrue to the values it describes and condones, because to be binding, morality must be ethnocentric. People today are 'spiritually unclad, unconnected, isolated, with no inherited or unconditional connection with anything or anyone'; they 'can be anything they want to be, but they have no particular reason to want to be anything in particular'.[14]

Daniel Bell has separated himself from neoconservatism and regards himself as a conservative only as regards one aspect of modern society – its cultural system. In this respect, however, he has elaborated interestingly on the work of both German and American neoconservatives. Since the decline of the Puritan temper that inspired early capitalist development, he says, the moral life of modernity has been left without transcendental guidelines. Culture has now become disjoined from economy and polity. Capitalism depends on a 'secular Puritanism' in the sphere of production, but has given way to imperatives of pleasure and play in the area of consumption. Liberalism (once more, in the American sense) countenances individual freedom and experimentation in art and literature as well as in economic life. Yet such experimentation, in Bell's eyes, when it enters the areas of family life, sexuality, and moral activity more generally, produces a rampant individualism that threatens the social fabric and creates emptiness. 'Nothing is forbidden' and 'everything is to be explored': 'the lack of a rooted moral belief system is the cultural contradiction of the society, the deepest challenge to its survival.'[15]

Neoliberalism

Neoconservatism may 'claim the future', but it is the New Right that over recent years has been the truly radical force in conservative politics. The ideas of the New Right are better described as neoliberalism rather than neoconservatism, since economic markets play such a large role in them. For the neoliberals, capitalistic enterprise is no longer regarded as the source of the problems of modern civilization. Quite the opposite: it is the core of all that is good about it. A competitive market system not only maximizes economic efficiency, it is the main guarantor of individual freedom and of social solidarity. In contrast to Old Conservatism, the neoliberals admire economic individualism; and they see such individualism as the key to the success of democracy within the context of a minimal state. Their leading thinker, F. A. Hayek, explicitly refused to call himself a conservative. Some of Hayek's followers, none the less, have tried to have their cake and eat it, referring to Hayek's ideas as 'conservative liberalism'.[16]

For neoliberal authors, the source of order in society is to be found neither mainly in tradition, nor in rational calculation and planning, whether by the state or anybody else. Society does have in a certain sense an organic quality; however, this trait comes from the spontaneous and unintended coordination of many individuals acting for their own motives. Well-functioning markets are the prime example, and main institutional anchor, of spontaneous social order. Such social order is not limited to the economic arena: as Milton and Rose Friedman put it, 'Economic activity is by no means the only area of human life in which a complex and sophisticated structure arises as an unintended consequence of a large number of individuals cooperating while each pursues his own self-interest.'[17]

The idea of spontaneous coordination – coordination without commands – as portrayed by Hayek has a definite connection to Oakeshott's conception of tradition. The indispensability of 'knowledge stored in habits and in practice' is for Hayek a key reason why command economies cannot work. The information signals provided by pricing in competitive economic conditions cannot be generated by central authorities. The explanation for this is not, or not only, that the information required is too complex or changing; it is because the knowledge needed is essentially practical and local, 'given in use'. Yet in Hayek's view such local knowledge is not really traditional; it is the tacit knowhow which individuals build up through the experience of handling problems on the spot. Hayek is a universalist, believing that the benefits of the liberal society can be extended to the whole of humankind.

The restricted role allocated to government in New Right

doctrines follows quite directly from the theory of spontaneous order. The main object of government is not to 'produce any particular services or products to be consumed by the citizens, but rather to see that the mechanism which regulates the production of goods and services is kept in working order'.[18] The message to governments from the competitive economy is: keep out! Even when prompted by the noblest of motives, government intervention is liable to create, if not tyranny (although this was the case in Communist regimes), then at least bureaucratic inefficiency. To this analysis neoliberals often add the conclusions of the Virginia school of public choice theory. In the era of the welfare state, governments tend to get overloaded or over-extended; in such a situation, government activity becomes dogged by the equivalent of business failure, without the disciplining mechanisms that markets provide to eliminate the less efficient.

What exactly are the connections between markets and democracy, seen from the vantage point of neoliberalism? Various differing views exist, but the leading theme is that markets create the basic conditions of individual freedom and are more important to democracy than the constitution of the state itself. Attempts to 'correct' market forces suppress the freedoms which market relations promote. Socialism, it is said, has nowhere been democratic, even in the Scandinavian countries, and it cannot be made so. For at the heart of socialism, in the words of Arthur Seldon, is the belief 'that government knows better than individuals. The essence of capitalism . . . is that it allows individuals to take the risks of living their lives as they see best.'[19] Capitalism, based on inexorable market forces, takes no account of people's social origins, skin colour or accent. Far from encouraging egoism, the single-minded pursuit of profit is a source of moral strength because it excludes political partiality or social prejudice. Voice and exit are possible in market settings in ways that can be mimicked, but not replaced, by political processes.

Social justice, Hayek and others have argued, cannot be achieved through the state – indeed Hayek claims that the idea of social justice is incoherent. Whatever the virtues of some types of welfare institutions, the limitations of the welfare state, according to neoliberal critics, are glaring and there for all to see. Among other flaws, it benefits the more affluent rather than the less and creates an unholy mixture of bureaucratic monstrosities and welfare dependency.

In New Right thinking, property and hierarchy have a different complexion from earlier versions of conservatism. Old Conservatism saw these as means of resistance to commodification, to the advance of commerce – and to democracy. For the neoliberals, property ownership (home-owning, share-holding) is to be encouraged precisely as a mode of ensuring participation in the market system. Hierarchy persists, but it is not the sort (esteemed in Old Conservatism) which allows the transmission of inherited privilege across the generations. Movement up the social scale, including the acquisition of property, in a market society is to be open to all with the will to success and the determination to compete.

Competitive individualism, however, according to the neoliberals, is not infinitely expandable. Certain contexts of social life stand outside, and in identifying these New Right authors tend to draw freely on American neoconservatism. A minimal state has to be a strong state in order to enforce the laws on which competition depends, protect against external enemies and foster integrating sentiments of nationalism. The New Right sees much evidence of moral decay in family life. The family, like the state, has to be strong, and where it has become weak family bonds must be re-established. The decline of the family has been attributed to various sources: to the sexual permissiveness introduced in the 1960s, lax parents, the rise of feminism and the spread of overt homosexuality. However, a connection is also frequently drawn between the growth of the welfare state and family disintegration. Welfare institutions, it is said, accustom people to expect from the state forms of support that in earlier generations were provided by family groups; welfare provisions allow single-parent families, as against the traditional family, to proliferate.

Although the decline in the moral authority of the family, according to New Right authors, is general – and needs to be reversed – it has affected the authority of the father in particular. Family responsibilities are a source of the moral regulation of men, who otherwise tend to be errant – shirking responsibilities not only in the home but also in the marketplace. In the sphere of the family at least, unintended consequences do not produce the beneficient and spontaneous order they are held to do elsewhere. The welfare state has allowed some fathers to abandon responsibility for the support of their wives and children. Men without women, in George Gilder's words, are 'destructive both to themselves and society'; if men 'cannot be providers, they have to resort to the muscle and the phallus'.[20] The development of an excluded underclass, having many 'circulating males' and many women lone heads of households, together with rising levels of crime, are expressions of, and causally influenced by, family disintegration.

Conservatism and neoliberalism

Advocates of New Right views see themselves as the inheritors of two centuries of conservative thought – as not only having brought conservatism up-to-date (if that is not an oxymoron), but also as having triumphed over rival perspectives of political theory and practice. After all, the rise to prominence of the neoliberals has coincided – and, some would claim, helped bring about – the demise of Keynesianism in the West and of Communism in the East.

Yet have the ideas of the New Right anything to do with conservatism at all? The question has quite rightly preoccupied many conservatives, as well as critics from the left, and is of more than semantic or historical interest. For neoliberals in some countries there is little need to find legitimacy in prior conservative thinking – on the contrary, there is a demand to be dissociated from such thinking where it became tainted through association with fascism. In Britain, however, such considerations do not apply; here the New Right, which has enjoyed a sustained period of power, has a strong interest in claiming continuity with earlier perspectives. And a good deal of ink, or computer printout, has been devoted to showing this to be so. One of the most sophisticated of such discussions is that offered by Shirley Letwin – who concerns herself with Thatcherism – and I shall treat it as paradigmatic. For Letwin not only provides an interesting characterization of neoliberalism, but also concerns herself with rebutting critics who have fastened on some of its paradoxes.

Letwin distinguishes Thatcherism[21] from 'middle way' Toryism but also from the views of 'true' laissez-faire liberals. The middle way Tory is not an Old Conservative. What the middle way Tory wishes to preserve is the result of the socialist movement: planning, economic controls and large-scale spending on welfare. Thatcherism is a crusade to free the 'vigorous virtues' of self-reliance and individual initiative from the cloying hand of bureaucracy and the 'Establishment'.

There are some 'superficial similarities', Letwin accepts, between this outlook and the views of the laissez-faire liberal. Both dislike the various vested interests that have fostered dependency, and place great reliance on the liberating influence of capitalistic enterprise. But the liberal favours a free market everywhere – as Bell complains, liberalism then becomes moral libertarianism, scornful of all forms of authority. The Thatcherite refuses this connection: what he or she wishes to see is the moral regeneration of the individual, or families, and of the national community. The values concerned here, Letwin says, have always been part of conservatism – it is middle way Toryism which, in the heyday of the welfare state, was an interruption of more long-standing conservative traditions.

According to Letwin, economic considerations are secondary to a programme of moral regeneration. The privatizing of state-owned industries, for example, helps increase economic efficiency; but, more important, the 'vigorous virtues' are promoted by privatization, which makes the ownership of share-holding property a possibility for millions. Widespread property ownership enhances 'personal energy and adventurousness, critical components of the vigorous virtues'. The extension of ownership also helps to promote the well-being of the family. Marx decried the fact that in a bourgeois society the family is reduced to a 'relation of property'; but to the neoliberal this is just the source of its strength. The ownership of property, and its transmission across the generations, gives the family its continuity. Moreover, a family which has a joint stake in commonly held property is likely also to have a strong sense of solidarity.

Such a way of thinking about the family, Letwin says, is one connecting point between the vigorous virtues and established themes of conservatism. The link between family sentiment and family holdings of property, she argues, has long been accepted as a commonplace in Toryism – it stretches right back to medieval times. But there are other ways too of showing that the New Right has revived conservatism rather than departed from it – in respect, for instance, of the role of the state.

Thatcherism, Letwin argues, does not, as laissez-faire liberals do, seek to minimize all state intervention in economic and social life. Rather, it distinguishes two senses of intervention, one to be rejected, the other to be regarded positively. A market economy is incompatible with state intervention in the form of overall planning or corporatism; but it actively demands the strong hand of the state in respect of the maintenance of law and order, the fostering of national ideals and the capability for defence. Thatcherism was a programme for radical change in many areas – but it recognized the importance of tradition in other contexts. It sought to attack 'entrenched practices' rather than traditions. The vigorous virtues, as portrayed by Letwin, turn out to be themselves part of such traditions, particularly when understood in the context of British history. Neoliberalism thus is supposedly in a direct line of continuity with Old Conservatism of the British variety, which has long emphasized the importance of a sturdy moral individualism. It is strange, Letwin avers, that this morality 'should have persisted for so long without being identified': it took the arrival of Thatcherism to make it (retrospectively) clear.

This very British individualism, according to her, is not selfishness. According to 'the British morality . . . there need be no conflict between society and individuals bent on cultivating their individuality . . . Society is . . . the cradle rather than the coffin of individuality.' From this viewpoint there flows a rejection of hierarchy, of the prejudice that some types of calling are inferior to others. When neoliberals claim that business skills are as worthy of respect as those of lawyers or poets, they return to 'the traditional British morality'.

How plausible is such an attempt to distance the New Right from liberalism and tie it to conservative traditions? The short answer is: it isn't very plausible at all. In the first place, neither in Britain nor anywhere else was Old Conservatism in favour of moral individualism, which it saw as the enemy of social solidarity. Such 'vigorous virtues' were the stock in trade of those who fought against Old Conservatism, in the name of bourgeois values or in fact as advocates of syndicalism. A strong state was valued by conservatives because it protected hierarchy, not because it created conditions under which all forms of work were regarded as of equivalent worth. It might very well be true that 'society is the cradle of individuality', but it was the critics of conservatives – and of laissez-faire liberalism – not conservatives themselves, who advocated this view.

It is illogical to accept much of the teaching of classical liberalism, as the neoliberals do, and yet to insist on the essential role of national sentiments and a strong state. Markets have no intrinsic connection with nation-states, whose boundaries they constantly transgress. If markets ignore social and cultural differences between individuals, so also do they ignore differences between nations. The spread of transnational capitalism (as many liberal thinkers hoped) should, according to liberal theory, do away for the need for warfare. If 'defence' is an inherent necessity of the 'strong state', this is nothing to do directly with markets, but with the position of states within the nation-state system.

New Right authors are fond of tracing the supposed decline of the family and other moral institutions to permissiveness spread by intellectuals or leftists. Yet as an explanation of 'family disintegration' this view is fatuous. Structural changes affecting the family, and other areas of social life outside the sphere of paid labour, are stimulated by the very influences which the New Right, in its neoliberal guise, promotes. If one is going to advocate individualism and individual initiative in the economic sphere, it makes no sense not to extend these to other domains as well, including that of the family. There is a damaging contradiction at the core of neoliberal thought. On the one hand, in encouraging the free play of market forces, neoliberal political philosophy unleashes detraditionalizing influences of a quite far-reaching kind. On the other hand, the very traditional symbols which these influences help to dissolve are held to be essential to social solidarity. It is not surprising that New Right doctrines mix liberal freedoms and authoritarianism – even fundamentalism – in an uneasy and unstable fashion. Letwin's assertion that 'nothing in human arrangements is inevitable, that what seems irreversible today may be reversed tomorrow' – as clear an expression as one could find of the principle that all that is solid melts into air – stands in blunt opposition to a professed adherence to traditional social forms.[22]

The 'strong state' is supposed to sanction the legal rules that allow markets their necessary free play; within the economic system itself, however, the New Right accepts the economism of classical liberal thought. It thereby ignores, or cannot cope with, that 'non-contractual element in contract' which Durkheim, drawing in fact on conservative ideas, long ago identified. Market institutions, as an Oakeshottian conservative would also argue, cannot prosper in an autonomous way. They imply norms and mechanisms of trust, which can be protected by law but only to a limited degree produced by legal formulations. They are certainly not inherent in the economic contract itself, viewed in isolation from a wider nexus of social institutions.

There is another basic respect in which neoliberalism diverges from the suppositions of conservative thought. According to most forms of conservatism, the world escapes our attempts to subject it to the encompassing rule of human reason – which is why we have so often to rely on tradition. The New Right recognizes imperfectibility in this sense in the realm of government, at least as regards economic planning. Yet it does not do so in respect of markets, which are understood as frictionless machines guaranteeing endless economic growth.[23]

Conservatism and social change

Why has neoliberalism achieved such prominence in recent years? New Right authors, of course, have an interpretation of their own successes. Their ideas, they say, diagnosed the failures of socialist-inspired collectivism and, even more significant, showed what remedies needed to be taken to overcome them. Socialist doctrines led to an overextension of government and the crippling of the vigorous virtues. To counter these problems the free flourishing of markets was required, plus a renewal of the hard core moral institutions of family and state.

The New Right did indeed address changes which have affected the industrialized societies over the past few decades. However, for reasons I shall develop more fully later, it did not, and could not, provide an accurate interpretation of what these changes were. In giving a new respectability to the long-ignored ideas of Ludwig von Mises and Hayek, the neoliberals believed they had perceived flaws intrinsic to all types of collectivism. In fact, if one means by collectivism the welfare state plus macroeconomic planning, these worked well in their own terms for a substantial time. In the 'golden age', there was a lengthy period of overall economic growth, in which the tendencies of capitalism towards cycles of boom and depression, and towards economic polarization, were fairly well controlled.

This situation changed when, and because, what came (somewhat inaccurately) to be called Keynesianism came to an end. Keynesianism became ineffective as a result of the twin and interconnected influences of intensified globalization and the transformation of everyday life. Globalization means much more than the internationalizing of economic competition, important though this is. Influenced by the development of instantaneous electronic communication, the 'new globalization' has created a new communications order. Twenty-four-hour global money markets, together with the 'computerizing of money', among other major changes in global systems, date from this time.

Globalizing influences have been directly bound up with far-reaching changes happening in the tissue of social life. They have helped set in play pervasive processes of detraditionalization in everyday social activity. Detraditionalization in turn means an acceleration of the reflexivity of lay populations. Keynesianism worked tolerably well in a world of *simple modernization*; but it could not survive in a world of *reflexive modernization* – a world of intensified social reflexivity.[24] Reflexive citizens, responding to a new social universe of global uncertainties, become aware of, and may subvert, the economic incentives that are supposed to mobilize their behaviour. Keynesianism, like some forms of policy which helped structure the welfare state, presumes a citizenry with more stable lifestyle habits than are characteristic of a globalized universe of high reflexivity.

The theories of the New Right address these basic transmutations in a partial and paradoxical way. The impact of globalization, with its manufactured uncertainties, is understood in terms of the need to deregulate markets. The transformation of daily life is grasped only via a dogmatic stress on traditional values in the family and elsewhere. Detraditionalization in these domains is fiercely condemned, even though the unconditional endorsement of market forces actively helps further it.

Given the aporias of neoliberalism, does it make sense to return to one version or another of philosophic conservatism? Some have suggested so, and not just on the basis of proposing a revival of 'middle way' or 'one nation' Toryism. Thus John Gray has argued that the New Right has succumbed to a misplaced rationalism, inherited from classical liberal thought, and to an 'unhistorical dogmatism', combined with an 'ignorant neglect of the verities of an older conservative philosophy'. The neoliberals imagine that they can establish universal principles of political life; and they discard Oakeshott's insight that political activity is a conversation and an art. New Right theories do not see that civil society depends on the sustaining of a 'common culture'. 'It is only by strengthening the resources of a common culture . . . that we can hope to renew the institutions of civil society across the generations. To assume that we can rely on a regime of abstract rules is the merest folly.'

The neoliberal argument for the market is, in Gray's words, not only that 'it allows for innovation and novelty in thought and practice in a way that collective decisions cannot'; but that 'it allows practitioners of different traditions and values to live in peaceful coexistence.' The philosophic conservative, however, recognizes that markets have distinctive limitations. The New Right suppresses 'the insights into markets as kaleidic, sometimes chaotic processes, susceptible to massive endogenous dislocation through speculative panics and the subjectivity of expectations'.

Gray emphasizes the connections between philosophic conservatism and ecological issues. Conservative thought has generally been hostile to green politics, which has been seen as 'anticapitalist propaganda under another flag'. Yet rather than being linked to the left, Gray says, a concern for the integrity of nature stands close to conservative themes. Both conservatism and green philosophies are marked by a scepticism about progress and a belief that economic growth for its own sake is dangerous, or even disastrous; the understanding that those who are living have a responsibility to forge perspectives relating dead generations of the past to those as yet unborn; and the conviction that individuals can only flourish within communal forms of life.

Accepting these ideas, Gray recognizes, implies a rethinking of conservative philosophy and policies, particularly as portrayed in the outlook of the New Right. 'The deepest need' which people have is for 'a network of common practices and inherited traditions that confer on them the blessing of a settled identity'. Conservative thought must become allied to, or even integrated with, green political ideals if we are to be able to cope with a world in which continuous economic growth is no longer sustainable – a world which is not far off, or is perhaps imminent, so far as the economically developed societies are concerned.

Market principles for Gray remain central, but they should be separated, he argues, from an endorsement of capitalism as such. For capitalism (much as Marx argued) depends on unending economic accumulation; any faltering of economic growth is interpreted as a flaw in the system. Moreover, he continues, the legitimacy of the modern political order is much too closely tied to continuous growth for its own good, something which underlines its fragile character:

> This is a feature of Western insitutions that should be profoundly distasteful to all true conservatives, for whom the legitimacy of institutions, and the authority of government, have (or should have) ethical and spiritual foundations, whereby they can weather even protracted periods of economic hardship. The dependency of Western capitalism on uninterrupted economic growth for its political legitimacy has allowed it to evade addressing its chief defects, which account for its systemic tendency to instability; the insecurity that it generates for ordinary people by its prodigious technological virtuosity and inherently innovative character; and the maldistribution of capital whereby this insecurity is compounded . . . Conservatives need to explore, with greens and others, as yet unthought-of dilemmas of life in societies which are no longer buoyed up by the prospect of incessant economic growth or by modernist pseudo-religions of endless world-improvement.[25]

Radical thoughts indeed – and quite different in most ways, as the author properly asserts, from the radicalism of the New Right. How valid is such an interpretation of conservatism, however? And does it avoid the paradoxes of New Right theories?

Conservatism and the concept of tradition

While it may be agreed that the concepts of authority, allegiance and tradition are vital to conservatism, it would be difficult to see each of these as on a par. Tradition is surely the most basic idea here, in the absence of which the other notions would lose their cogency. For it is not just any form of authority with which conservatives are concerned, but authority informed and legitimized by traditional symbols. And allegiance is not just a matter of belonging to some corporate body or another; it refers to an affiliation with groups organized on a basis of tradition rather than conscious, rational association.

Although the idea of tradition is so closely bound up with conservatism, the concept, surprisingly, has been very little discussed by conservatives themselves. It occupies such a central position in most conservative thinking, probably, that it is virtually taken for granted. What is tradition and why, according to conservatives, is it to be defended?

When conservatives discuss why the past should have a firm hold over the present, and why established symbols or modes of life should be protected, they often speak – as has been mentioned – of the test of time.[26] Scruton, for example, says that practices worth preserving 'must have the weight of a successful history . . . of something that has flourished'. He also offers two further criteria. Such practices must 'engage the loyalty of their participants, in the deep sense of moulding their idea of what they are and should be', and 'they must point to something durable, something which survives and gives meaning to the acts that emerge from it.'[27] These considerations, he says, rule out the idea that there could be traditions of torture, crime or revolution.

Quite plainly, however, they do not. Public executions, which often involved extreme tortures, flourished for many centuries in Europe and elsewhere. They were certainly bound up with creating loyalty and with norms and values about how one should act, forming as they did part of the framework of law and order; and they were very much to do with sustaining enduring patterns of meaning. So far as revolutions go, the Soviet Union, for a considerable period, was a society that met these criteria – and those in Russia today who wish to go back to the old ways are commonly, and perhaps accurately, called conservatives. At least one book has been written which tried to invoke philosophic conservatism to defend both Communism and the welfare state.[28]

Sometimes the test of time thesis involves a sort of more or less explicit evolutionism. Items of behaviour or symbols that have survived for a long while (although how much is a long while?) have done so for a reason, that reason being that they correspond to individual or social needs of some kind. Yet functionalist interpretations based on the idea of social needs are, to say the least, logically suspect.[29] And in any case they don't exclude those survivals with which conservatives would not want to be associated.

Oakeshott doesn't offer much guidance on this matter. Tradition for him is bound up with tacit knowledge, knowledge that is art, and which cannot be put into words because it is essentially practical. This insight is undeniably important, but doesn't provide a sufficient definition of tradition, or why certain traditions are valuable. Many skills, like being able to type or to ride a bicycle, involve tacit knowledge of a practical kind, but they are not thereby traditions. Whenever Oakeshott contrasts 'technical' with 'traditional' rather than simply 'practical' knowledge, he draws in a notion of continuity or inheritance; and this sits uneasily alongside his observation that everything is temporary.

It will help to explore these problems further if we look more directly at the concept of tradition itself. In understanding what tradition is, we should first of all try to grasp where its authority comes from, the means whereby it is able to claim allegiance. The distinctive quality of tradition, which separates it from custom or habit as well as from technical or expert knowledge, is that it presumes an idea of *ritual* or *revealed truth* – and this defining trait is also the origin of its authority.[30] What is 'hallowed' about traditions is not the past but the wisdom they incorporate. Such wisdom may or may not be functionally effective or 'technically accurate'; these traits do not specify it as traditional. Ritual truth is displayed in its enactment, in the repetition of practical formulae.

It is not its embeddedness in practice which makes something traditional, but the fact that certain ritual actions specify its truth. Traditions always have guardians of some kind or another: priests, wise men, elders, patriarchal fathers, have privileged access to ritual truth, to the wisdom of tradition. The past is essential to tradition, but not because to be traditional a trait of behaviour must persist over an indefinite period of time. Rather, the reason is that traditional wisdom has to be passed on in a practical fashion, as an apprenticeship.

In the current period, processes of detraditionalization bite more deeply than ever before, affecting the industrialized parts of the world in particular, but making themselves felt everywhere. The transformation of tradition is not only paralleled by, but converges with, the disappearance of 'nature'. Nature – a physical environment of human action existing independently of that action – has all but dissolved; the problems of environmental degradation which perturb us today come from the transformation of the natural into the social and cultural. Consider, for example, reproduction, so intimately bound up with the family as an institution. As a result of the introduction of a diversity of reproductive technologies, many happenings which used to be given – part of nature and traditionally-given ways of doing things – become subject to independent decision-making. They are no longer a 'horizon' of human activity but become caught up in the social world. Traditions used to be 'horizons' of our activity in a similar sense.

Which is more 'natural', a situation where a woman has twenty pregnancies, and some of her children die at birth or shortly afterwards, or one where she has two pregnancies and both children survive? We have to decide today, as individuals and collective humanity, what nature is and how we should organize our lives in relation to it. Much the same holds for tradition.

Let me put this point in a provocative fashion. We can no

longer – or should not aim to – defend traditions in the traditional way, because this produces fundamentalism. Once this situation has come about, even the most sophisticated form of conservatism, philosophical conservatism, becomes incoherent. In a world of instantaneous communication, affected by powerful globalizing influences, cultural cosmopolitanism is an unavoidable part of our lives. Defending tradition in the traditional way means asserting its ritual truth – its separateness and specialness – whereas moral and cultural communication are the only ground on which cosmopolitanism can stand.

Fundamentalism, I would propose, is in fact *nothing other* than tradition defended in the traditional way – but in response to novel circumstances of global communication. It is not therefore limited to the sphere of religion; fundamentalisms can arise wherever traditions are under threat or are being eroded. There can be fundamentalisms, for example, of the family, gender and ethnicity (and even ecological fundamentalisms). Fundamentalism in a world of cosmopolitan communication is always potentially dangerous. For it is a refusal of dialogue in circumstances where such dialogue is the only mode of mutual accommodation. There is a direct connection here between forms of violence that at first sight seem entirely heterogeneous. Much private and public violence of men against women comes from a sort of gender fundamentalism – a refusal of communication in social conditions where patriarchal traditions are under challenge. In this sense it is not in principle different from the violence between exclusionary ethnic groups.

Do those who do not become fundamentalists have to acquiesce in the disappearance of tradition? I don't think so; traditions, in some guises and in some contexts, surely do need to be defended today, even if not in the traditional way. Traditions need to be saved, or recovered – I shall suggest later on – in so far as they provide generalizable sources of solidarity. Is tradition protected in the service of wider social values still tradition? It is, and it isn't – in much the same way as is true of the naturalness of lapsed nature. Succouring traditions means preserving a continuity with the past which would otherwise be lost and doing so as a way of achieving a continuity with the future as well. Safeguarding traditions, however, like safeguarding 'nature', takes on a new colouring when their defence can no longer be mainly intrinsic.

In a situation where change has long ceased to be all progress, if ever it was, and where what progress is has become eminently disputable, the preservation and renewal of tradition, as well as of environmental resources, take on a particular urgency. Tradition, like nature, used to be, as it were, an external framework for human activity which 'took' many decisions for us. But now we have to decide *about* tradition: what to try to sustain and what to discard. And tradition itself, while often important and valuable, can be of very little help in this.

As understood in the usual ways, therefore, conservatism has collapsed or become self-contradictory. Some of its key ideas, however, acquire a new relevance when removed from their original contexts. We should all become conservatives now, I shall argue – but not in the conservative way. The trite observation that there is no longer a right or a left takes on a new intellectual and practical power in present-day social conditions. Distinctions between right and left have of course always been to some extent confused or ambiguous, and radicalism has never been an exclusive property of the left. The differentiation between the two, however, had some cogency throughout the long phase of the development of modern institutions marked by simple modernization.

Crudely put, the left – and most liberals – were for modernization, a break with the past, promising a more equal and humane social order – and the right was against it, harking back to earlier regimes. In the conditions of developed reflexivity which exist today, there is no such clear divide. It is not the need for a radical political programme that disappears – this is not the 'end of history'. Conservatism in the shape of neoconservatism and philosophic conservatism can be drawn on positively, if critically, to help to shape such a programme. In a new context, and in unconservative ways, we might assert again the old slogan mentioned before: too conservative not to be radical! Or to put it the other way around: too radical not to be conservative!

Freed from an intrinsic connection to either left or right, radicalism reverts to its original meaning as daring: it means being prepared to contemplate bold solutions to social and political problems. Radicalism is not, however, here valued for its own sake but instead is tempered by that awareness of the importance of continuity on which philosophic conservatism insists.

2

Socialism: the Retreat from Radicalism

Socialism was born out of the dissolution of the *ancien régime* just as surely as conservatism was created from the attempt to protect it. For some two centuries since, socialism has been the standard-bearer of 'progressivism', the notion that there is a direction to history and that appropriate sorts of political intervention can help us locate it as well as speed up the journey. The literature of socialism is full of talk about 'the path to be followed', 'the forward march of socialism', the 'road to socialism' and so forth. The more radical forms of socialist thought have long argued that there is only forward or back: either humanity advances in its journey or it is likely to relapse into barbarism. For socialists, the past is not comforting; it is valued at most because it has provided the means whereby we can actively move on to grasp and appropriate the future.

How extraordinary, therefore, is the situation socialists find themselves in today! For even if they disagreed fiercely with one another about what the future society would be like, socialists shared the conviction that they were in the vanguard of history. To socialists, others either, like the conservatives, looked back wistfully to social forms the world would never see again or, like the liberals, advocated types of social and political order that were only staging posts on the way to full emancipation.

With the fall of Communism, although certainly not for this reason alone, all this is in tatters. Long accustomed to thinking of itself as the avant-garde, socialism has suddenly become

archaic, consigned to the past it once despised. 'The idea of
"burying socialism"', it has been said, 'is a fantasy of some
conservative politicians.'[1] However, perhaps the fantasy has
become real.

Unlike conservatives, socialists have never been loath to set
down their ideas on paper, or deterred by reasons of philosophy
from doing so. On the contrary, socialist ideas have frequently
been expounded at very great length. In spite of, or more
probably because of, the existence of this mountainous literature,
the identity of socialism is elusive. Socialism, it has been
said, 'stands for the values of freedom, equality, community,
brotherhood, social justice, the classless society, cooperation,
progress, peace, prosperity, abundance, happiness'. Just as
great a diversity of values can be found when socialist ideals are
stated negatively. Socialists 'are opposed to oppression, exploitation, inequality, strife, war, injustice, poverty, misery and
dehumanisation'.[2]

Hardly surprising, then, that some commentators have concluded that socialism is all things to all people; or, like Schumpeter, have argued that socialism is so 'culturally indeterminate'
that it cannot be defined save in purely economic terms.[3] In view
of its great diversity, any endeavour to characterize socialist
thought with broad strokes is problematic, but I shall seek to do
so all the same. I shan't be concerned to cover all the main
dimensions of socialist doctrines, but only to pick out certain
elements relevant to the status of socialism today.

Socialism and the question of history

Like liberalism, socialism sets itself against tradition and in this
sense is an heir to the Enlightenment. Socialism depends on a
recovery of the human from the sway of the transcendent, and
from this point of view it is not hard to see why Marx followed
on so closely from Hegel. History does not express the will of
God, but is the result of the active struggles, and creativity, of
human beings themselves. The human authorship of history,
however, has been hidden by religious dogma and by the dead
hand of tradition. The task ahead for humanity is to take hold of

its own social development and direct it in a conscious way. We are, or can become, the masters of our own destiny.

This stance involves a view *of* history and of nature too. History is a resource, to be shaped to human purposes, but so also is nature. Given the importance of ecological issues today, many have looked retrospectively at socialist thought so as to discern there some basic ecological concerns; but one should probably accept at the outset that the dominant forms of socialist doctrine have no place for nature as a 'partner' of humanity. Nature is looked at above all in an instrumental way.

The relation of socialism to history is described in its pithiest form in one of Marx's aphorisms. Human beings, Marx says, 'only set themselves such problems as they can resolve'. Simple in formulation, the theorem helped to give Marxism its enormous intellectual power, as well as the practical appeal which it held for so long. Marx, as it were, urged the Owl of Minerva into premature flight. For Hegel, history has a pattern, a teleology; but these can only be discerned retrospectively. Marx projected this teleology towards the future. He did so in a way that linked metaphysics, sociology and politics. The metaphysical idea was that history, in its more consequential and revolutionary moments, is made by the oppressed. Marx gave the dialectic of master and slave sociological clothing by grounding it in class struggle. In turn class struggle, promoting the victory of the proletariat as the 'universal class', became the means of a general emancipation from the burdens of the past – from a history made by human beings, but not in a self-conscious way.

Marx's historical scheme was interpreted very differently by his followers and largely rejected by many socialists, particularly those who favoured evolutionary rather than revolutionary socialism. Yet the notion that the humanly created problems of history must be humanly resolvable was common to all. (Not only conservatism, but liberalism also has tended to be more sceptical about this assumption.)

For centuries, socialists have argued, human beings were 'separated' from their history, which was something that happened to them rather than a human product; and nature was like an alien force because its motive powers were understood only through the action of gods or spirits. It seemed an entirely reasonable assumption to socialists that the more we can understand our own social life, and the more we come properly to understand nature, the more (as collective humanity) we shall be able to master both.

The fact that socialists claim to be an avant-garde has had a series of theoretical and political consequences. It has often endorsed a more or less open eurocentrism, or the conviction that the only things worth fighting for are those that are 'modern'. It has sometimes bred a distinct ruthlessness otherwise incompatible with the values socialists claim to hold. As in the domain of art, the avant-garde may come to scorn the attitudes and conduct of the masses, who almost inevitably have to be 'led' down the 'road' to socialism. The idea of the 'vanguard party' – like the avant-garde, a suspiciously military metaphor – has been criticized as an undemocratic addition to socialism for which Lenin was responsible. Yet some such notion is surely intrinsic to socialism, because of its assumption that it is in the 'forefront of history'. It is one aspect of a tensionful relation that exists between socialist thought and democracy, to which further reference needs to be made later.

One major strand of socialism – which has given rise to a variety of different doctrines – is the theme of equality. In this respect socialism radicalizes some of the ideas introduced in the American and French revolutions; but it also draws on styles of radicalism that have a much longer history. Durkheim's classic analysis of socialism provides a good sense of how and why this is so. Durkheim showed that socialism is concerned with two distinct sets of issues, one longstanding and the other much more recent. On the one hand, socialism stresses the primacy of the community over the individual and draws on what Durkheim calls 'communism'. Communism is a body of thought that can be traced back to classical times. It typically takes the form of utopian writings, such as those produced by Plato, Thomas More or Tommaso Campanella. According to communist writers, private property is a social evil; the accumulation of personally owned wealth is a moral danger which must be minimized as far as possible. Thus, as Durkheim represents Plato, 'wealth and all that relates to it is the primary source of public consumption. It is the thing that, stimulating individual egoisms, sets citizens to struggling and unleashes the internal conflicts which ruin states.'

Communism makes a virtue of radical egalitarianism. It seeks, in a more recent terminology, to 'level down' and is inspired by asceticism: the private must not be allowed to dominate over the communal and egoism should be eliminated almost completely. Communism is based on the regulation of consumption, not production. It is essentially an ethical order, seeing egalitarianism less as an end in itself than as a source of necessary moral control which protects the weak against the strong. 'To regulate individual consumption in such a way that it is everywhere equal and everywhere moderate – that is the formula of communism.'

Socialism, Durkheim argues, was the heir to communism, which it partly absorbed but from which it also remained distinct. For socialism, unlike communism, was a product of a particular time and place, a response to the political and industrial revolutions of the late eighteenth century and after. Socialism has its intellectual origins in the Enlightenment, and the *philosophes* were interested in reason rather than equality. In Peter Gay's words: 'Seeking to distinguish themselves, the *philosophes* had little desire to level all distinctions; seeking to be respected, they had no intention of destroying respectability.'[4]

There is a line of direct descent here, Durkheim points out, from the *philosophes* to the liberal political theorists and political economists of the nineteenth century. For these latter writers the production of wealth became seen as basic to individual happiness and to social life more generally. Emancipation came to mean the freeing of the forces of production from the constraints of tradition in a similar way to the liberation of reason from the limitations of established precept and dogma. According to the socialists, however, while the liberal theorists were right to emphasize the central role of economic activity in the social order, they failed to understand that industrial activity must be coordinated in a direct way. Socialism is concerned above all with production rather than consumption. It advocates 'the connection of all economic functions, or of certain of them, which are at the present time diffuse, to the directing and conscious centres of society'.[5] This does not imply, Durkheim stresses, that the economy should be subordinated to political control; rather, the economy and state become merged, so that 'politics' eventually disappears.

The tension that Durkheim diagnosed between ideals of equality and the directive control of economic activity constantly resurfaces in the history of socialism. Marx spotted the problem early on – and fervently denounced all types of 'utopian socialism' – but his resolution of it was ambiguous. He rejected the suggestion that wealth or income should be equalized and always saw the production of material prosperity as desirable rather than as a source of moral harm.

Yet if the centralized control of production is not mainly directed towards redistribution, does that mean that socialism has nothing to do with egalitarianism at all? In some of his writings, Marx sought to cope with the difficulty by introducing secondhand slogans whose full implications were never developed; for example, 'from each according to his ability, to each according to his needs!' He presumably believed that the disappearance of classes, and therefore of private property, in a socialist society would *ipso facto* diminish inequalities. But he nowhere adequately resolved the issue.

Durkheim's analysis suggests that the theme of equality is 'loose' in the development of socialist doctrines. It is inspired by ideals, including conceptions of justice, that have no generic connection with the core notion of the replacement of 'irrational' market forces by economic reason. Class division cannot provide the missing link, at least not completely, because as understood in most forms of socialism, and particularly Marx's version, class is not primarily about economic inequality but about exploitation. Marx's theory of class tends to link it more to the 'conscious control' pole of socialism than to the 'egalitarian' one; the main point about a class society as compared to a classless one is that the former does not allow the rational control of economic life.

For all branches of socialism the conscious control of production supposedly tends to be promoted by the very maturation of capitalism, although some have viewed this in a much more deterministic way than others. The *locus classicus* is again Marx, if only because Marx gave a technical explanation of the incipient socialization of the market. In its early phases of development, he accepted, the capitalistic economy involves competition between many independent producers. In premodern societies there was a direct and conscious tie between production and consumption – products were either bartered or bought and sold in the local marketplace, where producer and consumer came into direct contact. With the development of modern capitalism this tie between producers and consumers is severed; they are connected primarily by the interaction of price and profit. Labour power itself becomes a commodity to be bought and sold on the market; those forced to sell their labour power to employers to make a living are limited by the conditions of the labour contract as to the economic returns they can achieve. According to one's interpretation of Marx, capitalism produces either the absolute or the relative immiseration of the working class.

At the same time, although not for the same reasons, the capitalist economy is subject to recurrent periods of boom and crisis. During periods of economic depression there is large-scale unemployment. Although Marx argued that the existence of the 'industrial reserve army' is an important stabilizing factor in capitalism, he also clearly thought of it as irrational when viewed against the background of a possible socialist society, which would not have this fluctuating character. It is not an effective way to run an industrial economy for hundreds of thousands, even millions of people to be out of work, and plant idle, while many go without goods they need or desire.

According to Marx the very tendency of the capitalist economy to crisis leads towards its socialization – although not, without a revolution, to socialism. In crisis situations large firms tend to survive, and eventually to grow, at the expense of small ones, which are driven out of business. The socialization of production is of two kinds. Through a process of the concentration of capital, giant firms emerge which have monopolistic or oligopolistic control over their sector of industry, on a national and perhaps even on a world scale. Capital also becomes centralized: markets are increasingly subject to intervention by state banks and other government agencies. As these processes advance, so more conscious ties are reintroduced between production and consumption: large corporations and centralized financial organizations are able to influence the conditions under which markets function. This situation Marx calls 'capitalism without the capitalist'; it is capitalism with its contradictions become manifest, and on the point of its transcendence by socialism.

Socialists have quarrelled interminably over the details of Marx's account, but his view of the characteristic process of the development of capitalism, or something like it, is indispensable to socialist politics. Marx himself thought the triumph of socialism over capitalism 'inevitable' on the basis noted earlier – the choice is either socialism, or a retrograde collapse into barbarism. He also claimed that, when coupled to the theory of the revolutionary proletariat, this analysis represented his main original contribution, since he drew on orthodox political economy for much of the rest. The driving impulse of capitalism to expand, destroying other social and economic systems, produces both its polarizing tendencies and limits its historical life.

Conscious control means economic planning, which to be effective even in principle has to be largely centralized. In socialist theory, this forms a 'cybernetic model' of economic organization. The socialist economy (not the state, which 'disappears') is regulated through a 'higher order intelligence', the economic brain, which controls 'lower order' economic inputs and outputs. As one prominent author of the earlier part of the century put it, production and distribution will be regulated by 'the local, regional, or national commissars', who 'shape, with conscious foresight, the whole economic life of the communities of which they are the appointed representatives and leaders, in accordance with the needs of their members'.[6]

Socialists have argued that such an arrangement will encourage rather than inhibit diversity. In the words of Karl Kautsky, 'the greatest diversity and possibility of change will rule . . . The most manifold forms of property in the means of production – national, municipal, cooperatives of consumption and production, and private – can exist beside each other in a socialist society.'[7]

Right from the beginning some critics anticipated that things would not work out in this way. Capitalism, wrote Max Weber and Eugen Böhm-Bawerk, uses markets as signalling devices; attempts at conscious control of economic life, at least beyond a certain point, create not only economic inefficiency but rule by bureaucrats. More extreme versions of such arguments were later developed by authors such as Mises, Lionel Robbins and Hayek, with writers such as Oskar Lange on the opposing side, speaking up for socialism. In Von Mises's words, 'as soon as one gives up the conception of a freely established monetary price for goods of a higher order, rational production becomes completely impossible. Every step that takes us away from private ownership of the means of production and from the use of money also takes us away from rational economics.'[8]

Many socialists, particularly those of a more reformist temper, have accepted that central planning has major limitations and dangers if developed too far – however 'too far' might be defined. Most came to be supporters of the 'mixed economy'. While Keynesianism dominated in the West and Soviet Communism in the East, the views of Mises and the others of like mind were regarded by them as so extreme as to be eccentric. As one enthusiast wrote in the late 1940s, 'we are all *Planners* now . . . The collapse of the popular faith in *laissez-faire* has proceeded with spectacular rapidity . . . all over the world since the War.'[9] The conscious direction of economic life seemed, as Marx had declared, simply to replace the irrational by the rational.

Socialism and democracy

As befits a doctrine influenced so strongly by the American and French revolutions, socialism is closely tied up with ideals of democracy. Yet the relation of socialism to democracy is ambiguous and paradoxical. In most versions of socialism, 'democracy' plainly does not only mean liberal democracy, for socialists have normally been critical of the shortcomings of 'bourgeois' political institutions. From there onwards, one might be tempted to say, as in the case of equality, all is muddle. Marx's ideas about democracy, for example, have been subject to notoriously divergent interpretations.

A few main threads, however, can fairly readily be sorted out. Marx's critique of bourgeois democracy was essentially twofold. The democracy of his time he saw as a sham because it fell far short of its own claims to universality. The democratic rights supposedly open to everyone were in fact available only to the privileged few – adult, male owners of property. From this point of view it was a relatively easy theoretical step for Marx to connect such a situation with capitalistic class power. The capitalist state, in his view, could only tolerate the enfranchisement of 'its own' – the capitalist class and its hangers-on. A full generalization of democratic prerogatives simply could not be achieved in a capitalistic society. Thus some of Marx's followers were able to downgrade the importance of democracy in pursuit of a 'revolution first' perspective. Reformist socialism by definition refused this route, claiming that universal democratic rights could, and would have to be, achieved as part of the very process of transforming capitalism.

Indeed, reformist socialism saw an anti-revolutionary philosophy as a necessary defence against the potential corruption of socialism into an authoritarian system of rule. In the eyes of Sidney Webb, for example, socialism was inherently gradualist: 'No philosopher now looks for anything but the gradual evolution of the new order from the old, without breach of continuity or abrupt change of the entire social tissue at any point during the process.' And he added, 'important organic changes can only be . . . democratic, and thus acceptable to a majority of the people.'[10] Somewhat later on, T. H. Marshall made political rights, understood in much the same way, a key part of his account of the progressive formation of citizenship rights with the advance of socialism.

The fact that bourgeois democratic rights did become generalized within a capitalistic society (although certainly, as the reformist socialists anticipated, changing that society along the way) did not bring liberal and socialist theory together. For the reason why, we have to turn to the second strand of Marx's critique of democracy. This runs roughly as follows. Even if universalized, the prerogatives of bourgeois democracy are still at best partial – as rights of political participation they leave a lot to be desired. Here the theme of inequality enters. How can a society be democratic when resources are distributed so unequally that formal rights lose much of their meaning? The celebrated 'freedom of everyone to live in Mayfair', if they so wish, is not a generalizable freedom.

More reformist socialists diverge from Marx on this point.

Formal freedoms of political participation, they argue, can lead to real change in the distribution of resources, and in power, in situations that fall well short of revolution. For such freedoms are the basis of collective action which can redress pre-existing inequalities; this is the view, for example, of Marshall.

Liberal democracy is representative democracy and admits of no form of direct participation by those who are governed in processes of government. It is confined to the political domain: in the realm of production, the worker has no rights over his or her fate once having entered the gates of the workplace each day. Although Marx had no developed theory of participatory democracy, his musings on the programme of the Paris Commune do contain some hints about it. In a socialist society, Marx seems to have envisaged, forms of participatory democracy could be set up alongside, or more probably as part of, a merging of political and industrial democracy.

In spite of the favourable remarks he sometimes made about it, Marx probably did not expect multiparty democracy to survive in a socialist order. For him, after all, and for very many of his followers afterwards, political parties are expressions of class interests; they should disappear when class society is overcome. In spite of the attempts of some interpreters of Marx to downplay it, the Rousseauian element in Marx's views on democracy seems strong and is difficult, if not impossible, to reconcile with political pluralism. For Marx, democratization in a socialist society is one aspect of the disappearance of the state. A substantive democracy would return power to civil society, but therefore 'abolish' it along with the state itself. The difficulties to which this sort of position gives rise are well known and do not need to be explored in detail here. Well before the Soviet Union had tried to translate it into practice by developing the system of Soviets, its limitations and paradoxes had been indicated by Durkheim. Who is to protect democratic rights or define obligations in a democratic way, Durkheim quite properly asked, if the state is pulled down into civil society? This is a recipe either for a vacillating and impotent populism or – as became the case in the USSR – for authoritarianism.

Socialist critiques of liberal democracy have not lost their interest or relevance today. The thesis that 'liberal democracy is not enough' remains important – further processes of democratization, as will be discussed below, are possible and even demanded in modern societies if social cohesion is effectively to be preserved and squared with the advance of individual rights and obligations.

As in other areas, however, socialist thought – revolutionary or more reformist – is better equipped for critique than it is for reconstruction. The tension here between economic coordination and egalitarianism reveals itself as crucial. The Rousseauian features of Marx's thought, with all the inadequacies to which they give rise, mesh closely with his emphasis that socialism means replacing the irrationalities of capitalist economic enterprise with the directive control of economic life. Those socialists, on the other hand, who have leaned towards the egalitarian pole have either favoured anarchism over democracy or have seen political power as an instrument to be used to produce socioeconomic levelling – carried to its extreme, one might argue, in the policies of Pol Pot.

Reformist socialism, almost by definition, has accepted the importance of democracy for socialist goals, but the tension between central economic regulation and equality appears just as strongly among reformist socialists as among their more revolutionary counterparts. Democracy is taken to be of core importance to socialism, but is extraneous to it theoretically. Democracy essentially offers a framework within which socialist parties can peacefully rise to power and implement their programmes of change. Extending democracy means 'involving the people' in this way; but the dilemma of how to reconcile the 'rational direction' of economic life with equality remains. The ambiguities of the welfare state, as I shall seek to show later, reflect this tension.

Revolutionary socialism

The question of 'revolution versus reform' was one of the main fault-lines of socialism for many years, indeed, throughout most of its history. Marx was certainly a revolutionary, but he was relatively uninterested in revolution itself; the actual revolutionary process was in his eyes only the point of transition confirming basic changes that had already occurred in society. Others have seen revolution as a cathartic experience, some even arguing that bloody revolution is preferable to more peaceful transitions because it would more thoroughly do away with the detritus of past history. The hold of the idea of revolution, bloody or otherwise, has to be understood in relation to the Enlightenment, in which the project of 'clearing away the past' is central. Socialist revolution is to complete the process begun by preceding bour-geois revolutions, an escape from the past into a humanly determined future.

The attractiveness of the idea of revolution to those who have fallen under its sway, it has been said by some critics, comes from its chiliastic qualities and from a certain Romanticism. Yet it would be possible to argue exactly the opposite. What is compelling about the concept of revolution – once interpreted, not in its old sense of a return, but as a leap forward – is that it is a concentrated moment of Enlightenment release from tradition and inherited authority. In the less ecstatic forms of revolutionary socialism, including Marx's own writings, there is a clear theoret-ical explanation of the importance of revolution. Whether or not it happens through active battles on the streets, revolution is the expression of a 'Gestalt switch', a transition from one type of society to another.

This is why, to the revolutionary socialist, reformism is always suspect and might even be counterproductive. For halfway reforms can act as a palliative, deflecting energies that might otherwise produce more radical transitions. A whole generation of revolutionary activists saw the welfare state, for example, in these terms. Over the past two decades we have become so accustomed to critiques of the welfare state coming from the right, and its defence on the part of the left, that it has almost been forgotten that the welfare state used to pit left against left. The history of such clashes goes back at least as far as Marx and Engels, who felt let down not just by the timidities of most socialists in their adopted country, Britain, but by the large numbers of the working class who resolutely turned their minds away from revolution.

Revolution for many socialists was the leading edge of socialism in much the same way as socialism was supposedly in 'the vanguard of history'. Loss of the idea of revolution, as socialist revolution at any rate – for it is an aspiration that has surely died – is one of the main factors responsible for the 'shrinkage' of socialism which is visible everywhere today. Revolution stood for colour, boldness, the drama of a history seized hold of in the most forceful way possible. The activities of the reformists, by contrast, seemed timid and inadequate. Yet it is the 'revolutionary societies' which have crumbled, their vanguard troops packed away in history's lumber room.

Why did 'Western Marxists' take so long to see what the right had been telling them for many years – that Soviet Communism was economically hidebound and politically totalitarian? The answer to this question is that in fact they did see these things, or many of them did, and in some ways well before most critics from the liberal centre, if not from the right. Some Western Marxists were from the beginning savagely critical of the new society being constructed in Russia; they included the followers of Trotsky, but also several of the most prominent members of the Frankfurt School and numerous 'humanistic Marxists'. During the period when Keynesianism was in the ascendancy in the Western countries, the Soviet economy showed high growth rates. Many non-Marxist observers in the West, including its political leaders, took quite seriously Khrushchev's boast that 'we will bury you' because Soviet growth rates would outstrip those of the West. Herbert Marcuse's *Soviet Marxism*, first published in 1959, makes sobering reading alongside such views.[11]

In spite of its disaffection with the Soviet Union, Western Marxism was able to prosper intellectually in the postwar period for various reasons. One was that it devoted much of its energies to the critique of capitalism. Most Marxist authors saw the welfare state either as a positive barrier to the achievement of full socialism, or as only a halfway house on the route towards it. They were clear that the socialist society of the future would not be much, or at all, like the Soviet Union, but were as reluctant as Marx himself had been to specify the nature of this society in any detail. Another was that, for some while, when they did look for models of socialism, they were able to find them in the Third World. Mao's China, Castro's Cuba, and occasionally a few other revolutionary Third World countries, inspired the hopes of some Western Marxists – until the shortcomings of these societies became evident.

A further prop of Western Marxism was the theory of capitalist imperialism and Third World dependency. Socialist revolution was claimed to be the only way in which Third World countries could break free from their inferior position in the global capitalist order. If China and Cuba couldn't necessarily show the way to the future for the Western world itself, they could at least demonstrate to other less developed countries how they might prise themselves free from economic stagnation. Here there was something of a close allegiance between Western and Soviet Marxism, because Western Marxists saw Soviet support for Third World revolutionary movements as a progressive force.

The failure of socialism as a means of Third World development has been as much of a hammer-blow for Western Marxism as any of the developments in the more industrialized parts of the world. After the disappearance of Marxism, China turned to the introduction of capitalistic forms of economic enterprise and initiated a period of rapid economic development. Socialist states in Africa and elsewhere foundered and later it became clear that Cuban social reforms were dependent on large-scale Soviet economic support for whatever successes they achieved. Perhaps most important of all, the rapid development of the Far Eastern 'tigers' showed that Third World countries could initiate rapid and successful economic development through their own efforts – and within a capitalistic framework.

Revolutionary socialism, Soviet-style – its political brutalisms apart – worked as an economic theory for much the same time, and for much the same reasons, as Keynesianism. It offered a schema of economic development closely bound up with the state, in a context of simple modernization. In the Soviet Union, the power vested in the state was employed to generate processes of forced industrialization which, although they later came back to haunt the economy, made possible a break with the pre-existing semi-feudal order. The Soviet Union closed itself off from the rest of the international economy, or attempted to do so, and concentrated on areas of commerce confined to its 'imperial domain' of Eastern Europe.

Limits of the cybernetic model

The cybernetic model implicit in socialism as a whole, and developed in its most advanced way in Soviet Communism, I have suggested, was reasonably effective as a means of generating economic development in conditions of simple modernization. Reflexive modernization, coupled to globalization, introduces quite different social and economic circumstances.

If this view is correct, the idea of New Right authors that Mises and others were correct all along about the inherent defects of socialist planning must be treated with caution. Mises's main arguments against Soviet-type planning presume the inevitability of the incentive of self-enrichment, or the maximizing of profit and rent by all economic actors. His thesis also turns on knowledge and initiative. In a complex economy innumerable exchanges take place all the time, in terms of which prices have somehow to be set. This happens in circumstances subject to constant change. No 'intelligent centre', even with the most acutely insightful body of planners, could determine the proper prices of assets brought to the marketplace. Market pricing, coupled to other market mechanisms, generate information that not even a supercomputer (talked of at one point by Lange) could possibly provide. Attempts to subject markets to any sort of directive control will therefore damage their functioning.

Hayek contributed in a significant way to the elaboration of this view: markets bring into play knowledge of a practical, tacit kind. They are devices for discovering and making use of local knowledge for the potential benefit of all. It is not, or not only, because of its complex and mutable nature that the information provided by prices in competitive markets cannot be taken over by a guiding intelligence; it is because the knowledge involved is 'knowledge given to us only in use', knowledge 'stored in habits and in practice'. What is at issue as regards economic planning is the impossibility of turning essentially practical knowledge into a matter of economic calculation; many decisions, to be taken effectively, have to be made 'on the ground' through the use of tacit knowledge and practical skill. Successful planning on a comprehensive scale is shown to be an 'epistemic impossibility'.[12]

Here there are some close similarities to Oakeshott's discussion of tradition: 'knowing how' always precedes 'knowing that', and while the former can stand alone, the latter cannot.

For Oakeshott and Hayek, such practical knowledge depends on tradition – or, perhaps, is tradition. However, there is an inconsistency here, because no matter how flexible they might be, traditions are surely not going to provide the sort of innovative, quick-on-the-feet reactions involved in economic decision-making in fluctuating information environments. We could thus make something of an opposite argument. Some kinds of central economic planning were effective in the phase of simple modernization because of the influence of tradition and custom rather than in spite of it. Directive economic control can be successful, in other words, when people have relatively stable preferences and where their level of reflexive involvement with wider social and economic processes is relatively low.

Practical, local knowledge – and the autonomy which goes along with it – does indeed become vitally important in a detraditionalizing world. This is so because the reflexive individual (as citizen and consumer) is a 'moving target' who possesses local knowledge as well as a good deal of the information available to potential central planners themselves; and because this very reflexivity informs modes of action and reaction grounded in local practices. The Hayek–Oakeshott position is substantiated on this point, save that such practices are not usually traditional; and where they are traditional, traditional qualities are sustained or renewed in a reflexive way.

In sum, although not solely for the reasons given by Hayek and the others, the idea that the 'irrationalities' of capitalist enterprise can be overcome by the socializing of production can no longer be defended. With its dissolution, the radical hopes for so long carried by socialism are as dead as the Old Conservatism that once opposed them. A modern economy can tolerate, and prosper under, a good deal of central planning only so long as certain conditions hold – so long as it is primarily a national economy; social life is segmentalized rather than penetrated extensively by globalizing influences; and the degree of institutional reflexivity is not high. As these circumstances alter, Keynesianism falters and Soviet-type economies stagnate.

The 'epistemological objection' which Mises and Hayek registered against centralized planning is valid, but it takes on full force only when certain profound social changes take place. The argument from complexity is telling, but it is not conclusive. Even in the most complicated of economic circumstances, planning can very often achieve outcomes superior to those produced by markets and is required to protect situations or values that the market is likely to destroy. Planning of many sorts, whether conducted by states, business firms, or other groups remains an essential element of capitalistic functioning – as the critics of radical free market philosophies have consistently emphasized. Markets make possible bottom-up decision-making which is very often the condition of economic efficiency. Yet the importance of bottom-up decision-making, autonomy and decentralization is not confined to the domain of markets alone; in an era of high reflexivity, these make advances in other areas too. The cybernetic model of economic regulation declines along with the hierarchical model of bureaucratic efficiency.

If welfare socialism has become conservative and Communism is no more, might there still remain a case for a 'Third Way' – for 'market socialism'? Certainly many of the dissidents in Eastern Europe who helped bring down the Communist system thought so; they did not want to replace Communism with capitalism. And certain forms of market socialism continue to have their articulate defenders. I shan't attempt in this context to engage with what has become a complicated literature on the subject. There are good reasons, in my view, to argue that market socialism isn't a realistic possibility. I shall mention some of these very briefly but I don't pretend they would convince those who aren't already sceptical.

Third Way conceptions, which have often been influenced by the idea that Scandinavian social democracy could become a more fully fledged socialism, usually allocate a central role to worker collectives. In the Swedish debate about the Meidner Plan it was suggested that workers should be able to accumulate funds in business or corporate sectors in such a way as eventually to eliminate the shareholder. Workers would own shares in worker cooperatives and would have the right to elect managers;

in contrast to ordinary shareholdings, workers' shares could not be bought and sold on open markets.

There seems no reason to doubt that workers' cooperatives might prosper under some circumstances and for a certain time. The suggestion, however, that such successes could be generalized to the whole, or most, of the economic order is not at all convincing. If market pricing is necessary for efficiency in respect of other assets, including labour power, capital cannot be made exempt; the difficulties created in centrally planned economies would simply reappear. For no market criteria or discipline would be available to mobilize the effective use of accumulated investment capital.

Other problems are also fairly obvious. The regular election of managers might sometimes have economically beneficial outcomes; but in many situations it would not do so. Capital stored in enterprises would tend to become risk-aversive and firms might stagnate just as they did in the Soviet Union. There would be little motivation to take on new workers in existing collectives, because each person's shareholding would be reduced; there would be little mobility out of the cooperatives because the individuals concerned would not be able to take their shares with them. Market socialism would exhibit 'massive structural unemployment, technological stagnation, a chaotic political auction of capital and recurrent episodes of authoritarian intervention by the central government to prevent or redirect the abuses of the worker-cooperatives . . . market socialism is an unhappy halfway house between socialist central planning and the key institutions of market capitalism.'[13]

There is no Third Way of this sort, and with this realization the history of socialism as the avant-garde of political theory comes to a close.

Socialism and the welfare state

Socialism turned defensive becomes concentrated on the welfare state, the core concern of the reformist socialists. In interpreting the welfare state from the point of view of reformist socialism, I shall concentrate on two sources: T. H. Marshall's account, already briefly alluded to, of the development of citizenship; and the text that was once the bible of some groups in the British Labour Party, Anthony Crosland's *The Future of Socialism* (whose title I echo in this book).

According to Marshall, two opposing sets of influences have been at work in modern societies since their inception: the polarizing effects of the capitalist economy on the one side, and the integrating effects of citizenship on the other. Capitalist class divisions set large groupings of people apart from one another but (contrary to Marx, or to the usual interpretations of Marx) citizenship tends to produce social cohesion, because citizenship rights are held by virtually all members of the national community. Legal and political rights, which taken together form Marx's 'bourgeois rights', provide the freedoms, and the means of countervailing power, used to help secure 'social' or welfare rights. The creation of social rights, according to Marshall, is almost completely a phenomenon of the twentieth century. In the early development of capitalism, those who were unable to work in paid employment, or whose wages were very low, forfeited most of their prerogatives. Paupers placed in the workhouse were treated almost as criminals.

The achieving of political citizenship rights, Marshall says, has allowed the working class sufficient strength to make its voice heard. The outcome, in essence, is the welfare state. The welfare state is a class compromise which stops things well short of the revolution Marx predicted (and Marshall feared). In Marshall's words:

> In the twentieth century, citizenship and the capitalist class system have been at war . . . The expansion of social rights is no longer merely an attempt to abate the obvious nuisance of destitution in the lowest ranks of society . . . It is no longer content to raise the floor-level in the basement of the social edifice, leaving the superstructure as it was. It has begun to remodel the whole building.[14]

For a long while the most effective, or most listened to, critics of this position were Marxists. What Marshall had documented, they claimed, was an unstable state of affairs that could not in the longer term endure. Welfare institutions might mitigate some of the worst excesses of capitalist class divisions, and cover up some of the irrationalities of capitalistic markets, but at some point the strains of the compromise would become too great – only in a socialist society could such tensions be fully resolved. The strains *did* eventually become too great, but not primarily because of the factors pointed to by these critics; and the subsequent generation of critics came not from the left but from the right.

Marshall sought to distance himself from Marxism, while still adopting some of its premises. Crosland's starting point was similar. Many Marxists, he pointed out, reject the possibility of creating effective forms of welfare within capitalism; they believe that capitalism must first be overthrown. To show their views to be false, Crosland analysed the capitalist class system and the theory of capitalist collapse in some detail. Marx, he concluded, 'has little or nothing to offer the contemporary socialist, either in respect of practical policy, or of the correct analysis of our society, or even of the right conceptual tools or framework.'

Capitalism, in Crosland's view, does not lead to the immiseration of the working class, absolute or relative. The capital-owning class has not increased its power, as Marx thought it would; on the contrary, it has lost much of it. The state has taken over many of the decisions and resources that previously lay in the hands of private capital, as a result of the combined effects of nationalization and the growth of welfare institutions. Full employment – at that date thought quite unproblematic – also shifted the balance of power, according to Crosland, from management to labour. As a result a country like Britain can no longer properly be called a capitalist society at all.

If capitalism has disappeared, what need is there for socialism? Socialism, Crosland concludes – like so many before him – has no precise meaning. The only common characteristic of socialist doctrines is their ethical content. Socialism is the pursuit of ideas of social cooperation, universal welfare, and equality – ideas brought together by a condemnation of the evils and injustices of capitalism. It is based on the critique of individualism and depends on a 'belief in group action and "participation", and collective responsibility for social welfare'.

The welfare state, according to Crosland, has already gone quite a way towards achieving these objectives. The

> full-employment welfare state . . . is a society of exceptional merit and quality by historical standards, and by comparison with pre-war capitalism. It would have seemed a paradise to many early socialist pioneers. Poverty and insecurity are in the process of disappearing. Living standards are rising rapidly; the fear of unemployment is steadily weakening; and the ordinary young worker has hopes for the future which would never have entered his father's head.

Yet there is still some way further to travel – towards yet greater equality, fewer class divisions and less 'avoidable social distress'. Further economic redistribution of wealth is called for; but the main point of future policies, Crosland argues, must be to reduce 'social' inequalities and conflicts. 'Social resentment' comes mainly from a situation in which people are not able to find a place in society commensurate with their talents – where those in positions of wealth or power can perpetuate their privileges across the generations. Equal opportunity is not enough. Greater social equality would mean a more egalitarian educational system, a reduction in inherited wealth and the further reorganization of industry. 'High-level industrial democracy', by which Crosland means mainly corporatism, should be fostered. Further nationalization of basic industries is recommended, although Crosland recognizes that it is no panacea – nationalized industries, like those in private ownership, can become inefficient and some sort of competition is generally worthwhile.

Crosland's discussion concludes with something of an abrupt change of gear, a call for a critique of the more sober versions of socialism, a requirement for more 'liberty and gaiety in private life':

> We need not only higher exports and old-age pensions, but more open-air cafés, brighter and gayer streets at night, later closing-hours for public houses, more local repertory theatres, better and more hospitable hoteliers and restaurateurs, brighter and cleaner eating-houses, more riverside cafés, more pleasure-gardens on the

Battersea model, more murals and pictures in public places, better designs for furniture and pottery and women's clothes[!], statues in the centre of new housing-estates[?], better designed street-lamps and telephone kiosks and so on *ad infinitum*.

For 'we do not want to enter the age of abundance, only to find that we don't have the values which might teach us how to enjoy it.'[15]

A preliminary assessment

Over the several decades since the work of Marshall and Crosland was first published, by and large the economic changes they expected and advocated have not occurred – as all of us now know. Full employment is a distant memory in most Western countries, and the welfare systems they took to be firmly established look distinctly fragile. The neoliberals appropriated the future-oriented radicalism which was once the hallmark of the bolder forms of socialist thinking – and which, in spite of his concluding flourish, is noticeably muted in Crosland's discussion. Today, as noted in the opening chapter, the conservative has become radical and the radical conservative. The main emphasis of socialist conservatism has turned towards a protection of the now embattled welfare state.

What went wrong? When they were first written, the ideas of Marshall and Crosland were more penetratingly attacked from the left rather than the right and aspects of this critique retain their interest and importance today. Marshall wrote of the development of citizenship rights as a sort of evolutionary process, much as Crosland did about the consolidating of the welfare state. Citizenship rights, and some of the main features of welfare institutions, however, have not just 'evolved'. They have been achieved in some part as a result of active struggle – and they are consequently much more a focus for tension and conflict than either of these writers suggests. Marshall's 'legal rights', for example, are not a once-and-for-all achievement. How far they are real rather than formal rights for certain marginal groups, how they should be interpreted – these are questions intrinsic to modern democratic politics, not only stages in the formation of the welfare state. They are bound up with issues of civic order that are considerably more complex than is implied in Marshall's account.

Marshall's 'economic citizenship rights' and Crosland's 'economic successes' of the welfare state do not represent a means of softening class divisions in the way suggested. Rights of welfare are a pivot of class divisions and of various structural conflicts, rather than dissolving or muting them. On this point Marshall and Crosland listened too closely to Marx in the very process of opposing him. The welfare state is neither the result of beneficent government (Marshall and Crosland) nor an instrument used to keep the working class in its place (Marxism). It is a tensionful combination of those two strands of socialism of which Durkheim spoke. One strand, that represented by Keynesianism, was concerned with the directive control of economic life; the other was concerned with the protection of the economically under-privileged. For some while global economic circumstances made this combination not only tolerable, but even propitious. When these circumstances altered the edifice started to decay.

For reasons that will be explored in subsequent chapters, neither the welfare state nor the more general aim of the conscious socialization of economic life can be defended in ways which, until relatively recently, made sense. The following considerations are relevant here:

1 The limits of the conception of economic citizenship advanced by Marshall are by now thoroughly exposed. Legal and political rights cannot be taken as 'established' and as a stable basis of 'social rights'. They imply instead a battle for democracy, involving whole sections of the population (such as women) who had not yet at Marshall's time fully broken away from their traditional statuses. 'Economic citizenship' was seen by Marshall in too passive and also in too patronizing a way; and the connection between citizenship and the nation-state was taken for granted rather than energetically explored.

2 Global economic competition, much intensified, gives a new centrality to productivity, whether of capital or labour, understood as a marginal capacity instead of an overall total. The circumstances that have brought this about will have to be analysed later in more detail. This development has the conse-

quence, however, of making attempts to use the welfare state as a redistributive mechanism even more difficult than before. Redistributive policies are likely to backfire, reducing levels of wealth creation, therefore risking suboptimal outcomes even for those who are supposed to benefit most from them.

3 Although the details are endlessly debated, the welfare state has been less than wholly effective in countering poverty and bad patches in individuals' incomes over the life-cycle. The conclusion that 'almost all public expenditure on the social services . . . benefits the better off to a greater extent than the poor' is one most researchers have reached. Direct transfer of income everywhere seems to have been the main form of assistance redressing the position of the long-term underprivileged.

4 The welfare state is tied to an implicit or more open model of traditional family and gender systems – or, more accurately, what these are assumed to be. Welfare programmes have been aimed mainly at supporting male participation in the paid labour force, with a 'second tier' of household programmes oriented towards families without a male breadwinner. Welfare systems after 1945 were set up at a time when women's participation in labour force was still relatively low and domestic chores went ignored in the statistics of 'work'. Those in the 'masculine sectors' of the welfare state were treated as the principal bearers of rights and purchasers of consumer services, while those in the 'feminine' sectors were regarded as dependent clients – this situation reflected, and probably helped sustain, the patriarchal family.

5 While this is in some ways a highly controversial matter – partly at least because of its unscrupulous use by some neoliberal authors – welfare dependency, as a set of attitudes and a culture rather than as simply an economic condition, is a real phenomenon. Instead of integrating individuals into the wider society in the ways Marshall and Crosland anticipated, welfare provisions sometimes lead, if not to 'passivity', then to a situation where welfare recipients become alienated from the broader social order.

6 The fact that the welfare state becomes a focus of conflict as much as reducing it puts limits on the fiscal resources that can be generated to fund its services. This issue has been thoroughly aired since the mid-1970s and although their proposed remedies

for the situation differ, there is some measure of agreement between right and left critics of the welfare state about its structural limitations. The 'taxpayer's revolt' places limits on the resources governments can muster to pay for the welfare state in circumstances where they have to compete for marginal votes in the electoral system. This squeeze tends to get tighter rather than to relax. As levels of voter dealignment grow, the parties can rely less and less on their established supporters alone and have to capture those in the middle; a resistance develops to paying marginal rates of tax once broadly acceptable to those who carried the burden.

7 As New Right authors have stressed, welfare state bureaucracies tend to become inflexible and impersonal. They can appear to those towards whom they channel resources as indifferent, or even actively hostile, 'authorities' over whom individuals have no control. Nationalized industries are often inefficient and wasteful; welfare agencies become unresponsive to the needs of those they are supposed to succour.

8 A mature welfare state, with a fairly high degree of nationalization of industry, once seemed a means of securing full employment – understood, however, as the paid work of men. As women enter the paid labour force in increasing numbers, and non-paid tasks of various kinds, including housework, are increasingly recognized as work, 'full employment' becomes a problematic notion. Moreover, high rates of unemployment understood in a quite orthodox sense add to the financial difficulties of the welfare state because of payments claimed by those out of work.

9 The pattern of welfare payments alters in relation to changes in class divisions (some of these associated with the growing affluence of those in stable paid employment), demographic changes, changes affecting the family, such as increasing divorce rates, and other factors. These shifts influence the fiscal problems of the welfare state, and partly add to the responsibilities it must shoulder. For example, demographic changes mean that a substantial proportion of the population at any one time is over the normal age of retirement, and may be entitled to claim benefits from the state.

10 Last, but definitely not least, welfare institutions only touch

on some aspects of individuals' lives to which radical politics might be thought relevant. This observation connects to some of the objections conservatives have put forward against socialism. The welfare state confines itself largely to economic matters and leaves other issues aside, including emotional, moral and cultural concerns. The conservative seeks to deal with these things mainly through the defence of tradition. Given their progressive orientation, socialists cannot take this tack. Thus, in general, socialists have been ill-prepared to cope with issues of life politics, although these are actually intrinsic to questions of welfare.

Such an absence is quite evident in Crosland's analysis. The concluding section of Crosland's book, in which he discusses how people might develop fulfilling lives in a socialist society, is almost completely disconnected from the arguments of the bulk of the work. It reads as an afterthought, a declaration that socialists are not the killjoys that many of their opponents have taken them to be. The tone is that of a personal manifesto, rather than of a series of conclusions flowing from the theoretical framework of the study.

In the light of this formidable list of problems, it is hardly surprising that discussion of the welfare state by socialists today has switched to the defensive. Such a strategy is not just a reaction to the attacks of the neoliberals, or to their policies where they have been in power; it is a sobriety enforced by the problems which the welfare state faces.

3

The Social Revolutions of our Time

If the terms right and left no longer have the meaning they once did, and each political perspective is in its own way exhausted, it is because our relationship (as individuals and as humanity as a whole) to modern social development has shifted. We live today in a world of manufactured uncertainty, where risk differs sharply from earlier periods in the development of modern institutions. This is partly a matter of scope. Some risks now are 'high-consequence' risks – the dangers they represent potentially affect everyone, or large numbers of people, across the face of the globe. Equally important, however, is the contrast in their origins. Manufactured uncertainty refers to risks created by the very developments the Enlightenment inspired – our conscious intrusion into our own history and our interventions into nature.

The high-consequence risks which face us in the present day, and many other risk environments of a less extensive sort, are social in origin. The risks associated with global warming, the punctured ozone layer, large-scale pollution or desertification are the result of human activities. They go along with a diversity of other humanly produced risks, such as that of large-scale war, the disruption of the global economy, the over-population of the planet, or 'techno-epidemics' – illnesses generated by technological influences, such as those producing pollution of air, water or food.

In some areas of human activity, of course, levels of security are higher than they used to be. Thus journeys that could once be undertaken by only the most intrepid of explorers, in the face of numerous hazards, can now be made by anyone (with the ability to pay) in comfort and relative safety. But new uncertainties also open up almost everywhere. The uncertainties inherent in high-consequence risks are perhaps particularly worrying, because we have little or no way of 'testing them out'. We cannot learn from them and move on, because if things go wrong the results are likely to be cataclysmic. With these we are condemned to grapple for the indefinite future. We can suspect that the correct strategies have been pursued only when certain events do not happen, rather than when others do; and for a long while all we shall be able to say effectively is: so far, so good.[1]

High-consequence risks are at some distance from our individual lives. Urgent though they may in fact be, in most matters of everyday life they seem remote. Our daily actions are nevertheless thoroughly infected by manufactured uncertainties of a less inclusive kind. For on an individual or collective, as well as a global level, the accumulation of reflexively ordered knowledge creates open and problematic futures which we have, as it were, to 'work on' as we go along in the present. As we do so, we influence processes of change, but full control of them chronically eludes our grasp.

Recognizing this, some have recently suggested that human beings should again treat as external that which we have sought to master. The Promethean outlook which so influenced Marx should be more or less abandoned in the face of the insuperable complexity of society and nature. A drawing-back from the ambitions of the Enlightenment is surely necessary. Yet the social and material worlds are now largely reflexively organized; there is no way of withdrawing from such reflexive engagement, however conscious we might be of the problematic consequences it can have and the paradoxes to which it gives rise. The 'new medievalism' has right on its side in so far as it recognizes that manufactured risk cannot be dealt with exclusively in terms of the further development of technical knowledge. The problems posed by such risk are irreducibly political and moral. Thus the decision to build a nuclear power station cannot be a purely technical one, made in terms of neutral risk assessment. There is an issue of political prudence, in John Locke's sense, here. Even

the risk of accidental damage cannot be exactly calculated, let
alone risks of terrorism, the use of reactor plutonium for war or,
by definition, as yet unknown polluting elements which might
affect the lives of future generations.

Simple and reflexive modernization

The creation of a world of manufactured uncertainty is the result
of the long-term development of the industrial order. Yet for a
long while its characteristics were suppressed by the dominance
of simple modernization. In such modernization, capitalist or
industrial evolution seems a predictable process, even if understood in a revolutionary way in the manner of Marx. Science and
the technological advances associated with it are generally
accepted as embodying claims to authoritative truth; while industrial growth has a clear 'direction'.

Reflexive modernization responds to different circumstances.
It has its origins in the profound social changes briefly referred
to in the introduction and which need to be spelled out more
fully here: the impact of globalization; changes happening in
everyday and personal life; and the emergence of a post-
traditional society. These influences flow from Western modernity, but now affect the world as a whole – and they refract back
to start to reshape modernization at its points of origin.

The current period of globalization is not simply a continuation
of the expansion of capitalism and of the West. If one wanted to
fix its specific point of origin, it would be the first successful
broadcast transmission made via satellite. From this time
onwards, instantaneous electronic communication across the
globe is not only possible, but almost immediately begins to enter
the lives of many millions. Not only can everyone now see the
same images at the same time; instantaneous global communication penetrates the tissue of everyday experience and starts to
restructure it – although becoming restructured in turn, as a
continuous process.

Globalization is not the same as the development of a 'world
system', and it is not just 'out there' – to do with very large-scale
influences. It is also an 'in here' phenomenon, directly bound up

with the circumstances of local life. We shouldn't think of globalization as a unitary process tending in a single direction, but as a complex set of changes with mixed and quite often contradictory outcomes. Globalization implies the idea of a world community, but does not produce it; such a community is signalled as much by the globalization of 'bads' as by integrative influences.

Globalizing influences are fracturing as well as unifying, create new forms of stratification, and often produce opposing consequences in different regions or localities. These events and changes no longer pass just from the West to the rest. Thus the industrial development of the East is directly bound up with the deindustrialization of the older industries in the heart of the core countries in the global order. Two areas that exist directly alongside one another, or groups living in close proximity, may be caught up in quite different globalizing systems, producing bizarre physical juxtapositions. The sweatshop worker may be just across the street from a wealthy financial centre.

On the cultural level, globalization tends to produce cultural diasporas. Communities of taste, habit and belief frequently become detached from place and from the confines of the nation also. Diasporic cultural traits are quite often standardizing, and as such influenced by mass advertising and cultural commodification. Styles of dress, from suits to blue jeans, taste in music, films or even religion take on global dimensions. Cultural diasporas are no longer carried solely through the physical movement of peoples and their cultures, important though this still is. Even – and perhaps sometimes particularly – in situations of poverty people become involved in diasporic cultural interchanges. As elsewhere in globalizing processes, however, there is not a one-way movement towards cultural homogeneity. Globalization leads also to an insistence on diversity, a search to recover lost local traditions, and an emphasis on local cultural identity – seen in a renewal of local nationalisms and ethnicities.

Globalizing influences tend to evacuate out local contexts of action, which have to be reflexively reordered by those affected – although those reorderings also, conversely, affect globalization as well. Major changes therefore occur in the very warp and weave of everyday life, affecting even the constitution of our personal identities. The self becomes a reflexive project and, increasingly, the body also. Individuals cannot rest content with an identity that is simply handed down, inherited, or built on a traditional status. A person's identity has in large part to be discovered, constructed, actively sustained. Like the self, the body is no longer accepted as 'fate', as the physical baggage that comes along with the self. We have more and more to decide not just who to be, and how to act, but how to look to the outside world.

The growth in food disorders is a negative index of the advance of these developments on the level of everyday life. Anorexia, bulimia and other food pathologies still tend to be concentrated in First World countries, but are now also starting to appear in Third World societies too. In many parts of the world people starve for no fault of their own, but because they live in conditions of extreme poverty. Their emaciated bodies bear witness to the intensity of global inequalities. The shrunken body of the anorexic looks physically identical, but reflects very different social and material circumstances. The anorexic is 'starving to death in a sea of abundance'. Anorexia happens in a world where, for very large numbers of people, for the first time in history, copious quantities of food are available, well beyond what is necessary to meet basic nutritional needs.[2]

Anorexia and bulimia do not come only from a Western emphasis on slimness, but from the fact that eating habits are formed in terms of a diversity of choices about foodstuffs. There is a close and obvious association here with globalization. The invention of container transport and new ways of the freezing of foods – innovations dating from only a few decades ago – meant that foods could be stored for long periods and shipped all over the world. Since that date, all those living in more affluent countries and regions have been on a diet; that is to say, they have to make active decisions about how and what to eat, in respect of foodstuffs available more or less all the year. Deciding what to eat is also deciding 'how to be' in respect of the body – and for individuals subject to specific social tensions, particularly young women, the iron self-discipline of anorexia results.[3]

Anorexia is a defensive reaction to the effects of manufactured uncertainty on everyday life. Our day-to-day lives, one can say, have become experimental in a manner which parellels the 'grand experiment' of modernity as a whole. In many situations of social life we cannot choose but to choose among alternatives – even if we should choose to remain 'traditional'. 'Everyday experiments' become an intrinsic part of our daily activities, in contexts in which information coming from a diversity of sources – local knowledge, tradition, science and mass communications – must in some way be made sense of and utilized. Tradition more and more must be contemplated, defended, sifted through, in relation to the awareness that there exists a variety of other ways of doing things.

The experimental character of daily life, it is important to see, is constitutive. How we tackle the decisions that have to be made in the course of our actions helps structure the very institutions we are reacting to. Nowhere is this more obvious than in the field of personal relations. Individuals have to decide today not only when and whom to marry, but whether to marry at all. 'Having a child' need not any longer have anything to do with marriage, and is a precious and difficult decision for both men and women, far from the circumstances of the past when such a thing, in many situations, seemed more or less natural. One even has to settle what one's 'sexuality' is, as well as grasp what 'relationships' are and how they might best be constructed. All these things are not decisions made about given contexts of action; they help define and reshape, in a mobile way, what those contexts are and become.

The evacuation of local contexts of action – the 'disembedding' of activities – can be understood as implying processes of intensified detraditionalization. We are the first generation to live in a thoroughly post-traditional society, a term that is in many ways preferable to 'postmodern'. A post-traditional society is not a national society – we are speaking here of a global cosmopolitan order. Nor is it a society in which traditions cease to exist; in many respects there are impulses, or pressures, towards the sustaining or the recovery of traditions. It is a society, however, in which tradition changes its status. In the context of a globalizing, cosmopolitan order, traditions are constantly brought into contact with one another and forced to 'declare themselves'.

The modern social order came into being in the context of a break with the past. The 'two great revolutions' which initiated the modern period each in their way were detraditionalizing forces. The spread of capitalistic production uprooted many local communities and dissolved many local customs and practices. The universalizing codes of democracy treat political constitutions as having to be made, not as inherited from the past. Yet the stabilizing of simple modernization depended also on the remoulding of tradition. New traditions were invented, such as those of nationalism and renewed forms of religion. Other traditional traits, such as those affecting gender and the family, became recast during the late eighteenth and the nineteenth centuries.

The world marked by simple modernization was a culturally diverse one. Its cultural diversity, however, depended in a substantial way on the continuance of geographical segregation. This was true even within the developed countries. Working-class communities associated with certain types of industry, for example, came into being only after the industrial revolution, but often established their own local traditions. Today we see these traditions breaking down again, or becoming altered, almost everywhere.

At a time of thoroughgoing detraditionalization, those who hold to traditions have to ask themselves, and are asked by others, why. Globalization here intersects with active struggles and confrontations. Thus feminist movements have challenged traditional conceptions of, and practices involved with, gender. They have sought to bring into public discourse that which remained latent in gender traditions. 'Femininity' is an open matter; and now masculinity, for so long something taken for granted, has been opened to scrutiny.

The profound influence of detraditionalizing influences explains why the concept and the existence of fundamentalism have become so important. The fundamentalist, as I have said, is someone who seeks to defend tradition in the traditional way – in circumstances where that defence has become intrinsically problematic. Fundamentalism's 'insistence' on tradition and its emphasis on 'purity' are only understandable in these terms.

The term fundamentalism was first applied, in a religious context, at about the turn of the century, to refer to a defence of Protestant orthodoxy against the encroachments of modern thought.[4] It has only come into wider usage over the past thirty years or so – something that expresses the very recency of the detraditionalizing forces to which it corresponds.

Fundamentalism is not a long-term reaction to modernity, as the quite recent nature of its development indicates. The defence of tradition only tends to take on the shrill tone it assumes today in the context of detraditionalization, globalization and diasporic cultural interchanges. The point about fundamentalism is not its defence of tradition as such, but the manner of its defence in relation to a world of interrogation and dialogue. Defending tradition in the traditional way means asserting its ritual truth in circumstances in which it is beleaguered. Refusing the discursive engagements which a world of cosmopolitan communication tends to enforce, fundamentalism is protecting a *principle* as much as a set of particular doctrines. This is why fundamentalist positions can arise even in religions (like Hinduism and Buddhism) which have hitherto been very ecumenical and tolerant of other beliefs.

If this view is correct, the concept of fundamentalism should not be applied only to the area of religion. Fundamentalisms – defending tradition in the traditional way – can arise in any basic domain of social life subject to detraditionalization. These include ethnic relations, nationalism, gender and the family. Religious fundamentalisms, as is well known, tend to overlap with these other contexts. A Protestant fundamentalist, for example, is likely to have strong beliefs about the need to preserve 'traditional' forms of the nation, family and so forth. Yet the fact that the notion of fundamentalism can be applied so widely has nothing directly to do with the spill-over of religious beliefs into these fields. It comes from the fact that these are all contexts occupied by tradition, but which are now becoming discursively forced into the open.

Detraditionalization not only affects the social world, but influences, as it is influenced by, the transformation of nature. Tradition, like nature, used to be an 'external' context of social life, something that was given and largely unchallengeable. The end of nature – as the natural – coincides with the end of tradition – as the traditional.

Social reflexivity is both condition and outcome of a post-traditional society. Decisions have to be taken on the basis of a more or less continuous reflection on the conditions of one's action. 'Reflexivity' here refers to the use of information about the conditions of activity as a means of regularly reordering and redefining what that activity is. It concerns a universe of action where social observers are themselves socially observed; and it is today truly global in scope. Anyone who doubts that such is the case might do well to consider the changing status of anthropology. In the era of simple modernization, stamped by the dominance of the West, anthropology was the study of peoples who, by and large, did not answer back. An anthropologist would visit an alien culture; on his or her return, a monograph would be written and deposited in the library.

Such a situation no longer holds. In the depths of the jungle, anthropologists are likely to encounter native peoples who are familiar with some anthropological ideas or even texts. Ethnologies are used to interpret local cultures, reconstruct lost traditional skills and habits, and count as evidence in courts of law. Such phenomena are often important in power struggles. Thus the idea of the Australian 'aboriginal' or the North American 'Indian' was a Western one, but these constructs have been deployed by those to whom they refer to intervene in local and national politics – and even in disputes before international courts.

Revived or protected traditions, as we all know, can easily degenerate into kitsch – reflexive awareness of this ever-present possibility is actually one of the driving forces of fundamentalism. Thus the novelist Yukio Mishima made a celebrated, if futile, attempt to revive declining Samurai values and practices in postwar Japan. The endeavour, which culminated in his ritual suicide, seemed somewhat absurd to most Japanese, but had a certain dignity. One couldn't, probably, say the same of the inhabitants of Suya Mura, a Japanese village made famous (in Japan as well as elsewhere) by an anthropological study written by John Embree. Embree's wife revisited the area where she had carried out the fieldwork with her husband some fifty years earlier. She found that the villagers were less interested in reminiscing than in making use of her presence in their attempts to turn the municipality into a tourist spot – as 'Japan's anthropological village'.[5]

In a society of high reflexivity the regular appropriation of expertise – in all its many forms – tends to replace the guidance of tradition. This is by definition an energetic society, not a passive one. Even where they stick by traditions, or recreate them, individuals, groups and collectivities are more or less compelled to take an active stance towards the conditions of their existence. Not just social movements, but self-help groups of all kinds, are a distinctive feature of a post-traditional order – they may be purely local, but often have globalizing implications and participate in global diasporas.

Structural consequences

The driving expansionism of capitalistic enterprise continues to fuel globalizing processes, as it has done in the past. Yet capitalism – as will be discussed further below – was never the sole influence on globalization, and today its impact across the world is more complex and many-sided than was previously the case.

With the fall of the Soviet Union and the redirection of economic growth mechanisms in China and other remaining Communist societies, there is a world capitalist economy in a more complete sense than ever before. However, that economy is much more thoroughly infused with reflexive mechanisms than it once was; and it is increasingly decentred, no matter what power Western states and agencies continue to hold over what was 'the periphery'. Socialist theorists of 'the development of underdevelopment' had an easy target to blame for the ills of the world – the influence of capitalism. However critical one might still want to be of unfettered processes of capitalist enterprise, that target has now become much more elusive. Conspiracy-style theories of global disparities don't have the purchase they once seemed, to some observers at least, to have.

The global spread of the capitalist economy is a major influence on the difficulties of the welfare state in the affluent countries and very substantially affects class relations, in ways to be explored later. When not counterbalanced by other forces, capitalism retains its tendency to produce polarizations of income, both within and between different countries. Those states which are able to fund developed welfare systems are able to hold off this tendency with considerable success, but only at the cost of increasing social and fiscal strain.

Neoliberal interpretations of economic development insist that the paring down of welfare provisions is the necessary condition of competitiveness in a globalizing economy. According to such interpretations, either a Pareto-type effect pertains in economic growth processes in open economies, combined with 'trickle down'; or widening inequalities are simply the price to be paid for competitiveness. Much hangs on whether or not such a view is correct, for it is the key argument advanced to insist that leftist thinkers have paid insufficient attention to supply-side considerations in their analysis of the 'welfare state compromise'.

I shall suggest in subsequent chapters that the terms of reference of this debate need to be thoroughly revised. Here it is enough to note that widening economic inequalities within societies are not, certainly not necessarily, the condition of increasing overall prosperity. On the contrary, increasing equality can accompany fast economic growth, as measured by conventional indices, and very possibly may actively contribute to it. Thus in the Asian economies which have leaped to prominence over the past three or four decades, the incomes of lower-paid workers have grown both in absolute terms and relative to executives and entrepreneurs. South Korea and Taiwan, for example, have developed rapidly from the mid-1960s at the same time as the gap between rich and poor has narrowed; while in many African and Latin American countries, conversely, economic stagnation has been accompanied by a decline in the relative income of those at the bottom.

We have to be careful about what increasing equalization means here, for reasons I shall subsequently go into at some length. The successful Asian countries do not rely on Western-style welfare state mechanisms to create equalization, but instead provide means for poorer groups actively to improve their life circumstances. Because of their sheer numbers, poorer people in the aggregate have much greater resources than the rich. Moreover, in the Asian economies poorer people 'save' by investing in others with whom they are closely linked, in family or friendship networks. The payoff of 'investments' of this form is to be found in increased social solidarity – but these probably also have important implications for economic productivity. In societies where the gap between rich and poor is very large, such 'investments' tend not to be made.

The globalizing of capitalist economic relations would seem on the face of things to leave large business corporations in a dominant position within the economies of states and in the world economy as a whole. And they do indeed wield great power, able as they are to move capital investments from place to place, often with scant regard to the impact on the lives of local populations affected. At the same time, the demonizing of the large corporations, so popular among some sections of the left at one time, does not make much sense now.

Globalizing influences tend to break down the formation of monopolies or oligopolies such as are often found within national economies. The celebrated propensity of capitalist production towards monopoly probably depended in fact on collaborative connections between the state and capital which are now being undermined. Like other organizations, the large companies face an economic environment hostile to fixed bureaucratic orders. It doesn't follow, as some have suggested, that the giant corporations are likely to become wholly dismembered, but it would be difficult to argue that present-day economic conditions are leading to an untramelled extension of their economic or social power.

The big companies influence new forms of social and economic regionalization, but they are not necessarily the main agents involved. Changing patterns of regionalization respond to wider aspects of globalization or, more accurately, to shifting relations of the local and global. As elsewhere, processes of regionalization are dialectical; many pre-existing local communities disintegrate or become substantially restructured, but these self-same changes also promote local communal mobilization.

The combined effects of globalization and social reflexivity alter the character of stratification systems within the economically developed societies as well as elsewhere. Much has been made in the recent sociological literature of the consequences of the shrinking of blue-collar work and the concomitant rise in the proportions of people in white-collar and professional occupations – changes which intersect in a complex way with the widespread entry of women into the paid labour force. Such changes are undeniably of great importance, affecting as they do the class system and also the political life of modern societies; and these changes are themselves heavily affected by globalization.

Equally important, however, is the fact that the growth of social reflexivity produces forms of 'double discrimination' affecting the underprivileged. To the effects of material deprivation are added a disqualification from reflexive incorporation in the wider social order. Exclusionary mechanisms here are normally both social and psychological. In other words, they concern not only subjection to modes of power coming from the technical control of knowledge-based systems, but also attack the integrity of the self: this is something about which I shall have a good deal to say in later chapters.

The advent of life politics

The political outlook of the left – and therefore, in counter-reaction, the right – has always centred on a notion of emancipation. Emancipation means freedom, or rather freedoms of various kinds: freedom from tradition, from the shackles of the past; freedom from arbitrary power; and freedom from the constraints of material poverty or deprivation. Emancipatory politics is a politics of life chances. It is about enhancing autonomy of action.

Emancipatory politics obviously remains important to any radical political programme. It is joined today, however, by a series of concerns coming from the changes just described – from detraditionalization plus the disappearance of nature. These concerns raise issues of life politics. Life politics, and the disputes and struggles connected with it, are about how we should live in a world where everything that used to be natural (or traditional) now has in some sense to be chosen, or decided about.

Life politics is a politics of identity as well as of choice. One reason why debates between right and left have become so often unappealing to many of the lay population is that they simply don't address these new fields of action. It would be a basic error to see life politics as only a concern of the more affluent. In some respects, in fact, the contrary is true. Some of the poorest groups today (and not only in the developed societies) come up against problems of detraditionalization most sharply. Thus women are now leaving marriages in large numbers, and in conjunction with this assertion of autonomy are recasting their lives. Many, however, become part of the 'new poor', especially if they are lone-parent heads of households. Cast down economically, they are also called on to pioneer new forms of domestic life and kin relations.

Life politics is not, or not only, a politics of the personal; the factors involved have become generic to many aspects of social life, including some of very wide span indeed. Ecological and feminist concerns are of major importance in life-political struggles, but they certainly do not exhaust them. Instead, thinking in life-political terms helps explain just why they have come to such prominence. They are reactions to, and engagements with, a world precisely where tradition is no longer traditional, and nature no longer natural.

Life politics also covers quite orthodox areas of political involvement: for example, work and economic activity. Like so many other areas of social life, work was until recently experienced by many as fate. Most men could expect to be in the paid labour force for much of their lives, while women were often confined to the domestic milieu. Protest against such 'fate' was first of all mostly emancipatory in impulse. This was true of the union movement, dominated by men, which developed most strongly among manual workers, who more than anyone else experienced work as a given set of conditions, offering little autonomy of action. It was also true of the earlier forms of feminism.

In current times, even among more deprived groups, work is now rarely approached as fate (unemployment, perversely, more often is). There is a wide reflexive awareness that what counts as 'work' is much more broadly defined than it used to be, and that work is a problematic and contested notion. Given changes in the class structure, fewer people automatically follow the occupations of their parents or those typical of homogeneous working communities. The involvement of large numbers of women in the labour force has made it clear that there are decisions to be made, and priorities allocated, not just in respect of trying to get one job rather than another, but as concerns what place work should have compared to other life values. Many other factors are also relevant. For example, the fact that many younger people spend years in higher education breaks the 'natural' transition between school and work. Many students now roam the world before attempting to enter the labour market. And older people may do much the same at a later phase of their lives.

Life politics is about the challenges that face collective humanity, not just about how individuals should take decisions when confronted with many more options than they had before. It has been said by some that the ecological crisis is to us today what capitalistic crises were to earlier forms of industrialized society. There is something in this idea, but expressed in such a way it is not compelling. Capitalism, after all, has not been overcome, as the socialists hoped and anticipated; moreover, the ecological issues which perturb us cannot be understood as matters concerning only the environment. They are rather a signal, as well as an expression, of the centrality of life-political problems. They pose with particular force the questions we must face when 'progress' has become sharply double-edged, when we have new responsibilities to future generations, and when there are ethical dilemmas that mechanisms of constant economic growth either cause us to put to one side or make us repress.

Social change and the role of active trust

A detraditionalizing social order is one in which the population becomes more active and reflexive, although the meaning of 'reflexive' should be properly understood. Where the past has lost its hold, or becomes one 'reason' among others for doing what one does, pre-existing habits are only a limited guide to action; while the future, open to numerous 'scenarios', becomes of compelling interest. At issue here, in the context of manufactured uncertainty, is the question of generating active trust – trust in others or in institutions (including political institutions) that has to be actively produced and negotiated.

Active trust, taken in conjunction with a society of clever people, implies a conception of generative politics, closely bound up with life-political concerns. I use the concept to make a contrast with orthodox ideas of both left and right. Generative politics implies a number of circumstances:

1 Fostering the conditions under which desired outcomes – leaving what is desired, and by whom, for the moment as a black box – can be achieved, without determining those desires, or bringing about those outcomes, 'from the top'.
2 Creating situations in which active trust can be built and sustained, whether in institutions of government as such, or in related agencies.
3 According autonomy to those affected by specific programmes or policies – and in fact developing such autonomy in many contexts.
4 Generating resources that enhance autonomy, including material wealth; what is at issue here are resources promoting productivity in the broad sense noted above.
5 The decentralization of political power. Decentralization is the condition of political effectiveness because of the requirement for bottom-up information flow as well as the recognition of autonomy. The push and pull between decentralization and the political centre, however, is not a zero–sum game. Decentralization can sometimes enhance the authority of the centre, either because of political trade-offs or because it creates increased legitimacy.

Thus described, generative politics is by no means limited to the formal political sphere but spans a range of domains where political questions arise and must be responded to. Active trust is closely bound up with such a conception of generative politics.

No longer depending on pregiven alignments, it is more contingent, and contextual, than most earlier forms of trust relations.
It does not necessarily imply equality, but it is not compatible
with deference arising from traditional forms of status. Active
trust demands the increased 'visibility' of social relations, but
also acts to increase such visibility.

Under reflexive modernization much of the population lives in
the same 'discursive space'; political issues form one type of item
in a diversity of reflexive engagements with (or disengagements
from) the wider world. Some authors argue that political policy
issues have become so complex that they can only be mastered
by a few specialists. Yet looked at another way there has never
been a time when information about current events and problems
has been more publicly debated, in a chronic fashion, than in the
present day.

The contingent and negotiated nature of active trust does not
mean that support for established political parties becomes more
volatile, although this may be the case in some contexts. General
issues of compliance do, however, come to the forefront. Where
the national polity has become only one among many points of
reference for the individual's life, many people might not 'listen'
much to what is going on in the (orthodox) political sphere.
'Tuning out' may nevertheless go along with a specific alertness
to questions the individual deems consequential. Appearances
sometimes to the contrary, many may be much more concerned
about how they are governed than in the period of simple
modernization.

The possibility that one can also 'tune in' at any point, and
disregard politics most or all of the rest of the time, is no doubt a
plus point for liberal democracy. As Norberto Bobbio says,
systems that seek to be 'too democratic', which extend the formal
polity into many areas of life, actually become *un*democratic.[6] In
a world of clever people, however, most people most of the time
know most of what the government knows. This situation may
serve to block off policies a government wants to initiate, but it
may also mean that, when a tuning-in occurs, more support is
forthcoming than was anticipated.

A major influence here is the diffuse impact of 'abstract
systems' – systems of expertise of all kinds – on our lives in the

present day. Under the double impact of globalization and detraditionalizing influences, many aspects of daily life become evacuated of locally developed skills and invaded by expert systems of knowledge. The revolutionary changes of our time are not happening so much in the orthodox political domain as along the fault-lines of the interaction of local and global transformations. One is speaking here of something more profound than the impact of technological change on people's lives, far-reaching though that is. Abstract systems include technology, but also any form of expert knowledge that substitutes for indigenous local arts or capacities.

The increasing role that expertise plays in social life intertwines with reflexivity; expertise is no longer the sole prerogative of experts. No one can in any case be an expert in more than a very narrow area. Every expert is a layperson in the face of the multiplicity of other abstract systems that influence his or her life; yet every lay individual can also, in principle and often in practice, appropriate expert knowledge to be applied in the context of social activities. All forms of expertise presume active trust, since every claim to authority is made alongside those of other authorities, and experts themselves often disagree with one another.

The Saint-Simonian vision of the future, which helped to inspire socialism, envisaged that political life would become directed by experts – in this case, scientists and engineers. For better or for worse, however, this idea has turned out to be an empty one. It only made sense at all in relation to simple modernization, where science and technology were supposed to generate unquestionable truths. Politics cannot be reduced to expertise; but also expertise can never sustain the claims to legitimacy possible in more traditional systems of authority.

This is so for various reasons. An expert has no more than a provisional claim to authority, because that expert's views may be contested by others with equivalent credentials. The state of knowledge in most areas shifts quite rapidly, so what is confidently asserted at one particular time may quickly become obsolete. In a socially reflexive era, moreover, expertise does not remain the sole province of the expert; any specialist claims to knowledge relevant to the practical tasks of social life will tend to be deflated through becoming, albeit often in an imperfect form, common currency. The prestige of science itself, so central to earlier phases of the development of modern institutions, becomes subverted by that very scepticism which is the motor of the scientific enterprise.

The practical importance of this last point is wide-ranging. A person with health problems, for example, might still turn first of all to the sphere of orthodox science and medical technology to resolve them, and follow the first diagnosis that comes along. Against a backdrop of active trust mechanisms, however, the choice might very well be to get a second or third opinion. Outside orthodox medicine a host of alternative treatments and therapies vie for attention. Sufferers considering any one of these are likely to find that they are also internally contested – there are many different kinds of psychotherapies, for example, some of which lay claim also to curing physical illnesses. There is no expert of all experts to lead the way.

The dilemmas thus provoked bite deep. Established ways of doing things – in matters of medicine, political allegiance, diet, sexuality and many others – may in various contexts be persisted with. Yet it is difficult not to be conscious that any lifestyle pattern – no matter how traditional – is only one among other possible forms of life. The contingency of active trust in such circumstances may often be muted by habit; but the ungrounded nature of habits, compared to more traditional types of activities, means that in situations of tension or crisis, personal or collective, trust might rapidly be withdrawn and invested elsewhere.

All these traits are to be found in the areas of personal and emotional life. In sexual involvements and in the relations between parents and children, trust must be generated through an active engagement with the other or others. For many people marriage has radically changed its character. It has become a public sign of the vesting of active trust. Only a few decades ago there was little rhetoric of 'commitment' in personal life. Once entered into, marriage was a 'natural' state – either one was married or one was not. Marriage already *was* a commitment, defined as such by social norms. 'Commitment' didn't need to be isolated out and discussed in the manner that has become so common in the present day.

The role of active trust in parent–child relations is perhaps not as obvious, but no less important for that. The authority of parents over children, among many groups at any rate, is much less of a given than it used to be – just the thing that provokes despair among more conservative authors. Whatever the wider implications of this change may be, this situation is one where parent–child relations are increasingly subject to negotiation on both sides. Children, even when very young, generally have much more autonomy in their relations with their elders than previously they did. It's not just by chance that a large volume of child sexual abuse has come to light in recent years, having presumably lain undisclosed before; or that there is now so much discussion, worldwide, of children's rights. What may seem to the conservative critic an objectionable decline in parental authority and filial obligation is more complex, and more hopeful, than such an essentially pessimistic interpretation would imply. The authority of parents over children is less arbitrary than it used to be; parents are more often called on to account for their actions, either by their children or by others. Many troubles and strains result, as they do in other areas of detraditionalization. Yet it does not follow that parental authority is always weakened; it may be enhanced when based more on consent than on the direct imposition of power.

The intrusion of abstract systems into social life, and the reactions this phenomenon conjures forth, do not affect local life and personal identity alone; these influences stretch right through to the most inclusive of global orders, including the various contexts of high-consequence risk.

Manufactured uncertainty and global risk environments

There are four main contexts in which we confront high-consequence risks coming from the extension of manufactured uncertainty. Each corresponds, as I shall try to show, to an institutional dimension of modernity.

The first concerns the impact of modern social development on the world's ecosystems. Our relation to the environment has become problematic in several ways. The material resources needed to sustain human life, and in particular the way of life of the industrialized parts of the world, look likely to become threatened in the medium-term future. The original report of the Club of Rome emphasized threats to non-sustainable resources, but at the present time more stress tends to be laid by environmentalists on the world's capacity to dispose of wastes. The list of dangers is well known: the probable development of global warming, as a result of the production of the so-called 'greenhouse gases'; the depletion of the ozone layer; destruction of the rain forests; desertification; and the poisoning of waters to a degree likely to inhibit the processes of regeneration they contain.

A second crisis concerns the development of poverty on a large scale – what has been described as the 'holocaust of poverty'. The statistics are not precise, but however they are calculated they disclose alarming levels of deprivation. Over 20 per cent of the world's population lives in conditions of absolute poverty, if such be defined as a situation where people cannot regularly meet their most basic subsistence needs.

The causes of global poverty are complex and the overall trend of change difficult to interpret. The days when global inequalities could simply be blamed on the spread of capitalism are certainly over, although there can be little doubt that capitalistic markets do often have a polarizing effect on distributions of wealth and income. It has also become evident that it is not always lack of economic development that brings about impoverishment, but sometimes such 'development' itself. A way of life which may have been very modest in economic terms, but which was self-sustaining and organized through local tradition becomes broken up when a development project – dam, plantation or factory – is introduced.[7]

People thus affected are likely to find themselves in a situation of relative poverty even if their material standards of life are somewhat improved; they are pitchforked into a society for which they are ill-prepared and in which they are marginalized. Relative poverty is a notoriously more elusive notion than absolute deprivation – some argue that all poverty is relative, giving the concept thereby an elastic definition. Judged by the usual measures, at any rate, including official designations of poverty, millions of people in the richest societies are also poor.

A third source of crisis is the widespread existence of weapons of mass destruction, together with other situations in which collective violence looms as a possibility. The ending of the Cold War has lessened the possibility of a nuclear confrontation that could have destroyed much of human life on the earth; it has not removed that threat altogether. There may be as many as fifteen countries which possess nuclear weapons. The number has expanded since the days of the Cold War, as a result of the new nuclear nations which have emerged with the break-up of the Soviet Union. The proliferation of nuclear weapons is a likely prospect given the large number of 'peaceful' reactors that exist capable of producing plutonium, and given the world trade that is carried on in the substance.

The problem of violence, how to lessen or prevent it, stands as one of the most difficult questions revealed by the disappearance of the superpower confrontation. As we all (reflexively) know, there is a new world order, but it looks almost as disturbing as the old. The problem is not just the accumulation of military hardware, but the exacerbation of local tensions in many different areas, tied in as they often are to nationalist, religious and ethnic divisions. It is evident in retrospect that the Cold War stand-off, overwhelmingly dangerous though it was, in some respects was a stabilizing force across many areas of the world.

In terms of scale, violence is above all a problem linked to the global military order; but it is of course also something that occurs in a multiplicity of more mundane situations. Male violence against women outside the context of war, for example, is a phenomenon of pervasive importance. If there is, as Marilyn French has claimed, a 'war against women', it is not one confined to any particular part of the globe.[8]

A fourth source of global crisis concerns the large-scale repression of democratic rights 'and the inability of increasing numbers of people to develop even a small part of their human potential'.[9] Military rule seems to be on the decline. Yet as of 1993 there were still over fifty military regimes in different parts of the world. According to Amnesty International, people were imprisoned for matters of conscience – solely because of their religion, language or ethnic origin – in more than eighty countries across the globe.

There are close connections here with the previous categories. The Cold War kept in place a hypocritical dialogue of 'democratic rights', during which time that concept became largely an empty one – a cloak for strategic superpower interests. Successive American governments made it clear that they would not tolerate regimes deemed incompatible with US interests – and others were actively destabilized where they were not seen to conform to these interests. The Soviet Union proclaimed its support for 'democracy' just as loudly as its global opponent; at the same time it also pursued policies governed mainly by geopolitical concerns.

The disappearance of the Cold War has served to make it clear that there are basic structural factors in global society which make for a denial of democratic rights. The repression of democracy was not just a Cold War phenomenon, or even one of political authoritarianism. Many people are 'unable to develop even a small part of their human potential' either because of enforced poverty or because of the restrictive nature of the circumstances in which they live.

The four sets of global 'bads' distinguished above relate to different institutional dimensions of modern civilization, as indicated in my first diagram.

(Capitalism)	Economic polarization	Ecological threats	(Industrialism)
(Surveillance)	Denial of democratic rights	Threat of large-scale war	(Means of violence)

The global spread of modernity, as the left always stressed (and left and right now agree on this) was driven in large part by the dynamism of capitalist enterprise. The modern world, however, is not solely *capitalistic*; it has other structuring dimensions as well, as I have tried to show at some length in other works. These dimensions include *industrialism*, as a mode of production driving our changing relation to material nature; control of military power and the *means of violence*, and control of information, or *surveillance*, as a means of generating administrative power.

Along each of these dimensions – and in relation to each of the four risk environments – the question that must be posed by political radicalism is: what alternative sociopolitical forms could potentially exist? I shall build most of the rest of the book around answers to that question suggested in my second diagram.

(Capitalism)	Post-scarcity economy	Humanized nature	(Industrialism)
(Surveillance)	Dialogic democracy	Negotiated power	(Means of violence)

(1) The notion of a post-scarcity economy, in a certain version at any rate, was a prominent idea within some versions of Marxism. It was long derided, in fact, as utopian by those concerned to advance the more 'realistic' economic option of the directive control of the economy. Now things have reversed themselves. The idea of subjecting economic life to central direction has lost its radical credentials. The concept of a post-scarcity economy, by contrast, as I shall try to show in a subsequent chapter, is no longer wholly utopian. Like the other political possibilities described here, it can be approached with an attitude of *utopian realism*; it has utopian features, yet is not unrealistic because it corresponds to observable trends.

The Marxist idea of a post-scarcity society was a vision of an era of universal abundance, in which scarcity would effectively disappear. In this guise it is indeed purely utopian and offers no purchase at all on a global situation where the conservation of resources, rather than their unlimited development, is what is called for. As I use it here, the concept of post-scarcity means something different; it refers to a situation, or more accurately a complex of situations, in which economic growth is no longer of overriding importance.

Post-scarcity doesn't mean the absence of scarcity – there will in any case always be 'positional' goods. Tendencies towards a post-scarcity economy emerge where accumulation processes are widely seen to *threaten or destroy valued ways of life*; where accumulation becomes manifestly *counterproductive in its own terms*, that is, where there is 'overdevelopment' leading to suboptimal economic, social or cultural consequences; and where in the domains of life politics individuals or groups take lifestyle decisions that *limit, or actively go against, maximizing economic returns*.

The attempt to counter economic inequality has been closely associated in the developed societies with the rise of the welfare state, the core concern of socialism turned defensive. And it is in the context of problems of welfare that I shall discuss issues of inequality in a subsequent chapter. However, such a discussion, I shall argue, cannot take place in isolation from wider problems of global poverty.

(2) The humanization of nature comprises ecology, but ecological issues have to be approached in the manner suggested by the analysis of detraditionalization. Nature has come to an end in a parallel way to tradition. The point at which the denaturing of nature effectively ended our 'natural environment' cannot be fixed in an exact way; but somewhere over the last century or so the age-old relation between human beings and nature was broken through and reversed. Instead of being concerned above all with what nature could do to us, we have now to worry about what we have done to nature.

To confront the problem of the humanization of nature means beginning from the existence of 'plastic nature' – nature as incorporated within a post-traditional order. Decisions about what to conserve, or to strive to recover, can rarely be decided by reference to what exists independently of human beings. Questions of resource depletion and environmental damage can sometimes be analysed in terms of how far they deviate from natural cycles of regeneration. In other respects, however – in respect of tradition as well as nature – conservation (or renewal, rebuilding) has to address the problem of how to accommodate to and interpret the past with respect to various projected futures.

(3) Large-scale warfare today threatens the environment in just as devastating a way as more pacific forms of technology. It was not always so; here there is a connection between industrialization and the waging of war. Industrialized weapons technologies

are capable of destroying vast areas of landscape or polluting the atmosphere of the earth as a whole. Even quite a limited nuclear exchange might create the conditions of a 'nuclear winter' – as with other high-consequence risks, no one really knows how likely this is. Other forms of industrial weaponry, such as chemical weapons, can be massively polluting. And who knows what another ten, twenty or a hundred years of further weapons development might bring?

If violence means the use of physical force to achieve one's ends, it is of course an everyday occurrence, not something linked only to military power or war. A normative political theory of violence cannot concern itself only with peace, or at any rate must generalize beyond a hypothetical situation of the absence of war. In today's world, I shall try to show, there is a new relation between violence, on the one hand, and the possibility of dialogic communication on the other; and this relation applies in principle to all forms of violence, from domestic violence to war.

(4) Could there ever be a social order free from violence? The idea, of course, is utopian. Yet the possibility of actively reducing levels of violence, in social domains ranging from the personal right through to the most global, is quite realistic – and, as in other areas of high-consequence risk, is surely necessary if humanity is to survive the dangerous period that now looms. The obverse of the use of force is negotiated power, a phenomenon which stands close to democracy. Democratization is bound up with the surveillance capacities of states and other organizations in the late modern world – the fourth dimension of modern institutions noted above. It is to the issue of democracy, its forms and possibilities, that I turn in the following chapter.

4

Two Theories of Democratization

The popularity of democracy

Suddenly everyone has discovered democracy! A passion for democratic government has long been a hallmark of liberal political philosophies, but Old Conservatism and revolutionary socialism always kept their distance. Are there any political thinkers today, however, who are not, in one sense or another, democrats?

Even those, such as some neoliberal authors, who have doubts about the effectiveness of formal democratic institutions have become advocates of democratization. For them the market democratizes where the democratic policy cannot reach. Universal enthusiasm for democracy, moreover, is not confined to the theoretical level. In many countries across the world as of the early 1990s moves have been made to try to replace authoritarian governments or single-party regimes with a plural party system. Over the period from 1989 to mid-1993, for example, more than twenty countries in Africa alone sought to introduce constitutionalism and democratic parliamentary institutions.

Why has democracy now become more or less universally popular? How should the concept of democracy best be understood? What are the prospects for its future development, as seen from the point of view of utopian realism?

Two contrasting approaches can be made to the first of these questions. One I shall call the orthodox approach – it is the view of Francis Fukuyama, but by no means limited to him alone. The orthodox view of democratization makes a virtue of, or in Fukuyama's case a philosophical case for, the disappearance of historical alternatives. Democracy has become universally popular in the present day simply because it is the best political system that humanity can come up with. And most nations and peoples now see this. Fascism failed long ago, Communism is no more and military rule cannot generate effective government. Liberal democracy, coupled to capitalism in the economic sphere, are what remains; some are enthusiastic about this situation, others (like Fukuyama) accept it only with a measure of resignation.

The orthodox view is not new. 'Two cheers for democracy', E. M. Forster's not so subtle way of putting things – this less than fervent enthusiasm for democracy was given solid sociological shape by Max Weber as early as the turn of the century. Weber was influenced by the critique of democracy and capitalistic production coming from Old Conservatism, although he did not accept it. Democracy allows populations to vote to decide who should rule them and, given certain conditions, can help generate good political leaders. It permits a certain amount of choice, which a one-party system by definition does not; and so do capitalistic markets as compared to a socialized economy. These things having been said, for Weber democracy is a dreary business and bourgeois society unheroic and mediocre.

Most of those who take the orthodox approach have long shaken themselves free from the aristocratic values of valour and adventure which coloured Weber's qualified appreciation of democracy. What distinguishes the orthodox account today is that it has only just *become* an orthodoxy, with the disintegration of Communism; and that it is applied to help explain that very disintegration.

This account might be described as a catching-up theory of democracy. The revolutions in Eastern Europe occurred, so it runs, because Communism became unacceptably authoritarian and was exposed as economically inefficient. It didn't have to be attacked from without, but largely crumbled from within. While previous rebellions against Communist autocracy in Eastern Europe had failed, the oppositional movements this time were successful (much more successful than they or anyone else had anticipated) because the system as a whole had reached such an advanced state of decay. Eastern Europe needed to catch up with the West and now has at least the opportunity to do so. The only question that remains according to the orthodox view – although it is a serious and difficult question – is when and whether the formerly Communist societies can catch up with the liberal democracies of the West. The same applies to the countries of the Third World. Will they be able to follow along the road – a 'road' which no longer leads to socialism – that the Western democracies have already trodden? For, as Marxists always liked to say of socialism, the alternatives are only liberal democracy plus capitalism, or stagnation.

Fukuyama's version of this view has a boldness and a sweep that its rivals lack. For Fukuyama liberal democracy marks the 'end point of mankind's ideological evolution' and the 'final form of human government'.

> From Latin America to Eastern Europe, from the Soviet Union to the Middle East and Asia, strong governments have been failing over the last two decades. And while they have not given way in all cases to stable liberal democracies, liberal democracy remains the only coherent political aspiration that spans different regions and cultures around the globe.[1]

Why have strong states become weak? Authoritarianism, whether of the right or the left, Fukuyama says, has failed because it could not develop a satisfactory legitimation of its own power. Such regimes do not have a fund of goodwill which can see them through difficult periods; they are not flexible in the way liberal democracies are. A remarkable feature of the decline of authoritarian government in the present period is the lack of bloodshed in the transitions that have taken place – including particularly those in Eastern Europe. This 'willing retreat from power', although usually provoked by specific critical situations, 'was ultimately made possible by a growing belief that democracy was the only legitimate source of authority in the modern world'. The economic impotence of the Soviet Union only in fact exposed its more fundamental weakness, its lack of legitimacy.

Unlike some other authors, who have seen liberalism and

democracy in some tension, Fukuyama regards the two components of liberal democracy as belonging closely together. Liberalism is the rule of law, the recognition of rights of free speech and the right freely to own property. Democracy is the right of all citizens to vote and form political associations. This right can be seen as one among other liberal rights – in fact, the most important one – hence the tie between liberalism and democracy. Democracy itself, however, can only be defined in a procedural way; it cannot be made substantive as the Communist states sought to do. A state is democratic 'if it grants its people the right to choose their own government through periodic secret-ballot, multi-party elections, on the basis of universal and equal adult suffrage'.

Similarly, there is a close and evident connection between liberal democracy and capitalism. This bond is not, as the neoliberals argue, an economic one. Here, Fukuyama says, we must return to Hegel. The universal advance of liberal democracy is bound up with the understanding of history as a 'struggle for recognition'. While the desire for recognition goes through various vicissitudes, in the bourgeois era it becomes built into liberal beliefs, as the acknowledgement that every individual has the right to live autonomously and with dignity. Combined with capitalism, liberal democracy creates a great deal of material abundance; yet what motivates democratization is not wealth but 'the completely non-material end of recognition of our freedom'. Liberal democracy 'recognizes' all human beings 'by granting and protecting their *rights*'. Liberal democracy and capitalism are bound to one another because economic development enhances the conditions of individual autonomy. Economic growth, energized by science and technology, demands a developed educational system; and universal education liberates 'a certain demand for recognition that did not exist among poorer and less educated people'.

Yet how satisfying to live in will this social universe of triumphant liberal democracy be? Fukuyama concludes in a manner reminiscent of Weber, drawing as Weber did on Nietzsche. Valour, heroism, nobility, even virtue – for Nietzsche these are attainable only in aristocratic societies. Bourgeois society means the rule of mediocrity – there is more than an echo of the Old Conservatism in what Fukuyama has to say. He also shows a certain similarity to more recent conservative critics of moral relativism. There may be nothing beyond liberal democracy, but such an order produces its own problems and inner frailties:

> Modern thought raises no barriers to a future nihilistic war against liberal democracy on the part of those brought up in its bosom. Relativism – the doctrine that maintains that all values are merely relative and which attacks all 'privileged perspectives' – must ultimately end up undermining democratic and tolerant values as well. Relativism is not a weapon that can be aimed selectively at the enemies one chooses. It fires indiscriminately, shooting out the legs of not only the 'absolutisms', dogmas, and certainties of the Western tradition, but that tradition's emphasis on tolerance, diversity, and freedom of thought as well.

Whatever one thinks of the 'struggle for recognition', Fukuyama's work differs in an important way from neoliberal interpretations of the ascendancy of democracy and capitalism. For he doesn't assume that economic individualism connects the two. It is not the pursuit of self-interest in competitive markets which accounts for the spread of democracy; democratization has largely independent origins, to do with a desire for autonomy and respect. This is a view I shall endorse in what follows; but in other respects Fukuyama's views have serious shortcomings.

Capitalism is connected to democracy for Fukuyama because it allows for a material autonomy which makes possible a generalizing of mutual respect. Fukuyama's position, however, assumes what he calls 'accumulation without end'. Yet surely 'accumulation without end' has its own contradictions, just as serious, or perhaps more serious, than those of liberal democracy? Ecological considerations have no real place in Fukuyama's discussion; all he says is that capitalism has not been as destructive of the environment as has Communism.

Moreover, it is not easy to see from Fukuyama's theory why democratization has accelerated so rapidly in very recent times. The processes he discusses are mostly much longer-term ones; we are all today heir to the 'bourgeois revolutions started over four hundred years ago'. Why, then, did it take the world so long to grasp this? The only answer offered by Fukuyama, or indeed by other proponents of the orthodox view, is that there were diversions along the way. Until recently too much attention was given to other, false, historical alternatives. Old Conservatism sought to block the development of bourgeois society, while Communism wanted to transcend it before it had even got fully off the ground. Rapid and general democratization had to wait until these blinkers were removed.

This explanation seems weak. So also is Fukuyama's interpretation of the travails to which liberal democracy is likely to become subject. The problem of value relativism is a very real one; but Fukuyama does not trace out its implications at all, either philosophically or sociologically. Is value relativism the product of liberal democracy, as he says, or is it more the result of the spread of capitalistic markets? For, as the neoliberals stress, the capitalistic economy is no respecter of morals or values, save for those intrinsic to contract.

The issue of nihilism that Fukuyama alludes to, like that of 'accumulation without end', might be more alarming than he thinks. If the neoconservative critics of relativism are correct, the destruction of the traditional virtues leads to a fundamental and perhaps irreparable decay of social solidarity. Fukuyama speaks mostly of the disappearance of values of heroism and manly struggle, which Weber also so admired. Yet the threat to the social order presented by bored and frustrated adventurers is probably much less than that offered by a rampant hedonism – or by the compulsive pursuit of material success turned sour.

The difficulties to which Fukuyama believes liberal democracy is subject he seems mostly to see as lying ahead, somewhere in the future, once democratization has become more thoroughly developed across the world. Yet liberal democratic polities seem in trouble almost everywhere in the here and now. In many liberal democracies we see what amounts to a large-scale alienation from, or at minimum an indifference to, political institutions. Voter preferences in most Western countries have become unstable. Many people feel that what goes on in party politics has little relevance to the problems, or opportunities, of their lives. Discontent with political leadership is so widespread as to be more than just a contingent phenomenon relative to a particular generation of leaders. Moreover, in spite of the fact that liberal democratic norms are universalizable, liberal democracy remains largely confined to the nation-state. This paradox, noted by Kant many years ago, becomes even more acute than it used to be given the new dialectics of globalization.

An alternative view

All these things provide good reason to be sceptical not only of Fukuyama's viewpoint, but of the orthodox account of democratization as a whole. I want to propose a different interpretation – one that I hope provides a more convincing explanation of why liberal democracy is becoming generalized, but which also indicates why at the same time it has come under strain.

Democratization processes today, in my view, should be understood in terms of the social changes I have described in the preceding chapter. Consider first of all the transformations in Eastern Europe. These, of course, were complex in origin and I want to comment only on certain aspects of them. As many observers (including Fukuyama) have noted, in some key respects the 1989 events didn't resemble earlier twentieth-century revolutions, and not only because they were made against socialism rather than in the name of it. They were not led by organized revolutionary parties, were mostly peaceful, and state power, as it were, melted away rather than having to be directly overthrown.

The influence of electronic communication on the 1989 changes has often been noted.[2] The sequence of events that took place, moving rapidly from country to country, probably could not have occurred without the instantaneity conferred by radio and especially television – given the ability of the latter medium to give a dramatic visual form to scattered happenings that could otherwise be understood only in an abstract fashion. Yet instantaneous electronic communication is only one aspect of, if also a major influence on, wider processes of globalization. And it is globalization, with its attendant transformations of everyday life, which surely underlies pressures towards democratization in the present day.

The 'weakness of strong states' of which Fukuyama speaks was not present from the origins of the Communist societies, but was created by changing conditions in the wider environment of global society. Democratization processes today are driven by the expansion of social reflexivity and detraditionalization. As reflexivity advances, the 'weakness of strong states' can be seen to have little to do with strong states specifically. Processes of global and local change affect all states, not necessarily weakening them in a unilateral way, but altering the status of the formal political domain.

Many of the most important changes which affect people's lives today do not originate in the formal political sphere and can only in some part be coped with by it. This is a crucial theme of this book. Such changes form the social revolutions of our time of which I spoke in the previous chapter; they press for, and themselves in some part represent, processes of democratization, but these democratizing influences and pressures cut across the political arena and destabilize the liberal democratic system as much as they reinforce it.

Part of the attraction of liberal democratic institutions is that they allow individuals and groups to free themselves from the political sphere, rather than that they create general conditions of legitimacy. On the one hand, large numbers of the population are reflexively better informed about the political domain than they were before; on the other, that domain becomes for them one among multiple points of reference, local and more global, in a cosmopolitan globalizing order. Liberal democratic systems, and the state more generally, are affected in basic ways by this situation.[3] It does not follow, however, that the 'weakness of states' becomes their strength, in a reversal of Fukuyama's theorem: that is, that the 'strongest' state is a 'minimal state' as described in neoliberal theory. Here lies the domain of generative politics, which needs to be related to a wider appraisal of democratizing traits than is provided where democracy means only liberal democracy.

Participation, representation, dialogue

Liberal democracy, I shall accept, with Weber and Bobbio, is essentially a system of representation. It is a form of government characterized by regular elections, universal suffrage, freedom of conscience, and the universal right to stand for office or to form political associations. Defined in such a way, democracy is normally understood in relation to pluralism and the expression of diverse interests.

Those who say two cheers for liberal democracy have considerable justification for so doing. The trend towards the universalizing of liberal democracy is undeniably important when placed in the context of the apparent decline of authoritarian or totalitarian regimes. Yet the limitations of liberal democratic systems are well enough known by now and have frequently been driven home by conservative and socialist critics alike. However it be organized, representative democracy means rule by groups distant from the ordinary voter and is often dominated by petty party-political concerns.

These endemic problems do not, I think, account for the travails of liberal democracy in the present day – for the fact that its emergence as the only game in town coincides with its ailing condition even in those societies where it is most firmly established. Nor do they provide much of a clue about how democratization might be further advanced; here the well-established debates pitting participation against representation offer little purchase.

We need to look in a different direction from this – towards what I have termed dialogic democracy. Dialogic democratization is not an extension of liberal democracy or even a complement to it; in so far as it proceeds, however, it creates forms of social interchange which can contribute substantially, perhaps even decisively, to the reconstructing of social solidarity. Dialogic democracy is not primarily about either the proliferation of *rights* or the representation of *interests*. Rather it concerns the furthering of *cultural cosmopolitanism* and is a prime building-block of that connection of autonomy and solidarity I have spoken about earlier.

Dialogic democracy is not centred on the state but, as I shall argue, refracts back on it in an important way. Situated in the context of globalization and social reflexivity, dialogic democracy encourages the *democratizing of democracy* within the sphere of the liberal democratic polity.

What is democracy?

A starting point for considering these issues is offered by what some have recently started to call 'deliberative democracy' – and have specifically contrasted to liberal democracy. Liberal democracy is a set of representative institutions, guided by certain values; deliberative democracy is a way of getting, or trying to get, agreement about policies in the political arena. The deliberative ideal, according to David Miller, for example, 'starts from the premise that political preferences will conflict and that the purpose of democratic institutions must be to resolve this conflict'. For such conflict resolution to be democratic, he says, echoing Jürgen Habermas, it must occur 'through an open and uncoerced discussion of the issue at stake with the aim of arriving at an agreed judgement'. It does not have to be the case that agreement is reached directly through such discussion. A vote might be taken; the important thing is that the participants reach a judgement on the basis of what they have heard and said.

The deliberative conception of democracy Miller distinguishes from an 'epistemic' one, sometimes attributed to Condorcet and Rousseau among others. The epistemic view of democracy asserts the existence of a general will and presumes that democratic procedures can realize it – that is to say, it holds that a correct or valid answer can be reached to questions facing the political community. Such a view, according to the proponents of deliberative democracy, sets an impossible standard for democratic institutions to meet. The deliberative approach accepts that there are many questions either which have no single correct answer, or where solutions are not thoroughly contested. In deliberative democracy, accord might be reached by various means. Those involved might agree on a norm or norms which guide the assessment of particular policy decisions; or they might agree on a procedure which can be applied to contentious cases. 'The emphasis in the deliberative conception is on the way in which a process of open discussion in which all points of view can be heard may legitimate the outcome when this is seen to reflect the discussion that has preceded it, not on deliberation as a discovery procedure in search of a correct answer.'[4]

Democracy in this conception is not defined by whether or not everyone participates in it, but by public deliberation over policy issues. In a representative system, the conditions of deliberative democracy could be met through ensuring the visibility of what elected representatives do. The normal electoral procedures would be in place to sustain the possibility of recall if members of wider publics objected either to how particular agreements were reached or to policies enacted on the basis of them.

This approach has some important implications for the democratization of democracy. In an increasingly reflexive social order, where people are also free to ignore politics when they so wish, political legitimacy will not readily be maintained simply because a democratic apparatus of voting, representation and parliaments happens to be in place. To create and preserve such legitimacy, the principles of deliberative democracy are likely to become more and more significant. In circumstances of simple modernization, where a population has relatively stable, and local, customs or habits, political legitimacy can depend in some part on traditional symbolism. No one worries too much about what goes on behind the scenes. All sorts of patronage and even downright corruption are able not only to survive but to become, within the political leadership, the accepted way of doing things. Taxation and other resources utilized by the governmental or state apparatus, for example, can be appropriated without much public accounting of where the money goes.

Parliaments and congressional assemblies in a liberal democratic system are supposed to be the public spaces where agreement is achieved on policy-making matters. Yet how open these are, as it were, to 'inspection' by the public is quite variable. They can become either dominated by the factionalism of party politics or become essentially private debating societies. Deliberative democratization would mean greater transparency in many areas of government – not least important, in the sphere of resource generation.

Miller's conception of deliberative democracy is confined to the formal political domain. We need today, however, to consider the possibility of much larger orders of actual and potential democratization. Such orders concern those two intersecting areas of change within which our lives today are becoming so fundamentally altered: everyday life, on the one hand, and globalizing systems on the other. In investigating democratization in these spheres it is worth keeping in mind the conventional association of democracy with deliberative assemblies; but it is the aspect of being open to deliberation, rather than where it occurs, which is most important. This is why I speak of democratization as the (actual and potential) extension of dialogic democracy – a situation where there is developed autonomy of communication, and where such communication forms a dialogue by means of which policies and activities are shaped.

Dialogic democracy is not the same as an ideal speech situation. In the first place, dialogic democratization is not linked to a transcendental philosophical theorem. I don't presume, as Habermas does, that such democratization is somehow implied by the very act of speech or dialogue. The potential for dialogic democracy is instead carried in the spread of social reflexivity as a condition both of day-to-day activities and the persistence of larger forms of collective organization. Second, dialogic democracy is not necessarily oriented to the achieving of consensus. Just as the theorists of deliberative democracy argue, the most 'political' of issues, inside and outside the formal political sphere, are precisely those which are likely to remain essentially contested. Dialogic democracy presumes only that dialogue in a public space provides a means of living along with the other in a relation of mutual *tolerance* – whether that 'other' be an individual or a global community of religious believers.

Dialogic democracy therefore stands in opposition to fundamentalisms of all types; this is indeed a major part of its importance in a social order of developed reflexivity. It doesn't imply that all divisions or conflicts can be overcome through dialogue – far from it. Nor does it mean that, in any system or relationship, dialogue has to be continuous. Dialogue should be understood as the capability to create active trust through an appreciation of the integrity of the other. Trust is a means of ordering social relations across time and space. It sustains that 'necessary silence' which allows individuals or groups to get on with their lives while still existing in a social relation with another or others.

Liberal democratic political theory is based on the idea that a strict separation must be maintained between state and civil society; and the fate of socialism would seem to have borne out this thesis. Socialism breached this principle by, as Bobbio has put it, trying to democratize too much. If most aspects of life are not kept out of the political domain, the state tends to reach down into them and become an autocracy.

Keeping state and civil society apart is indeed a major contribution of liberal democracy – as I have emphasized, it means that individuals can ignore the political arena when they wish so to do. Here one must go back again to the interconnected processes of globalization, reflexivity, and the transformation of day-to-day life. While these help bring about the widespread movement towards liberal democracy, they cannot in any way be *contained* within the orthodox political sphere. Discontent with liberal democratic institutions mounts at the very same time, and for much the same reasons, as those institutions become generalized. People become disillusioned with 'politics' because key areas of social life – some of them areas they are able reflexively to master, others of them areas which are sources of threat – no longer correspond to any accessible domains of political authority. Nor does consumer power, as the neoliberals suppose, substitute for such absent authority. Needs are conditioned by capitalist commodification just as much as they influence it through market choices. More important, technological innovation stimulated by capitalistic development alters basic aspects of social life; capitalist markets themselves provide no clue whatsoever about how these should be confronted or dealt with. In some respects liberal democracy, coupled to the welfare state, *adds to* these incapacities rather than alleviates them.

Dialogic democracies

Outside the formal political sphere, dialogic democracy today can be seen to advance in four connected areas – what happens in each of these reacts back on (and also often creates problems for) orthodox politics. In each case we can speak at the moment only of democratizing tendencies, generating opportunities for a renewal of political radicalism, but also surrounded by basic dilemmas, difficulties and countertendencies.

First, there is the arena of *personal life*, subject to so many changes today as a result of causes already noted. Detraditionalization and expanded reflexivity alter the pre-existing character of marriage, sexuality, friendship, the relations between parents and children, and kinship ties. To a large degree, although with many variations according to context, these changes, like all the others discussed here, refract around the world.

In personal life, the more a post-traditional society develops, the more there is a movement towards what can be called the *pure relationship* in sexual relations, marriage and the family. The pure relationship should be understood as an ideal type in the sociological sense; it is a limiting case, towards which actual social relations tend, rather than a complete description of any real context of activity. A pure relationship is one that is entered into and sustained for its own sake – for the rewards that association with another, or others, can bring.

Forming pure relationships and ensuring their continuity draws in an inherent way on active trust. In the various spheres of intimate life, getting to know and getting along with the other depends on an attribution of integrity. The relationship depends on who the other 'is' as a person, rather than on a specified social role, or on what the other individual 'does' in life. Thus marriage used to be – and of course in many empirical instances still is – a meshing of roles. What men did differed from what women did, so that marriage was intrinsically a division of labour. Marriage was often arranged, rather than initiated and sustained by the individuals involved. Marriage was rather like a state of nature.

Over the past half a century, particularly in Western countries, but to some extent across the world, marriage has changed in a fundamental way. It is, in principle at any rate, a meeting of equals rather than a patriarchal relation; it is an emotional tie, forged and sustained on a basis of personal attraction, sexuality and emotion, rather than for economic reasons; and it has actively to be 'made to work' by the marital couple.

The more marriage tends towards a pure relationship, the more it becomes precisely a public symbol of that relationship. One could not say that marriage is then insignificant, because its symbolic character may be socially important and it has a legally binding form. However, its 'success' comes to depend more and more on criteria that are the same for people who are together but not married – that is, on compatibility within the context of a mutually rewarding relationship. As marriage becomes emptied of its traditional content, so also does sexuality. In a post-traditional order, sexuality becomes 'plastic'; one has to decide, in effect, what one's sexuality is, and heterosexuality (in principle) is no longer a pregiven, 'natural' standard. The dynamics of same-sex sexual relationships may differ in some ways from heterosexual ones, but for the most part they depend on exactly the same emotional mechanisms.[5]

Whether in marriage or in other areas of personal life, to endure the pure relationship depends on an 'opening out' to the other – on cognitive and emotional communication. Individuals must 'give of' themselves for the relationship to continue; such giving is at the same time the very means of mobilizing active trust. To open out to the other, one must know oneself. A reflexivity of self – being in contact with one's own emotions – is the condition of forming an effective relationship with the other. Emotional communication, almost by definition, does not necessarily need to be talked about – it is lived. Yet the pure relationship also inevitably presupposes dialogue. It is a relationship sustained through the open discussion of 'policy issues', issues of mutual involvement and responsibility.

Hence there is a close tie between the pure relationship and dialogic democracy. Dialogue, between individuals who approach one another as equals, is a transactional quality central to their mutuality. There are remarkable parallels between what a good relationship looks like, as developed in the literature of marital and sexual therapy, and formal mechanisms of political democracy. Both depend on the development of what David Held calls a *principle of autonomy*. Within a wider polity, or in relationships, the individual must have the psychological and material autonomy needed to enter into effective communication with others. Dialogue, free from the use of coercion, and occupying a 'public space', is in both cases the means, not just of settling disputes, but of creating an atmosphere of mutual toler-ance. That is to say, the very framework of the democratic system – or of the relationship – is open to 'public' discussion.

How might all this apply to parent–child interaction: what evidence is there that the relations between parents and children tend towards pure relationships? Such evidence is to be found in clear trends towards 'negotiated authority' within the family – in some part this is the very tendency which rightist authors see as the disintegration of the authority of the parents altogether. Parents' authority here in fact becomes post-traditional; it is no longer a 'given', a fact of life for them and for children alike, but more actively negotiated on both sides. A child and parent approach one another as implicit equals, even if empirically the parent holds the greater authority.

A democratic parent–child relationship is one of counter-factually bargained authority. The parent in effect says to the child: if you were able to discuss our relationship with me as an adult would do, in a free and open way, you would accept my reasons for treating you as I do. Such a 'counterfactual demo-cracy' can even apply to the situation of a newborn infant, incapable of this kind of communication with its parents. To the degree to which it develops, a democracy of the emotions would have significant implications for the furtherance of formal, public democracy. Individuals who have a good understanding of their own emotional makeup, and who are able to communicate effectively with others on a personal basis, are likely to be well prepared for wider tasks of citizenship. Communication skills developed within the arenas of personal life might very well be generalizable across wider contexts.

The development of emotional democracy is a potential implied in the detraditionalizing of personal life; it is far from an inevitable consequence of it. The problems that rightist authors have pointed to in the areas of gender, sexuality and the family are all too real. It is by no means clear that such detraditionalization might not produce a disastrous decline in family solidarity, a world of short-term, fraught sexual encounters providing little enduring satisfaction, pockmarked with violence. On the other hand, a democracy of the emotions does correspond to observable trends in the various domains of everyday life, offering good cause for hope.

A *second* area of democratization, again of global spread, is the proliferation of social movements and self-help groups. Such movements and groups express, but also contribute to, the heightened reflexivity of local and global life today. Social movements have received a great deal of attention in the political and sociological literature. Yet, in terms of their numbers, their importance in the lives of many and their endurance over time, self-help groups are perhaps more significant.

It is obvious that neither social movements nor self-help groups are necessarily democratic in their aims; some such movements and groups, after all, have been dedicated to discrediting the whole framework of democratic institutions. Social movements are sometimes led by demagogues; such leaders may create a mass emotional identification that is the very antithesis of dialogic democracy.

Yet it makes sense to think of an intrinsic connection between democracy, social movements and self-help groups, coming in large part from the fact that (in principle) they open up spaces for public dialogue. A social movement, for example, can force into the discursive domain aspects of social conduct that previously went undiscussed, or were 'settled' by traditional practices. The feminist movement problematized female and male sexual identity through making them matters of public debate; ecological movements have achieved a similar result in relation to the environment.

Some kinds of social movements and self-help groups pioneer, and perhaps help sustain, democratizing influences by the very form of their social association. Thus Alcoholics Anonymous, for instance – certainly a group of global scope – has an organizational form that inhibits fixed hierarchies. It deliberately sets out to create the maximum of discursive space for its members; and it is also concerned with the development of autonomy.

Communication with others, produced by and contributing to increased self-understanding, is the means whereby the sufferer is able to overcome addiction.

Social movements, but especially self-help groups, may come to have a major role in democratizing the numerous areas of what Ulrich Beck calls 'subpolitics'. They frequently have a deep involvement, of course, with the arenas of emotional democracy in personal life. 'Self-help': in its broadest sense what does this mean if not the enhancement of autonomy? Self-help groups of many kinds have developed in relation to sexuality, personal relationships, marriage and the family.[6]

Self-help groups become important in many contexts where constant technological change, including the denaturing of nature, regularly outstrips democratic controls offered in the formal political domain. The area of reproductive technologies is a good case in point. Few changes have affected people's lives as much, particularly the lives of women. As everywhere else, possibilities of increased autonomy jostle with renewed forms of expropriation and domination. Self-help groups, however, have played a major role in wresting power from experts and in the lay retrieval of expertise more generally. Technological change facilitated the invasion of the perinatal experience of women by the medical profession, predominantly a male enclave. Those affected, however, have not sat passively by, but have actively organized themselves in ways making for a recovery of autonomy – in active dialogue with the 'experts'.

A *third* context of democratization is to be found in the organizational arena, where the combined influence of globalization and reflexivity is so marked. With the generalization of capitalism, as mentioned earlier, it looked as though the giant corporations would reign unchallenged in the world economy. Things have not turned out exactly that way. 'Corporate giants', it has been said,

> once walked tall and proud, bestriding the globe, champions of this century's miraculous economic growth. The goal of every ambitious company was to join them and, like them, be mighty enough to shrug off the blows which regularly toppled smaller rivals. But these are troubling times for the world's biggest

companies . . . The triumphs of mass production early in the century had given birth to most of the giant firms which came to tower over their industries. That bigger is better was rarely disputed . . . [but now many large firms are] scrapping layers of middle managers, cutting overheads and reorganising themselves into 'federations' of autonomous business units – that is, they are trying to become more like their smaller rivals . . . The era of corporate empire-building is over. An age of broader, fiercer global competition, with all its risks and uncertainties, has begun.[7]

Weber linked the effectiveness of large organizations, with their bureaucratic hierarchies, to universal principles of social rationality. His theory was clearly a cybernetic one, even if he used it to attack the aspirations of socialism. Bureaucracy for Weber is the most efficient form of organization because it concentrates information and power at the top; the lower down one is in an organization, the more fixed and delimited one's tasks tend to be.

It is not at all obvious that this form of organization is completely disappearing today, or that there will occur a wholesale transition towards decentralized and more flexible systems of authority, as many have claimed. All social change tends to be dialectical; a movement one way usually produces opposing trends also. So it is likely to be with organizations. In the economic sphere, for example, flexible authority for some probably means increasing constraint for others in different areas or contexts. Large corporations which come under attack may very well find ways of defending themselves; processes of decentralization in one sector might create renewed centralization in another.

Yet some of the changes now affecting organizations are likely to proceed further, and the overall direction of development seems clear. Democratizing processes within organizations are all the more striking because they fly in the face of what was the accepted wisdom about scale and bureaucratic organization up to no more than a generation ago. A post-bureaucratic organization can both harness social reflexivity and respond to situations of manufactured uncertainty much more effectively than a command system. Organizations structured in terms of active trust necessarily devolve responsibility and depend on an expanded dialogic space. A 'responsibility-based organization' recognizes that reflexivity produces a return to the need for local knowledge, even if such local knowledge is not ordinarily traditional.[8]

A *fourth* domain of dialogic democratization concerns the larger global order. For a long while democratizing influences on a world level were understood in the conventional terms of international relations theory. The 'international arena' was seen as 'above' the level of nation-states. In this conception, any tendencies towards democratization would involve the construction of political institutions of liberal democracy writ large. The 'empty' or 'anarchic' areas connecting nation-states, in other words, would have to be filled in. Such ideas have not become irrelevant, but look to be of more limited importance where globalization and social reflexivity are so deeply interrelated. For many globalizing connections do not flow through the nation-state, but in large part bypass it.

It is possible, indeed probable, that forms of representative democracy paralleling those established within states might come to exist globally. Thus Held's model of cosmopolitan democracy involves the establishing of regional parliaments covering whole continents and responsible to the ultimate authority of the United Nations. Without an advance of dialogic democracy, however, such organizations would become subject to the same limitations as state-based liberal democratic systems. On a global level, dialogic democratization would imply the democratizing of democracy, but also the spread of other dialogic mechanisms.

What might these be? They would involve, in some part, factors and influences already mentioned. Social movements and self-help groups of global spread have in many circumstances opened up dialogic spaces with states and business organizations. No government in the world, for example, can claim ignorance of ecological problems; and such problems are in effect today at the centre of worldwide dialogues involving a multiplicity of collective actors.

Potential dialogic space, however, is also opened up along all those points of contact which global cosmopolitanism brings between different cultures and traditions, whether these be decaying or resurgent. Here, as I shall argue in a subsequent chapter, there is likely to be a stark trade-off between dialogic democratization and violence. The issue of fundamentalism at this point raises itself with full force; for fundamentalism, I have suggested, can be understood exactly as a refusal of dialogue in a world where different traditions are brought into regular contact as never before.

Democracy and the problem of solidarity

In each of the spheres noted above, the development of dialogic democracy at the moment is more possibility than actuality. Yet identifying these contexts of potential democratization allows us to explore the connection of democracy with the creation of new solidarities.

On each side of the political spectrum today we see a fear of social disintegration and a call for a revival of community. If a radical politics in current times has to be restorative, can we rediscover the idea or reality of community in present-day social conditions? The auguries don't look good. After all, the destruction of community, and most forms of communal solidarity, have been firmly signalled in sociological thought for a long while. Community, as Durkheim and Ferdinand Tönnies argued at the turn of the century, has been replaced by association – by impersonal ties, organized through the economic division of labour. Durkheim believed that community could to some extent be re-established in the occupational sphere; unions and professional associations could provide sources of social solidarity lacking elsewhere. That has proved, however, to be an impractical dream.

A reconstruction of civil society, or aspects of it, might prove the answer – or so many say. Several problems exist, however, for those who call for a regenerating of civil society as a means for the rediscovery of community:

1 The idea of civil society, and its reality, was bound up with the state and its centralization. Indeed, I would say it was an *aspect* of that centralization, a set of reinvented traditions. How, therefore, could civil society be renewed in an era of detraditionalization where the state, especially in its most integrated form,

as a nation-state, comes up against intensified forms of globalization?

2 A renewal of civil society could prove dangerous rather than emancipatory. For it might encourage an upsurge of fundamentalisms, coupled to an increased potentiality for violence. One of the great successes of the nation-state was the high level of internal pacification it achieved, at least in the industrialized societies. Organized civil violence, in the shape of civil war, became very much the exception rather than the rule. Yet it may very well be that such internal pacification was achieved only against the background of chronic preparation for external war. Solidarity at home, clear-cut enemies abroad – this was after all the context in which rights of citizenship became expanded. Where states have no enemies, but only face diffuse threats, a potentially but not actually hostile international environment, disintegrative tendencies internally might again become strong.

3 There is a possible tension between democratization and a renewal of civil society. The development of abstract, universal rights, such as advocated in liberalism, does not create community, at a national or any other level. Indeed it has been suggested by some critics that a proliferation of rights invades communal orders of civil society and destroys them. The idea goes back to Tocqueville, who in a famous passage wrote of individuals in American society:

> Each of them, living apart, is as a stranger to the fate of the rest – his children and his private friends constitute to him the whole of mankind; as for the rest of his fellow-citizens, he is close to them, but he sees them not; he touches them, but he feels them not; he exists but in himself and for himself alone; and if his kindred still remain to him, he may be said at any rate to have lost his country.

The renewal of social solidarity is a conservative problem, fastened on by conservative critics of liberalism and leftism, but it does not admit of conservative solutions. For conservatives of all persuasions a sense of community has to come from the past, and gains its hold from the sense that the group, with its sedimented wisdoms, is greater than the individual. Community is inseparable from tradition; yet, as I have stressed, we cannot go back to tradition to resolve current social problems. Or we cannot do so, at least, where tradition is defended in the traditional way. It follows that we cannot go back to civil society either, in anything like *its* traditional form. For, as it is ordinarily understood, civil society was the product of social arrangements that no longer exist.

Tocqueville spoke for many others when he portrayed a decline of communal responsibility in the face of a coruscating egoism, a spectacle of isolated individuals 'incessantly endeavouring to procure the petty and paltry pleasures with which they glut their lives'.[9] Egoism, however, should be distinguished from individuation, which neither stems from it nor (necessarily) leads to it. The advance of social reflexivity means that individuals have no choice but to make choices; and these choices define who they are. People have to 'construct their own biographies' in order to sustain a coherent sense of self-identity. Yet they cannot do so without interacting with others and this very fact creates new solidarities. The key element here is the generating of trust, particularly via the transition to more active trust mechanisms.

The problem of social solidarity has to be understood against the background of the disappearance of 'cultural segmentalism' – the cultural cosmopolitanism that was preserved through geographical separation. Local communities in a segmental system function through exclusion, a differentiating of insiders from outsiders. They also depend on the infrastructural traditions of family and gender noted earlier. Those who think of 'community' only in a positive sense should remember the intrinsic limitations of such an order. Traditional communities can be, and normally have been, oppressive. Community in the form of mechanical solidarity crushes individual autonomy and exerts a compelling pressure towards conformism.

A return to cultural segmentalism means an increased likelihood of social disintegration – the very opposite of what calls for a revival of civil society are designed to achieve. Social solidarity can effectively be renewed only if it acknowledges autonomy and democratization – as well as the intrinsic influence of social reflexivity. Such a renewal must recognize obligations, not just rights. Obligation is not only important because it implies a 'vertical' connection with the needs of others; it matters because it refers also to the sustaining of ties with others over time.

Let us first of all consider how trust, obligation and solidarity might relate to one another in the various areas of personal life: the family, sexual involvements, friendship and kinship. In a post-traditional order, trust in personal relations depends on an assumption of the integrity of the other. It is based on a 'positive spiral' of difference. Getting to know the other, coming to rely on the other, presumes using difference as a means of developing positive emotional communication. It is active trust; compulsive dependence is a sign of an unhappy relation with the other. Trust in others generates solidarity across time as well as space: the other is someone on whom one can rely, that reliance becoming a mutual obligation. Intimacy here is not, as some have suggested, a substitute for community, or a degenerate form of it; it is the very medium whereby a sense of the communal is generated and continued.

When founded on active trust, obligation implies reciprocity. Obligations are binding because they are mutual, and this is what gives them their authority. I take it that this theorem applies as much to obligations between parents and children as between marriage partners, lovers or friends. One must emphasize that obligation here is based on the communication of difference, geared to an appreciation of integrity. Obligation does not come from rights. The rights one has in a relationship specify one's autonomy; they do not define one's obligations to the other. The enemy of obligation is moral fecklessness, since this trades off the integrity of the other. Obligations will stabilize relationships in so far as the condition of mutual integrity is met.

The interconnection of dialogic democracy, personal life and social solidarity, however, does not resolve wider questions of community, society and more globalized social systems. Here again the problem is not only the creation or sustaining of solidarities, but the avoidance or minimizing of conflicts, clashes and pariah-type effects where such solidarities *are* strong. The notion of dialogic democracy suggests several general contexts in which democratization might enhance social cohesion while avoiding such negative consequences. These might be portrayed, together with the democratizing of personal life, as follows:

Context	Domain of active trust
Personal relationships	Mutual obligation based on integrity and communication
Abstract systems	Social visibility and negotiated responsibilities
The state	Civil association (Oakeshott)
Global orders	Cosmopolitan communication

In the realm of abstract systems – the many expert systems that so influence our lives today – dialogic democracy focuses on issues of 'subpolitics', including in particular the impact of scientific and technological innovation in social life. Expertise remains uninterrogated so long as science remains a 'tradition' and so long as expertise is approached as though it were akin to 'traditional authority'. In a more reflexive social order, these assumptions in any case come under strain and start to break down. Yet the innovations of expertise are frequently disruptive and problematic in so far as the activities of experts are unaccountable, save to other experts. As Beck has commented, the non-accountability of 'subpolitics' results directly from the separation of theory and practice on which, until quite recently at least, scientific orthodoxy has always insisted. Lack of responsibility for consequences, disinterested testing of theories, freedom of research from any ethical constraints – these were the basis, not just of the claims of science to produce truth, but of the random impact of technology on the social order.[10]

There is no alternative to the rule of science and expertise; yet when our very everyday life has become experimental, the development of autonomy and the protection of solidarity means that equally there is no alternative to a dialogic engagement with them. Self-help groups and social movements, as mentioned before, can and do play an important part here. But so also do all those other agencies, including government and transnational agencies, which concern themselves with the filtering and regulation of expert claims to knowledge.

The 'opening out' of science has a real similarity to that 'opening out' characteristic of the generating of trust in personal life. In neither case is it incompatible with authority; and it does not necessarily threaten that independence which science must have if it is not to succumb to dogmatism. The opening out of science, in fact, is part and parcel *of* attempts to come to terms with problems of truth and responsibility – where claims to valid knowledge can no longer be said to rely on induction and to 'speak for themselves'. These are questions to which I shall return in a subsequent chapter.

I take it that, as in other areas, the relation between dialogic democracy and solidarity, as regards expert systems, centres on the question of trust. As opposed to 'acceptance of', or 'reliance on', expert authority, active trust presumes visibility and responsibility on both sides. Reflexive engagements with abstract systems may be puzzling and disturbing for lay individuals and resented by professionals. Yet they force both to confront issues of responsibility that otherwise remain latent.

Active trust is the enemy of fundamentalism to the degree to which it is established through difference – and this is exactly its connection with dialogic democracy. What applies to the 'difference' between expert and layperson applies also to the wider arenas of civic and global orders. In this respect we can turn profitably to Oakeshott's discussion of what he calls 'civil association'. Civil association depends on cultivating the 'civil condition' which Oakeshott, following Vico, speaks of as 'a relationship of human beings': this is not, he says, a ' "process" made up of functionally or causally related components; it is intelligent relationship enjoyed only in virtue of having been learned and understood.' Civil association 'is not organic, evolutionary, teleological, functional or syndromic relationship but an understood relationship of intelligent agents'. It is not, in other words, community writ large: that way, one might say, lie the dangers of xenophobic ethnicities or nationalisms.

Nor is the civil condition a market, which is a form of 'enterprise association'. The 'vernacular language of civil understanding and intercourse' isn't a language of commerce – or one of love or affection. The civil condition can be 'understood as agents acknowledging themselves to be *cives* in virtue of being related to one another in the recognition of a practice composed of rules . . .'[11] For Oakeshott, such rules take on the force of law when part of a formal canon; and they express the hold of tradition.

The central insights of Oakeshott's view that I want to stress concern the theses that civil association is not a community, and that the rules of which he speaks depend on 'intelligent relationship'. 'Intelligent relationship', I shall presume, whether Oakeshott himself intended this or not, means living along with others in a way that respects their autonomy. The civil condition in a post-traditional order in its most desirable forms of expression can be understood in a way which owes as much to John Dewey as to Oakeshott. A democratic order, Dewey argued, requires a 'socially generous' attitude of mind. 'Civic efficiency', he wrote, is 'neither more nor less than capacity to share in a give and take experience.'[12]

Civil association, in this reading, would depend on the 'positive appreciation of difference', but not on the conditions of active trust in personal relations writ large. And there would be an inherent tie between civil association and a cosmopolitan engagement with groups, ideas and contexts that have nothing immediately to do with the domain of the state. The New Right tends to insist that a cosmopolitan outlook is inevitably the enemy of commitment and obligation. For such critics, it is an attitude in which anything goes – and consequently where nothing has any particular value.

But why shouldn't one take cosmopolitanism – a sort of global generalization of civil association – to be almost the opposite? A cosmopolitan attitude would not insist that all values are equivalent, but would emphasize the responsibility that individuals and groups have for the ideas they hold and the practices in which they engage. The cosmopolitan is not someone who renounces commitments – in the manner, say, of the dilettante – but someone who is able to articulate the nature of those commitments, and assess their implications for those whose values are different.

Let me sum up briefly. Pressures towards democratization – which always face contrary influences – are created by the twin processes of globalization and institutional reflexivity. Detraditionalization disembeds local contexts of action and at the same time alters the character of the global order: even where they remain firmly adhered to, traditions are increasingly forced into contact with one another. Globalization, reflexivity and detraditionalization thus create 'dialogic spaces' that must in some way be filled. These are spaces which can be engaged with dialogically, invoking mechanisms of active trust – but which can also be occupied by fundamentalisms (as well, as we shall see later, by compulsive behaviour or addictions).

The domain of personal relations is a central arena of potential democratization – an area of extraordinarily rapid change, whose influence directly permeates more formal and public milieux. Since it concerns divisions of a very fundamental kind – between the sexes and between the generations – the possible democratization of personal life is of the first importance for many aspects of political reform today. The forms of social solidarity which it can generate, however, cannot be directly interpolated within wider institutional or political orders, the reason being that the trust mechanisms involved depend on the recognition of personal integrity.

Such integrity, of course, is highly important in public institutions, but it is not the prime source of solidarity there. In the other areas mentioned – abstract systems, the state and more global interconnections – the means of developing active trust have to be different. Visibility and responsibility are the guiding themes in these contexts, but organized in somewhat contrasting ways in each area. In relation to the impact of science, and more broadly of expert systems, dialogic democratization presumes the intrusion of the lay public, organizations and states into contexts which scientists themselves might like to claim as 'autonomous'. Such a phenomenon raises issues of a complicated kind and I shall confront them more fully in chapter 8.

Cosmopolitanism, as an attitude of mind and as an institutionalized phenomenon, is the connecting thread between the democratizing of democracy within the state and more global forms of interaction between states or other organizations. Civil association, although not exactly as described by Oakeshott, is in turn the condition of existence of a cosmopolitan state; this is (in principle) a state conceived of, not as a community but as people living in 'intelligent relationship' with one another. The famously Janus-faced character of nationalism comes from the fact that it straddles the divide between civil association and the conception of the state as a community with its own 'personality'. It isn't surprising, therefore, that in a post-traditional age nationalism stands close to aggressive fundamentalisms, embraced by neo-fascist groups as well as by other sorts of movements or collectivities.

Dialogic democracy on a more global level might begin to resemble civil association if there were to come about an extension of cosmopolitan democracy such as envisaged by Held. Without such a globalizing *cives*, communicative mechanisms of a cosmopolitan sort are inevitably quite limited and diffuse – although no less consequential for world society for all that. For obvious reasons, there is no arena in which the capability of dialogue to create and sustain active trust is more important.

Democracy, inequality and power

Democratization combats power, seeking to turn it into negotiated relationships, whether these be between equals or are relations of differential authority. Yet democracy, dialogic or otherwise, plainly has its limits. These limits concern especially the intrusive influence of inequality. Dialogue does not depend upon material equality, but it does presume that differential resources aren't used to prevent views being voiced or for a drastic skewing of the conditions of dialogic interchange. One of the great strengths of the critique of liberal democracy coming from the left has long been the demand that democracy be conjoined to programmes of economic equalization.

For many leftists, the welfare state has come to be a, even *the*, vehicle of such equalization. It has been theorized as an essential part of long-term processes of social emancipation, leading from political to economic equality – most notably in the work of T. H. Marshall. Marshall's views, influential though they have been, do not stand up to scrutiny. In place of his evolutionary theory of rights, we should see the domains of the civil order, polity and economy as separate institutional frameworks, with their own dilemmas and possibilities. The rights and prerogatives they yield to the less favoured groups in society can at no point be declared 'safe' – they are likely to be subject to more or less chronic tension and struggle.

The question of poverty is usually approached, particularly by supporters of the welfare state, as the other side of wealth. What could be more logical? Poverty is to be fought against, in this view, because it is an affront to norms of economic equality; reducing inequalities necessarily takes the form of redistributing wealth and income from the more affluent to the poor through systems of welfare. Such an emancipatory politics, however, is of little value if not driven by life-political considerations, for reasons I shall seek to make clear in the chapter which follows. This discussion needs to be placed in a wide context, for the welfare state is bound up with concerns other than poverty or inequality alone.

5
Contradictions of the Welfare State

Structural sources of the welfare state

Protecting the welfare state seems to many on the left essential to what a civilized society is all about; the needy and the sick are not abandoned to fend for themselves, but through the actions of government have the chance to lead satisfying lives. Yet this situation needs enquiring into, because welfare institutions have only partly been the creation of socialists – and more radical socialist thinkers, in fact, used to spend a lot of time criticizing them.

One of the problems with the term 'welfare state' is that it is not clear what is qualifying what. The approach of reformist socialism assumes that it is the state which organizes welfare: the state intervenes in the economy in order to render the social order more equitable. Suppose, however, that 'welfare' qualifies 'state'? In this case the modern state is in some part *defined* by such intervention, which might be part of its administrative form. This interpretation, which I think is the correct one, makes sense of the fact that welfare systems, at least until the period following the Second World War, did not originate from one particular side of the political spectrum.

Poverty, unemployment, sickness and so forth, according to such a view, are not just givens with which the state has to cope as best it can; they are constituted as part of the process of state formation, defined not by the state alone, but by conflicts and battles between state agencies and other organizations and groups. And this process of social constitution has been a long-term one, not limited to the past fifty or even hundred years. Thus 'pauperism' was not just a condition of individuals living in 'civil society', into which the state came to intervene, but became formed in and through such intervention – this very circumstance, in fact, helped establish 'civil society' as such. Civil society, to repeat a theme of the previous chapter, apparently the terrain on which welfare systems were established, was brought into being as part of their construction; it has never been simply a set of institutions 'outside' the state.

From the late seventeenth century onwards the 'discourse of the poor' in the industrializing countries was oriented towards national integration and the development of national wealth. 'Poverty' was not defined as the condition of being without resources, but emerged in relation to the needs of *industry* – the term 'industriousness' connected 'productive work' with a specific outlook on life. The poor were those who could not or would not work. The connection of pauperism with lack of moral education was very clear: 'work for those who will labour, punishment for those that will not, and bread for those who cannot.' Moral purposefulness in turn related directly to social well-being; for, as Matthew Hale put it, poverty 'leaves men tumultuous and unquiet' and combating poverty is 'an act of civil prudence and political wisdom'.[1]

Until the early nineteenth century, 'industry' was used only as an adverb and was opposed to pauperism without specific reference to capitalist production. The origins of the welfare state are not to be traced to attempts to define and police pauperism – although this endeavour certainly has had its enduring effects – but to the development of what Claus Offe has called 'active' versus 'passive' proletarianization.[2] Passive proletarianization is the dispossession of large numbers of people from agrarian or peasant occupations, where this process is either unwanted or resisted by them. Active proletarianization – a willingness to enter a labour contract – did not follow inevitably from the passive type, however. State intervention was a prime influence connecting the active and passive forms; and here we find the point at which the 'administrative state' started to become transformed into the 'welfare state'. This was not a matter of some mysterious functional compatibility between the state and capitalistic enterprise. It was the outcome of the realization on the part of state officials and industrialists that social policy was needed to protect individuals in non-market situations where traditional sources of support had largely perished; and to a lesser degree the outcome of the active mobilization of workers' movements to improve their conditions of life.

Various recent interpretations of the early history of welfare institutions, such as that of Abraham de Swaan, have emphasized that the welfare state 'was not the achievement of the organized working classes, nor the result of a capitalist conspiracy to pacify them . . .'[3] Its development 'was a gradual and often uninformed process propelled as much by ambitious politicians and rather visionary civil servants as by an abstract notion of a crumbling social order or fears of major social unrest'.[4] The basic elements of the welfare state in most Western countries were in place well before the Second World War, at a time, in Europe at any rate, when rightist governments were mostly in power. Part of the reason was the perceived need to deal with mass unemployment; but some key welfare measures came from the period of the Great War. Mobilizing the economy and society was the prime demand in wartime; the enhanced role of the state in the First World War introduced forms of social and economic provisions that were solidified and extended during the Second.

The structural sources of the welfare state are several. First, welfare institutions have their beginnings in the effort to create a society in which work, meaning paid labour in industry, has a central and defining role. Welfare measures, particularly social security, might appear to be concerned only with those who for one reason or another cannot enter the labour market; but in fact in their earlier and later history they are bound up with promoting 'industry' in the adverbial sense. Second, the welfare state has always been a national state and this connection is far from coincidental. One of the main factors impelling the development of welfare systems has been the desire on the part of governing authorities to promote national solidarity. From early days to late on, welfare systems were constructed as part of a more generalized process of state building. Who says welfare state says nation-state.

Third, the welfare state, from its first origins to the present time, has been concerned with the management of risk, efforts at risk management indeed being a basic part of what 'government' in general has become. Welfare schemes are a form of social insurance. Insurance refers to any risk-management scheme oriented towards coping with an open future – a means of dealing with (predictable) hazards. Social insurance is about the disposal of risks in a wealth-creating, future-oriented society – particularly, of course, those risks that are not 'subsumed' in the wage–labour relation.

This outlook reflected the early encounter of modernity with pre-existing forms of social order. For in pre-modern societies, poverty, like bad harvests, was simply something that 'happened' – an event in nature. The rise of the concept of social insurance reflected not so much novel perceptions of social injustice as the ascendancy of the idea that social and economic life can be *humanly controlled*. Critiques of classical economic theory, particularly in the shape of Keynesianism, were of course very important here, most notably in shaping responses to the Great Depression. For a period of several decades after the 1930s, the dominant economic orthodoxy saw the risk of large-scale unemployment as one that could effectively be managed.

The notion that welfare institutions should be understood as risk management systems fits closely with Goodin and Le Grand's convincing – although heterodox – interpretation of the reasons for the expansion of the welfare state after the Second World War. As they see it, pervasive uncertainty of a time of total war – a war which affected the civilian populations of most of the involved nations more directly than the First World War – 'led to a new popular demand for risk-spreading and broke down old barriers to it'.[5]

The experience of the war brought home to the population that risks were shared: after all, the bombs fell on everyone. Before the war, even after the Great Depression, most social security programmes were aimed at the chronic poor; the wartime experience had the consequence of shifting attention from income-specific to universalistic programmes. The poor were not so much 'always with us' as a testament to the misfortunes which could befall more or less everyone.

> Under [wartime] conditions, anyone's future might be your own. That forces each of us to reflect impartially upon the interests of all. Welfare states and suchlike constitute the appropriate institutional response. These responses get frozen and persist well beyond the moment of uncertainty that gave rise to them . . . Wartime uncertainty and risk-sharing seem to us to provide a particularly powerful explanation, not only of the origins, but also of the persistence and now the waning of the post-war welfare state.

An interpretation of social programmes as the sharing of risk fits closely with the themes of solidarity and the promotion of industriousness. Each of these other concerns became intensified in times of war. Thus towards the end of his report, Beveridge wrote:

> The prevention of want and the diminution and relief of disease – the special aim of the social services – are in fact a common interest to all citizens. It may be possible to secure a keener realisation of that fact in war than it is in peace, because war breeds national unity and readiness to sacrifice personal interests to the common cause . . .[6]

An emphasis on work is also particularly central in war conditions, when a collective effort is strongly fostered and there is 'more than' full employment – many are working longer hours than they would otherwise do.

Socialists and workers' organizations had long pressed for some of the programmes adopted during the maturation of the welfare state in the postwar period. Reformist socialism in power was the main vehicle of the enactment of welfare provisions. The socialists, however, adopted and nurtured a child which was not wholly their offspring. They were able to do so by reinterpreting the welfare state in terms of the twin imperatives of socialist thought: centralized direction of economic life and the pursuit of greater equality. By involving labour in the running of government, the welfare state became a symbol of a class compromise that apparently resolved the longstanding 'social problem' and at the same time guaranteed economic effectiveness.

Problems of welfare: work and class

Those who regard the post-1945 welfare state as a major achievement surely are right to do so. While there are notable differences between countries as to the level of the development and the broad social effects of welfare institutions, the progress made towards overcoming Beveridge's 'five evils' was remarkable. The problems the welfare state now faces, in its various versions in different societies, nevertheless lie very deep. They concern each of its main 'thematics': work, solidarity and risk management. Most interpreters of the travails of the welfare state have placed emphasis on the first two of these factors, but I shall stress the core significance of the third.

All three, however, raise important questions. The first concerns not only the nature of work in modern societies, but key questions of gender and the family. The second implies, among other things, a look at class analysis: the integrative effects of the welfare state supposedly concern especially the diminishing of class divisions. The third involves pressing further the theme of external versus manufactured risk.

The welfare state, as has been well documented, took for granted and even furthered the equation of work with paid employment in the labour market; it hence also presumed the patriarchal family. The achieving of full employment, one of the most important aims of socialist advocacy of welfare systems in particular, meant male employment. This was a model of work as fate (for men) and domesticity as fate (for women). It belonged to a time when gender identities had not yet been reflexively challenged and when 'non-standard' work, including domestic work, in official definitions of things didn't count as work at all.[7]

If such systems are out of line with a situation in which women have entered the paid labour force in very large numbers, so they are also with a society in which the centrality of industry is coming to be placed in question. The idea of full-time, permanent employment, as Patricia Hewitt observes, can be seen clearly in the social security system, employment law and policies for retirement and pensions. It pervades the culture of business, management and public life. It affects the organisation and strategies of trade unions as well as most discussion of full employment. It indirectly influences decisions in many other policy areas, including transport, leisure provision, child care and the care of elderly dependants. And it profoundly affects and depends upon the organisation of family life.[8]

Today the model of the permanent full-time worker becomes assaulted by a host of other competing modes of work organiz-ation – an expansion of part-time work, voluntary career breaks, self-employment and home-working. Even though they are quite often disguised pay-claims, efforts to achieve a shorter working week have in most countries led to fewer average working hours. In all these areas the ethos of 'industry' – or what I shall later call *productivism* – comes under strain.

The connection of welfare policies to the consolidating of the nation-state has rarely been thoroughly analysed in the literature. Yet this connection not only helps explain the rise of welfare systems, it is also a major source of the tensions with which they have become beset. The 'fulltime, permanent employment' model which dominated the expansion of welfare institutions was based on the economic centrality of mass production and the centralized organization of capital and wage labour. The welfare state was an integrated national state in which 'corporatism' enhanced – but also presumed – national solidarity. The new period of globalization attacks not only the economic basis of the welfare state but the commitment of its citizenry to the equation of wealth with national wealth. The state is less able to provide effective central control of economic life; at the same time, the sovereign capabilities of the nation become undermined through a mixture of globalization and social reflexivity.

The relation between the decline of the welfare state and the changing character of the global order of states was to some extent masked by the very political successes of the New Right. The neoliberals led the attack on the 'overloaded' welfare state in the name of freedom of competitive enterprise from bureau-cratic burdens and from enfeebled labour markets. Simultaneously, however, they not only defended the state and nation but called for a 'strong state' in the international arena. The paradoxical character of this position was soon noted by critics, and corresponded to the wider paradoxes of New Right political theory noted earlier. Yet for a while, where it was in power at any rate, the New Right was able to contain the contradiction and claim that an assault on the welfare state was compatible with strengthening the nation. In fact, the very same factors that were altering the position of the nation-state in the wider global system were helping to undermine the welfare institutions previously so closely bound up with national solidarity.

One of the most familiar theses about the stresses and strains of the welfare state is the argument that it has been undermined by its own successes. In other words, when the economic climate becomes adverse, those who have benefited most move to protect the position they have attained against more disadvantaged groups. The middle class 'taxpayers' revolt' comes from the selfish desire to protect a comfortable way of life, with middle-class groups biting the hand that originally fed them. As a result of the very expansion of welfare capitalism, the majority of the population in the developed societies enjoy a high standard of living. The members of that majority are able to opt out of, or no longer require, the welfare provisions that helped them get where they are. They form what Galbraith has called 'the Contented Majority, the Contented Electoral Majority or, more spaciously, the Culture of Contentment':

> The future for the contented majority is thought effectively within their personal command. Their anger is evident – and, indeed, can be strongly evident – only when there is a threat or possible threat to present well-being and future prospect – when government and the seemingly less deserving intrude or threaten to intrude their needs or demands . . . self-regard is, and predictably, the dominant, indeed the controlling mood of the contented majority.[9]

Conventional though it has become, this sort of argument is surely dubious. In the first place, one might speak of the existence of a culture of anxiety as much as one of contentment. A detraditionalizing order offers important forms of freedom for many, but it also creates many new sources of tension and problems – in daily life, nationally and globally. Middle-class or more affluent people are less distinctively protected from some of these forms of turbulence than they used to be. This is the case even on the economic level, where few occupations any longer offer safeguards against unemployment.

The response of the majority to this situation is not just a primitive holding on to what one has got. The fact that the more affluent on the whole tend to benefit more from the welfare state than poorer groups is not likely, in this reflexive world, to be something that escapes their awareness. If many have, in some part and in some ways at any rate, turned against the welfare state, the reasons are more complex than suggested by the culture of contentment thesis. The 'bureaucratic critique' of the welfare state is not confined to the neoliberal intellectuals; in circumstances where, in numerous aspects of life, one cannot choose not to choose, centrally organized systems of dispensation can come to be seen as an affront to autonomy even when they confer material benefits. Conversely, those who simply accept that they will live through such systems, who carry on in the old way, seem to refuse to accept the responsibilities that others must shoulder.

What is at issue here, then, is perhaps not so much an egoistic refusal to engage with the wider world, as a spreading consciousness that the world has changed rather dramatically, and with it the conditions of day-to-day existence. As their relation to the state, and to the nation, alters, the members of the supposedly contented majority take a more open and questioning attitude towards many aspects of their lives (no doubt this often goes along with a defensiveness too). They are conscious of the phenomenon of welfare dependency and react suspiciously, sometimes perhaps aggressively, to it. They are less prone to deference towards the state authorities, whether in the form of the political leadership or bureaucratic officialdom. Hence they are liable to question more and accept less, including the burdens of taxation – particularly where what they get from their 'investment' is not visible, but hidden away in the overall finances of big government. They are conscious also of the relative impotence of governments to control what they claim to govern, including their own national economies.

These things go along with quite basic changes in the class system on a broader level. Classes in current times affect the life chances of individuals in a more 'refracted' way than used to be the case, even until fairly recently. What Marx thought would be the basis of global political revolution, the development of class-based movements, proved to be more bound up with struggles within the nation-state. The links between class and collective social engagement have become quite sharply lessened over the period of the expansion of reflexive modernization. Class used to be connected to communal experience and action in several ways. One was through regional division and common occupational experience in the local area. Many such traditional communities, particularly working-class communities, have become broken up. New modes of regionalization, the result of globalized stratification divisions, rarely produce the same class solidarities.

A second factor relating class and social community was the sexual division of labour. Communal class action was not only primarily a male affair but was enhanced by the social invisibility of other types of work, including non-waged work. Gender divisions in work, paid and otherwise, as we know, do not often coincide with class boundaries. Finally, there used to be discernible cultural symbols related to class solidarity, from the cloth cap to the royal sceptre; these disappear or lose their mobilizing power as a result of detraditionalization.

Some of the consequences of these developments can be briefly enumerated:

1 Class for the most part is no longer experienced as class, but as constraints (and opportunities) emanating from a variety of sources. Class becomes individualized and expressed through the individual's 'biography'; it is experienced less and less as collective fate.

2 The individual relates to the class system not just as a producer but as a consumer. Lifestyle and taste, mobilized in an active way by individuals and groups, become as evident markers of social differentiation as position in the productive order.

3 Problems that may originate in, or be strongly influenced by,

class factors tend to be perceived 'laterally' rather than 'horizon-tally'. They are not experienced as coming from the past, but as a result of circumstances impinging on an individual or group at a particular time. The 'generational transmission belt' of class comes to be broken. It isn't that the class background of individuals becomes irrelevant to their life chances – far from it. Since, however, children rarely now follow the occupation of their parents, and may have virtually no knowledge of their parents' contexts of work, their experience tends to seem more *ab novo*.

4 Class is hence less of a 'lifetime experience' than it was before. A high proportion of people (especially men) who are in blue-collar occupations at any one time have been at some point, or can expect in the future to be, in a white-collar job. Many, however, will have interrupted careers as a result of periods of enforced unemployment. Nor does unemployment only affect those at the lower end of the class scale. Given globalized economic competition, and the speed-up of technological inno-vation, the experience of redundancy becomes common across the occupational spectrum.

5 The growth of the secondary economy notwithstanding, inclusion in or exclusion from the labour market counts for even more than it did before. Non-economic support networks, includ-ing traditional support sources such as kin groups or spouses – and the state – are not able to cope. The 'new poor' are those having a weak situation in the labour market, or excluded from it altogether.

The question of the underclass

The period during which the welfare state has become embattled, from about the mid-1970s to the present, has also been one during which levels of (relative) poverty have risen in most industrialized societies. How far has such poverty been created by welfare institutions, rather than alleviated by them? And in what sense, if any, do those who find themselves in a situation of chronic poverty form an underclass? These issues have now been the centre of fierce debates between right and left for some two decades.

The term 'underclass' originally had a fairly clear sociological meaning and a not particularly controversial one. It has become politicized, however, as a result of having been drawn into the centre of polemics about the virtues or otherwise of the welfare state. Some leftists refuse any longer to use the concept, not on the grounds that it doesn't describe a reality, but because of its association with rightist critiques of welfare.

Galbraith is one author on the left who accepts the existence of an underclass and who indeed asserts that it is 'deeply functional' for contemporary societies. The underclass in the United States, he says, consists of people who 'do not share the comfortable well-being of the prototypical American'. Its members are to be found 'in the centres of the great cities or, less visibly, on deprived farms, as rural migrant labour or in erstwhile mining communities'. The underclass is composed mainly 'of members of minority groups, blacks or people of Hispanic origin'. It consists of people prepared to take on tasks that the majority of the indigenous population refuse to do. Much the same situation, Galbraith argues, applies in the European countries as well. Onerous tasks relinquished by the native populations fall to immigrants from the southern Mediterranean, North Africa, South Asia and elsewhere.

In Galbraith's words, 'The modern community – the market system – requires such an underclass . . . and it must reach out to other countries to sustain and refresh it.' Yet the conditions under which this class lives breed crime, family breakdown and general social disorganization. Such a situation comes about mainly because barriers limit the chances of underclass members of upward social mobility. Racism and other influences prevent full assimilation.

The view from the right is quite different. The underclass is the creation of welfare dependency, which fixes and institutionalizes social and economic circumstances that would otherwise be much more fluid. Underclasses are not made up of victims of the market system, but of individuals who exclude themselves from that system, opting instead to make use of welfare state benefits. A life on welfare is one which tends to become devoid of moral regulation – hence the disintegration of stable communal and family life, something which, in the words of Charles Murray, is 'now contaminating entire neighbourhoods'.[10] People who take from the welfare system tend to scorn the wider social community rather than recognizing obligations to it. An aimless attitude invades their life as a whole, leading to irresponsible attitudes towards parenthood and towards property. High rates of illegitimacy, lone-parent households and criminality are the result.

Which of these conflicting interpretations, if either, is valid? And what evidence is there in any case that the development of underclasses is a real phenomenon?

How far a distinct underclass exists depends on quite conventional sociological indices – whether there are groups having life chances notably distinct from those of people in more favoured class situations. Studies in the United States do in fact indicate that a substantial proportion of the poor remain mired in poverty for a long while, and that their offspring do also. Surveying the available evidence, Wilson concludes that there is 'a firm basis for accepting the argument that a ghetto underclass has emerged and exhibits the problems of long-term poverty and welfare dependency'.[11] Much the same conclusion can be accepted for other industrialized countries, although the degree of 'class hardening' observed varies considerably.

A good deal hangs on assessing the conflict between left and right interpretations of the origins of underclasses for analysing wider issues of welfare. Galbraith's argument from functional necessity, one could say to begin with, seems weak. For a period of time a demand for labour sparked off immigration from Third World to developed countries. Yet some of the groups represented in underclasses, most notably American blacks, are not recent immigrants to the society in question. Moreover, it is not obvious how the long-term unemployed, who become experienced as a financial burden by the rest of the society, are functional for the social order.

The argument from the right, however, also comes up against basic objections. For instance, if welfare incentives lead to underclass joblessness and the breakup of family life, these trends should become reversed when welfare benefits decline, as they have done in many Western countries over the past twenty years.

This has not happened. Levels of joblessness among younger members of minority groups in US cities have reached calamitous proportions, but have also risen steeply in Britain and elsewhere. Structural unemployment, combined with an exodus of working-class and middle-class families from inner-city neighbourhoods – particularly pronounced in the United States – are the main influences. The processes involved then tend to become self-reinforcing:

> Thus, in a neighbourhood with a paucity of regularly employed families and with the overwhelming majority of families having spells of long-term joblessness, people experience a social isola-tion that excludes them from the job network system that per-meates other neighbourhoods and that is so important in learning about or being recommended for jobs that become available in various parts of the city. And as the prospects for employment diminish, other alternatives such as welfare and the underground economy are not only increasingly relied on, they come to be seen as a way of life.[12]

What happens is a sort of destructive spiral, which welfare programmes may sometimes contribute to rather than counter-act. There are very real similarities here with circumstances of more global poverty. A sequence of events is set in train which destroys local cultures and modes of self-reliance. Bureaucratic aid programmes can help in some ways to alleviate such a situation, but in other respects they may actually reinforce it. The result is ambivalence and psychic discomfort. Individuals become dependent on systems of provision which they recognize as alien and over which they have little control; it isn't surprising that they might tend to take a manipulative attitude towards them and may not feel in the least bit grateful for what the wider society has provided. For their dependence on that wider com-munity is bracketed with exclusion from full participation in it.

The social influences creating underclasses are structural before they are cultural, but once in play they may bring cultural demoralization of a profound kind. The debates between left and right on this issue in the present day are effectively a replay of the controversy created in the social sciences several decades ago by Oscar Lewis's notion of the culture of poverty. On the basis of his work in Latin America, Lewis suggested that, once they have become economically marginalized, people develop adaptive responses transmitted from generation to generation. The culture of poverty, according to Lewis, is 'a reaction of the poor to their marginal position in a class stratified, highly individuated, capitalistic society'. Even by the age of six or seven slum children 'have usually absorbed the basic values and attitudes of their subculture and are not psychologically geared to take full advantage of changing conditions or increased opportunities which may occur in their lifetime'.[13]

Welfare dependency can become linked to cultures of poverty; what we should be careful not to do is to suppose that the traits of cultures of poverty are wholly opposed to social and cultural attitudes found in the larger world. Impoverished groups may be structurally 'hidden away' from the more affluent, who rarely if ever visit the areas where poverty is concentrated; but in globalized social conditions their lives are not culturally isolated. Ethnic differences from the majority population are often bound up with the development of underclasses, and such differences may become a focus of cultural exclusion. However, these very differences often directly connect the poor to globalized cultural settings – in matters of custom, religion, dress or music. For immigrant populations, these may be attachments sustained with countries and cultures of origin; but they often form cultural diasporas, which may stretch very widely.

Underclasses are not just pockets of deprivation within national societies, they are fault-lines along which the Third World rubs up against the First. The social isolation which separates underprivileged groups from the rest of the social order within nations mirrors the division of the rich from the poor on a global scale – and is causally bound up with that division. First World poverty cannot be approached as though it had no connection with inequalities of a much broader scale. This is an issue that will have to be returned to in the following chapter.

The future of welfare: a preliminary orientation

The welfare state project has foundered partly because it came to embody what turned out to be the failing aspirations of socialism, and partly because of the impact of the wider social changes that form a preoccupation of this whole book. The 'class compromise' of welfare institutions could remain relatively stable only so long as conditions of simple modernization held good. These were circumstances in which 'industriousness' and paid work remained central to the social system; where class relations were closely linked to communal forms; where the nation-state was strong and even in some respects further developing its sovereign powers; and where risk could still be treated largely as external and to be coped with by quite orthodox programmes of social insurance. None of these conditions holds in the same way in conditions of intensifying globalization and social reflexivity.

One of the most important structural weaknesses of the postwar welfare state was contained in the tenuous relation between the promotion of economic efficiency and attempts at redistribution. Welfare systems proved not only incapable of bringing about much redistribution of wealth and income; the welfare state actually became in some part a vehicle helping to promote the interests of an expanding middle class. The class compromise wasn't directly between capital and the working class; it was a compromise which solidified the middle sectors of the social order.[14]

Redistribution is an ambiguous term. As socialists have understood it, the word refers to the reduction of economic inequality. The welfare state has not proved very effective in reaching this goal, largely because of the heavy beneficial involvement of the middle class in social programmes. Poverty has been alleviated not mainly by redistribution from the more affluent to the poor but because of overall increases in wealth which moved everyone up. This has been as true in the Scandinavian societies, with the most conspicuously developed welfare programmes, as elsewhere. Redistribution can however also refer to the sharing of risk. It is here that the successes of the welfare state have been most marked. What welfare programmes have effectively achieved is a generalization of social insurance, particularly across the life-cycle.

This success is very real and significant. It presumes, however, a relatively stable distribution of risk across society; and also that risk can be depoliticized, or dealt with by being 'contained'.[15] In an era of reflexive modernization these issues become much more problematic. Manufactured risk is unstable in relation to both human and natural environments of action. It can no longer be confronted in an actuarial way, through the control of the 'routine disorder' of environments, including the environment of capitalistic production as well as of nature.

The question of external versus manufactured risk, as I shall try to show, is fundamental to rethinking the issue of welfare, and its relation to the state, in the industrialized countries today. The welfare state did not originate as a socialist project, but became increasingly drawn into the orbit of socialism, at least of the reformist socialist type. As such, it reflects the paradoxes of socialist thought but, even more importantly, it is part of a now lapsed historical endeavour. For most socialists – and also for other, more reluctant, supporters – the welfare state seemed to point a way ahead to a controllable and egalitarian future, whether or not this was seen as a halfway house to 'full socialism' or to some version of communism. With the collapse of socialism's historical ambitions, we have to look at the welfare state in quite a different light – one reason why it is worth stressing its heterogeneous origins.

6

Generative Politics and Positive Welfare

Welfare systems and manufactured uncertainty

The connection of welfare systems with the control of risk, as suggested in the preceding chapter, is quite elemental. Behind the calculation of risk there stands nothing less than the whole weight of Enlightenment philosophy. For the idea of risk is integral to the endeavour to control the future and to harness history to human purposes. The notions of risk and 'accident' are closely related. In most premodern contexts there were misfortunes rather than accidents; misfortune was fate seen, as it were, from its downside. It was, literally, 'bad fortune'.

The term 'accident' was coined and popularized alongside the idea of the regularity of accidents.[1] Accidents stem from hazard, which can be identified and catalogued. They are bound up with the concept of the 'common life' – or with the state – because they have to be classified in terms of large populations. The notions of risk and accident imply an ethics. Events which happened 'naturally' used to include the good and the bad; whether given by God or not, there seemed no basis on which to correct them. The collective assessment of risk, by contrast, presumes and expresses a situation where remedy is both available and desirable.

The idea of risk by definition recognizes the limits of control. But (understood as external risk) it does so only by seeing those limits as both 'manageable' and as lying outside the purview of modernity itself. The seamless character of modernity's spread into social and natural domains thus continues in an uninterrupted way – or it does so long as risk can be coped with by orthodox methods of insurance.

Manufactured risk might seem to differ from external risk mainly in so far as it escapes or confounds insurance. Thus Ewald argues that high-consequence risks have certain characteristics which set them apart from risk as previously experienced or understood. They are risks the damage associated with which cannot be compensated for – because their long-term consequences are unknown and cannot be properly evaluated. They express 'a causality and a temporality that is so wide, diffuse and extended' that they escape orthodox modes of attribution. We don't know how to come to terms properly with threats like these.[2]

These observations are important and I shall have more to say about their implications later. But one shouldn't understand the transition from external to manufactured risk only in relation to the emergence of overwhelming hazards. As I have emphasized previously, the real contrast lies in the source of risk. It is just because it isn't external that manufactured uncertainty can't readily be dealt with in an actuarial way.

Manufactured uncertainty, as I have tried to stress throughout this book, enters deeply into everyday life – it is not, or not only, expressed in more directly globalized forms of risk. Day-to-day life expresses manufactured risk to the degree to which it becomes detraditionalized – in so far as the experience of nature and social norms 'as fate' diminishes. Manufactured uncertainty – risk actively confronted within frames of action organized in a reflexive way – suggests, for reasons I shall develop shortly, a conception of *positive welfare*, connected in an immediate way with both life politics and generative politics.

At least some of the institutions usually grouped together under the rubric 'welfare state' have emphasized positive aspects of self-development and social care. This has been true most obviously of the sphere of education. Yet as a system of social insurance the welfare state has been organized mainly in terms of external risk. Thus social security provisions essentially seek to cover all those circumstances in which individuals find themselves unable to achieve a certain basic level of income and resources. Social security measures, by and large, do not attribute fault to those who are the recipients of state aid; but by that very token neither do they imply the assumption of responsibilities on the part of those affected.

Most welfare measures in fact are designed to cope with events once they have happened, rather than at origin – a major source of 'state failure'.[3] The problems of the welfare state are normally seen in fiscal terms, and indeed this is how they present themselves electorally. Welfare institutions have become more and more costly; the taxpayers' revolt places decisive limits on how far the revenue of the state can be expanded to meet those needs. According to the views of leftist authors at any rate, this situation is a prime influence on the spread of poverty and the development of underclasses.

Things look rather different if we see the difficulties of the welfare state as resulting from a movement from external to manufactured uncertainty. It is not so much rising costs and inability to meet them that is at issue as resources being organized in ways which are more and more inappropriate to the problems they were set up to meet. Welfare systems designed for emancipatory ends become strained or ineffective where life-political issues loom increasingly large and where generative political programmes are needed to cope with them.

Manufactured uncertainty does not form part of the 'closed circle' of Enlightenment modernity: it presumes measures which are as much preventive or precautionary as ones implying the continuous development of technical knowledge. Yet the imponderable character of manufactured uncertainty means that such measures cannot always, or even characteristically, be simply instituted from the top. Reflexive engagement with expert systems – with all its forms of potential empowerment and all its dependencies and anxieties – becomes the necessary framework within which risk has to be approached, on an individual and on more global levels. Consider some relevant examples.

No one (at the moment, at least) knows the causes of cancer. Some medical specialists believe, however, that some 80 per cent of cancers are the result of environmental factors. The treatment of the illness could be seen solely in terms of alleviating its symptoms or finding a means of cure – and perhaps such will be at some point discovered. 'Treatment at source', however, involves us deeply in life politics. The risks of contracting cancer are likely to be minimized if the following lifestyle practices are observed: not smoking; avoiding undue exposure to strong sunlight; following certain diets rather than others; avoiding toxic substances at work or in the home; making use of early detection procedures.

Road accidents are a major source of mortality, injury and disability in modern societies: in these respects they are as significant as any of the major illnesses, particularly for younger age groups. As many observers have pointed out, high levels of death and injury on the roads are accepted by governments and by lay citizenry – with all the costs involved – almost without demur. Yet the incidence of mortality and injuries from road accidents could be brought down massively if more generative policies were initiated: cars made much safer than they are at present; lower speed limits rigorously enforced; improvements made in road design; measures taken to offer greater protection to other road users; and the use of public transport strongly promoted at the expense of the private vehicle.[4]

The third example seems on the face of the matter quite different from the first two. It is one I have mentioned a lot: the sphere of marriage and the family. Social security measures currently in place in most, or all, developed societies were constructed in an era not only when patriarchy went largely unchallenged, but when marriage was fate: marriage established one sort of life as appropriate for men and another as appropriate for women. Risk in both cases was – and usually still is – treated as effectively external. Yet where marriage has become a 'relationship', a commitment, for both sexes, and women are in the paid labour force in large numbers, such an orientation becomes quite inappropriate.

Social security systems for the most part at present treat problems of marriage and the family in terms of compensation for 'casualties'. A woman lone head of household, without sufficient direct means of support, receives economic benefits; her ex-husband or partner is required by the state to pay towards the maintenance of their children. A generative political approach would recognize the centrality of active trust in relationships today, and would concentrate on the conditions under which it could be created and sustained – even when partners separate rather than stay together. Such an approach would mix educational, regulative and material components. For example, many women leave their partners because of the violence they experience from them. A generative programme would be concerned above all to reduce the levels of such violence – something which can effectively be integrated with other forms of strategy concerned with repair of the family, for men who are violent towards women have quite commonly themselves been abused in one way or another as children.

As a further illustration, consider a generative approach to coping with crimes of violence. The cost of current methods of combating violent crime is very large. The response to such crime in most societies at the moment is a reactive one – most attention goes towards hospital care for victims, arrest, prosecution, defence and incarceration. Yet strategies which have been successfully applied to reduce levels of smoking, drunken driving and heart disease can also be applied to the main categories of violent crime. Such strategies can be divided into areas of primary, secondary and tertiary prevention.

Take the case of smoking as an example. Primary prevention targets people, especially young people, who don't smoke to prevent them from taking up the habit. Mostly, preventative attempts have focused on changing attitudes and social norms. Smoking was once considered glamorous and sophisticated; now, at least partly because of specific policy programmes, it is widely seen as unhealthy and offensive to non-smokers. In respect of violent crime, primary prevention strategies would mean attacking the idea of the 'superhero', along with other aspects of conventional masculinity. The glorifying of violence might at some point become as archaic as the glamorizing of smoking.

In the instance of smoking, secondary prevention strategies involve policies designed to help people stop the habit – the use of nicotine substitutes, group meetings, replacement therapies and so forth. With violence prevention, such strategies could take various forms. They could involve, for example, therapeutic programmes aimed at the many children who have been the victims of violence, or who characteristically resort to violence at school and elsewhere in their dealings with others.

Tertiary prevention means responding to the pathologies produced by smoking once they have developed. Even here it isn't sensible to think only in terms of external risk. Treatment for the physical effects of smoking needs to be geared to making sure that individuals subsequently alter their lifestyle habits. The same is true of violent crime. As we know, prisons often only serve to harden attitudes which supposedly they are designed to transform.

Positive welfare frequently demands the intervention of the state, but plainly cannot wholly be confined within its boundaries. A generative concern to improve conditions of health through the reduction of pollution, for instance, might require international, even global, cooperation. The intrinsic tie between 'welfare' and 'state' is therefore in some part broken.

Critics might object to all this as follows: aren't positive welfare programmes necessarily long-term, whereas current welfare institutions have to deal with the needy in the here and now? How would such programmes help with the fiscal difficulties of the welfare state, since they would seem much more expensive than the 'correctional' measures in place at the moment? And, perhaps most telling: how would a generative approach contribute to tackling problems of poverty and underprivilege?

Each of these questions, however, could be turned around. Some positive welfare programmes would necessarily be quite long-term: but that is to their advantage in a world where many processes of social and natural repair need to be undertaken. Yet there are many more short-term generative measures cheaper to institute and maintain than policies oriented to external risk. And some kinds of more long-term forms of positive welfare are both simple to introduce and cheap: a ban on the advertising of cigarettes is one example. Probation policies which promote the rehabilitation of offenders against the law, to take another example, may be much less expensive than keeping them in prison.

So far as poverty and underprivilege are concerned, a new approach is called for. Attempts at the redistribution of wealth or income through fiscal measures and orthodox welfare systems on the whole have not worked. This is true both within the welfare states of the industrialized countries and between the rich and impoverished nations of the world. Poverty probably can *only* be combated with some reasonable hope of success, I want to claim, through a conception of positive welfare based on the twin concerns of life politics and generative politics. I shall discuss this issue in some detail later; but it cannot be analysed with reference to the industrialized societies alone. Since welfare conditions are now so strongly affected by globalizing influences, there can no longer be any question of considering Western welfare states as though they can prosper independently of what goes on in the rest of the world. Or, to put it another way, were such an attempt made, not only would they become bastions of privilege, compelled to hold the Third World at bay by force, but within such states we would also see the increasing dislocation of areas of privilege from impoverished, and criminalized, under-class groups.

Arguments from global poverty

It might seem that no one who considers the future of the welfare state in the wealthy West would have anything to learn from the less developed parts of the world. The only problems worth tackling appear to be how the rich countries might be persuaded to give some of their wealth to help the global poor; and to specify what the poorer societies might be able to copy from welfare systems created in the wealthier states. I want to suggest, however, a counterposed strategy – that a radical politics of welfare, North and South, has much to learn from the experiences of the most deprived.

The Brandt reports, from the original international commission set up to investigate global poverty, envisaged a large-scale transfer of resources from North to South, to cope with expanding inequalities and with Third World debts.[5] This has not happened, something that isn't particularly surprising. One might point as a reason to the stinginess of the richer countries – parallel, as it were, to the supposed egoism of the 'contented majority' within those countries – but this would be to miss the shortcomings of the reports themselves.

As Paul Ekins points out, the Brandt reports reveal a preoccupation with states and the influences acting on them; with industrialization and economic growth as the meaning of 'development'; and with financial institutions and indicators in the remedies proposed.[6] The developing countries have in fact managed to acquire substantial external funding since the early 1970s – the source of their debts, since it was obtained through borrowing rather than from wealth transfers. Most, however, passed to the state authorities and was spent on such items as large capital projects, prestige buildings, luxury imports and armaments. Some also found its way into private bank accounts abroad. The Brandt reports neglect to discuss the failure to make productive use of foreign loans; yet why should large capital transfers meet with any different fate?

The Brandt argument for a transfer of funds from rich to poor depends on a notion of equity but also one of self-interest. Global inequalities are an affront to any reasonable sense of justice; reducing them, it is argued, will also help the prosperity of all, because a less impoverished South will offer more markets for the North to sell its goods. Yet this view is far from persuasive; by most measures the North profits extensively from the current arrangements. 'Third World resources are as cheaply available as in colonial days without the costs of foreign administrations.'[7] An agenda of more thoroughgoing reform, starting from the Third World end rather than the First World, is needed to break this deadlock.

Such a programme must place in question the very notion of development as economic growth, while still recognizing the enormous problems that global poverty presents. It has to be a challenge to modernity rather than an attempt to generalize it successfully everywhere. The battle lines are already drawn:

> On the one side are scientism, developmentalism and statism, backed by the big battalions of the establishment: modern technology, and the institutions of world capitalism and state power. On the other are the people, principally the 30 per cent of humanity that is disposable as far as the modern project is

concerned, but aided and abetted by many from the other 70 per cent who regard this project as ethically, socially and environmentally intolerable.[8]

What would an 'alternative development' look like? It would not be socialism, in the sense of centrally controlled economies that would opt out of the global capitalist order; as in the industrialized world, this is a solution proven only to worsen the situation it was supposed to redress. Nor would it be a series of schemes to be foisted on those supposedly due to gain from them. It would be a generative political programme, drawing on policies and activities already in existence in some or many places.

An alternative development would involve the following traits:

(1) This kind of development would draw on and further encourage *reflexive engagements* which, all over the world, indigenous social movements and self-help groups have already made with the forces transforming their lives. Take as an example the Seventh Generation Fund, developed by American Indian activists. Traditional Indian cultures, according to SGF leaders, have a great deal to offer to the dominant society of North America. The organization seeks to reconstruct the economic and political autonomy of Indian communities and to protect aspects of their cultural heritage. It is named after the Iroquois Indian practice of considering, before policy decisions are enacted, their potential impact on the seventh generation. Its object is to foster self-reliant economic development, which makes use of renewable resources and local skills to provide goods and services.

(2) Alternative development has *damage limitation* as a basic concern, whether this be in respect of local culture or of the environment. Modernization almost everywhere, together with its many benefits, has had harmful consequences; in many situations we cannot expect further modernization to cope with these, since it helped bring them about. This is one main point of connection of a radical politics of development with philosophic conservatism; conservation should be understood as in many cases a rational response to the destructiveness of modernity.

(3) It would regard *life-political questions* as central to emancipatory politics, rather than simply working the other way around. Emancipation can no longer be equated with simple modernization, but demands the confronting of questions of lifestyle and ethics. To speak of 'lifestyle' with regard to the poor and hungry of the world initially sounds odd; but a response to poverty today can no longer be regarded as purely economic. The question of 'how to live' in a globalizing milieu where local culture and environmental resources are being squandered has in fact a *particular* significance for the poor. A battle for autonomy, for self-reliance, is also a struggle to reconstitute the local as a prime way, sometimes the only way, of avoiding endemic deprivation and despair.

(4) It would promote *self-reliance* and *integrity* as the very means of development. Self-reliance may sometimes entail the promotion of markets, but it refers mainly to the reconstruction of local solidarities and support systems. Examples of self-reliant development abound today. An illustration is the Grameen Bank in Bangladesh. Its founder flouted conventional banking wisdom in holding that loans to the poor, given certain conditions, need not be charities – and need not expand into unpayable debts, as happened at the national level. Grameen aims to generate opportunities for local development among the landless rural poor. The majority of its borrowers are women; some villages do not accept men as members of the bank. The benefits thus far have been very considerable, and the bank has a 98 per cent repayment rate. It does not follow, of course, that specific examples like this can be generalized, given the diversity of societies across the world. Self-help programmes involving women farmers, for example, may work well in some contexts, but may be shortlived or impossible to set up in others.

(5) Alternative development distinguishes *two different sources* of the ecological crisis. The wealthy societies create environmental disasters by the promotion, or at least the toleration, of wasteful patterns of production and consumption. The environmentally harmful practices of the very poor are more secondary and defensive. Where they have probably carried on renewable production for generations, as they become displaced or margin-

alized they are forced to adopt more short-term and destructive practices in order to survive at all. It would be futile to blame the poor for a situation produced largely from elsewhere. Yet here is a situation where wealthy and poor, except in the very short term, have the same interests, because resources that are destroyed often cannot be replaced.

(6) Improving the *position of women* relative to that of men is a fundamental part of an alternative development. Women own less than 1 per cent of the world's wealth, and earn less than 10 per cent of global income; yet they do two-thirds of the world's work. Most of the differentials found within the industrialized regions apply in an even more acute way in more impoverished areas. Women's paid employment is heavily concentrated in the most peripheral sectors of the labour market, having the worst working conditions, low take-home pay and poor job security. Emancipatory politics, however, again has to be complemented by life-political concerns. For the issue is not only one of achieving greater equality between the sexes; changes in femininity and masculinity, and in associated patterns of behaviour, are both called for and are happening almost everywhere.

Involvement of women in labour markets may help to bring down levels of population growth, but by no means necessarily does so. The most important single factor influencing population growth is the local empowerment of women: their capability to take their own decisions in relation to reproduction.

(7) Health care is always problematic for the very poor. An alternative development stresses the primacy of *autonomous health care*; such health care has a place for Western scientific medicine, but is conscious also of its limitations and its counter-productive tendencies. Scientific medicine in very poor areas of necessity has to be regarded as one approach to health and sickness among others. David Werner's *Where There Is No Doctor* is perhaps the best-known health manual for health care in very poor communities. His approach is one open to very wide application, emphasizing the following:

— Health care is not only everyone's right, but everyone's responsibility.

— Informed self-care should be the main goal of any health programme or activity.
— Ordinary people provided with clear, simple information can prevent and treat most common health problems in their own homes – earlier, cheaper and often better than can doctors.
— Medical knowledge should not be the guarded secret of a select few, but should be freely shared by everyone.
— People with little formal education can be trusted as much as those with a lot. And they are just as clever.
— Basic health care should not be delivered but encouraged.[9]

(8) The *family* is often oppressive, particularly for women and children. Nevertheless, for the very poor everywhere family connections provide an emotional and material resource that no other institution can match. In particular, family ties offer social insurance for individuals, protecting them when times are especially difficult. To be sure, from the point of view of the wider global community this situation can rebound. People may want large families because the greater the number of children, particularly male children, the more their security for the future. The young will care for one when one is old. Yet even when family size comes down, and inequalities within the family are lessened, the family remains an important protective mantle. An alternative development would seek to sustain family ties while seeking to combat patriarchy and the exploitation of children.

(9) In the family and other domains, such a model of development would emphasize not only rights but responsibilities. Recognition of formal and substantive rights (such as rights of women and children) means also specifying concomitant obligations. Responsibility in fact accords closely with self-reliance. Where, as for example sometimes happens through the intervention of aid agencies, charity is delivered with no reciprocal expectations, the result can be dependency.

(10) It would be shortsighted to pretend that an alternative development could be organized purely in local terms. Such development also depends on intervention from 'big battalions' – states, businesses and international organizations. This intervention needs, however, to be generative in nature, sensitive to local

demands and protective of local interests. Without such sensitivity, development programmes can serve to exacerbate global inequalities rather than remedy them.

An alternative development

An alternative development: isn't that just what we see emerging – or struggling to emerge – within the more developed societies also? And isn't such an alternative development at the same time the only way in which it would be remotely possible for the reconstruction of welfare in the North to be compatible with increasing prosperity in the South? What is at issue here is the coming into being of a post-scarcity society – a process still perhaps led by those in the wealthier countries, but worldwide in its implications.

I do not equate a post-scarcity society with an end to economic growth; and it is not a social order in which most people have become wealthy enough to do what they please. A post-scarcity order, as noted earlier, starts to emerge where continuous economic growth becomes harmful or manifestly counterproductive; and where the ethos of productivism begins to be widely called into question, creating a pressure to realize and develop other life values.

So far as economic growth is concerned, many critics are inclined today to ask of the affluent countries, rhetorically, how much is enough?[10] How much is enough? The question seems to be one of environmental limits, of how much the earth can bear, and so in some part it is. It is above all, however – or so I shall argue – a question concerning life practices. The continuous production and consumption of goods has become the gearing mechanism of life for the affluent sectors of the world, while the poor struggle in a chronic way just to survive. 'Only population growth', one observer comments, 'rivals high consumption as a cause of ecological decline, and at least population growth is now viewed as a problem by many governments and citizens of the world. Consumption, in contrast, is almost universally seen as a good – indeed, increasingly it is the primary goal of national economic policy.'[11]

What has been called the 'global consumer class' includes about a fifth of the world's population, concentrated in the highly industrialized regions, and making up about a thousand million people. Its lifestyle habits have led to a large increase in the consumption of raw materials, but a much higher growth still in the consumption of goods and services. In the shops, a dazzling variety of goods, and shopping malls springing up everywhere; yet accompanying this affluence a situation where the affluent majority is encircled on a global level by the world's poor.

It is worth dwelling a while on the similarities between the problems afflicting state welfare within the industrialized sectors of the world and those affecting aid programmes established to alleviate Third World poverty. In each case attempts at assisting the underprivileged are often effective. Yet the criticisms made against aid programmes in the South, offered more often than not by leftist authors, strikingly mirror critiques of the welfare state suggested by those on the political right.

I have mentioned some examples in a preceding chapter. The construction of large dams in impoverished regions of the South, for instance, may have effects which echo on a much larger scale those associated with the building of large housing estates in poor areas in the industrialized countries in the 1960s and 1970s. Dams were at one time widely thought of as a major symbol of industrial development in Third World countries. They undoubtedly can bring certain benefits to the wider economy, but sometimes involve the displacement of many local people – in some cases many thousands – whose indigenous ways of life are destroyed and who often find themselves worse off, even in sheer economic terms, than before. Thus a study of more than fifty projects financed by the World Bank involving forced resettlement found not a single case in which those affected had reached the standard of living they had held before.[12]

Aid programmes, observers have pointed out – as has been said of welfare systems too – create bureaucracies which are quite often inefficient and have interests different from those they are designed to serve. Partly because of this fact benefits may not reach more than a proportion of those they are supposed to help. Where aid destroys local traditions and means of livelihood, recipients may not only become demoralized, but develop attitudes similar to those of welfare dependency in the economically advanced societies. Policies initiated with the best of intentions in both cases have perverse outcomes. In the case of aid, some have even spoken of 'aid that kills'.[13]

Let us consider for a moment two apparently quite different, and certainly disconnected, discussions relevant to these issues. The first comes from Charles Murray, one of the most prominent critics of the welfare state, and also one of the most controversial. Murray is a forceful advocate of the view that welfare systems create impoverished and demoralized underclasses. However, the debate about welfare, he argues, should move on from 'arguing about welfare cheats and begin considering what constitutes the good life for the people that the welfare state takes under its wing.' The point of human existence, he adds, is not just reaching a certain standard of living, but the achieving of definite life values. And such values can't effectively be sought after without 'a strong component of self-possession, of autonomy, of contributing to the community as well as receiving from it'. Such social arrangements, he says, can be established, but not within the context of current welfare institutions. They happen – and, according to Murray, they can only happen – in Burke's 'little platoons'.[14]

Murray, whose work has been influenced by experiences in rural Thailand, asks the question, what's wrong with being poor (once people are above levels of subsistence poverty)? Why should there be such a general concern to combat poverty? We seek to combat poverty, Murray argues, in order to expand the sum of human happiness. He rejects the idea that happiness is too imponderable to define in an objective fashion; it can be summed up as a 'lasting and justified satisfaction with one's life as a whole'. Adapting Abraham Maslow's hierarchy of human needs, Murray recognizes three enabling conditions relevant to the pursuit of happiness: material resources, security and self-respect. In his view, not much more than subsistence is required in the way of material resources if one is to pursue happiness. Drawing on survey materials from a range of countries concerning relationships between income and expressed happiness, he seeks to show that, after a certain quite low threshold, increasing levels of income do not lead to greater degrees of happiness or satisfaction with one's life. Security and self-respect, not wealth or income, are what count. One doesn't need much in the way of material goods to pursue happiness effectively, so long as other conditions are fulfilled. Poverty alone isn't necessarily to be feared or abominated; the key condition of the good life is what Murray, following Maslow, calls self-actualization.[15]

Murray doesn't consider the question of whether the affluent can learn from the poor and is far from advocating Durkheim's 'communism', in which poverty is positively extolled as against wealth. Yet Murray's arguments could be used to justify greater *equality* rather than the persistence of inequality. For the possession of wealth doesn't necessarily make one happy, any more than poverty as such is a source of misery. Why not, therefore, attempt to bring the conditions of life of rich and poor closer together, even if this isn't done through wealth or income transfers? So far as the pursuit of happiness is concerned, the real enemy, it could be argued, is neither poverty nor wealth, but productivism, as defined earlier.

Compare Murray's arguments with Serge Latouche's discussion of the situation of the global poor. The average per capita income of members of the richest societies in the world, Latouche points out, is some fifty times that of those in the poorest countries. Are people in the affluent countries fifty times happier than people in the impoverished regions, he asks rhetorically? Of course they aren't. Like Murray, he supposes that it is possible to live happily in quite frugal circumstances.

The world's poor, says Latouche, on the face of things seem to inhabit a 'planet of the shipwrecked', adrift on the shoals of modernity. Everywhere, within the economically developed societies as well as in the countries of the South, their ways of life contrast with that of the global 'consumer class'. Yet the 'society of the excluded', he argues, is not inevitably a disaster; on the contrary, notwithstanding all the hardships the poor face day in and day out, the 'informal society' is diverse and fertile in all 'its horrors and its marvels'.

The informal economy or sector makes up 60–80 per cent of urban employment in the Third World, even in those societies which do not rank among the poorest. How could one say that such a sector is 'secondary'? Perhaps, Latouche suggests, we should consider the hypothesis that the informal society does not just represent the detritus of modernity, and is instead an order on which modern institutions are in fact dependent. The culture of the excluded may be richer than consumerism in everything save material benefits; more than the source of 'another development', it may be the 'prefiguration of another society' on the other side of the modern.

Latouche's argument at this point strikingly echoes the critique of capitalism made by the neoconservatives. The expansion of modernity, he implies, depends on sources of symbolism and vital morality which productivism represses or pushes to the margins. The informal sector has two sides. On the one hand, the demoralized and the dispossessed, often terrorized by crime and in hock to the drug dealers; on the other, the survival and perhaps recreation of local traditions, a bursting variety of activities carried on by neo-artisans, living off their locally developed skills as well as catering to the needs of the neighbourhood.

The informal economy, in Latouche's words, is a set of 'strategies of global response to the spread of modern institutions', the reactions of people 'caught between lost traditions and an impossible modernity'. As such, it stands in a relation of both opposition and symbiosis to the modern order. Informal activity, whether or not it represents clearly discernible 'work', obeys a different logic from productivism. Where artisanal activities produce a surplus, it isn't invested in expanded production but tends to be used to bolster local loyalties and solidarities. The 'economic' here isn't separated off from the rest of life in the manner characteristic of formal economic enterprise. The alternative is not an alternative development, but an 'alternative *to* development'.

In Latouche's eyes the obsessive attempt to raise the living standards of the world's poor more often than not brings about a true impoverishment of their life. This is so in respect of social solidarity and even old age, sickness and death.

The societies of the Third World still hold many hidden treasures in the attitude which they maintain towards old and sick people. Sickness and old age are not natural curses which separate the individual from the world of the active, and which have to be

> cared for in isolation as though they were sources of shame . . .
> Experiences inherent in the human condition, and perhaps neces-
> sary, cannot be wholly denied; to deny their significance impover-
> ishes us.[16]

This phraseology is very resonant of some versions of conservatism and might suggest a purely backward-looking perspective.
Latouche insists not; the 'laboratory' of human inventiveness
represented by the informal sphere points towards the future,
not only towards the past. It is, as it were, another way of looking
at the limitations of modernity – but one which has important
'positives' in suggesting alternative ways of living in the world.

It is obvious that the social significance of poverty cannot be
assessed only in relation to the pursuit of happiness and no doubt
there are few today who would advocate poverty as a desirable
condition. Wealth may not necessarily bring happiness, but it
does often bring power and social prestige; those who are most
deprived on an economic level tend to be relatively powerless in
respect of some of the major influences affecting their lives. The
fact that the poor may sometimes be happy, if one rejects
Durkheimian communism, is not an argument in favour of
poverty. It can be made sense of only in terms of a broader
confrontation with productivism – with definitions, for example,
which understand welfare only as economic welfare.

The questions which then arise are: could it be that a move
towards a post-scarcity order discloses reactions against productivism compatible with the ideas suggested by Murray and
Latouche? And, if such be the case, what implications should be
drawn for the debates about the welfare state in the industrialized
societies and about Third World poverty? Analysing these problems means identifying some of the structural tensions now
affecting the affluent societies and considering how they relate to
the circumstances of manufactured uncertainty.

The structural diamond

Productivism, I shall assume, cannot be explained in terms of
consumerism; the reverse is the case. Consumerism has its roots

in, and indeed is a quite direct expression of, a productivist orientation to the world. It is, as it were, an active, mass exploration of life politics, but one carried out under the sway of productivism rather than driven by a critique of it. In a post-scarcity order the dominating influence of paid work and of economic concerns is placed in question. An orientation to consumerism already breaks away from the idea of work as the standard-bearer of moral meaning (or, rather, as a substitute for such meaning). But the need to make life choices is expressed only in a distorted and narrow way as the purchase of goods and services.

The welfare state, for reasons already mentioned, is deeply locked into productivism, which is in turn locked into established lifestyle patterns and habits – these including in particular a division of gender roles. Risk management can be treated as largely external where such roles are relatively fixed and a certain nexus of institutional conditions sets the lives of the population for long periods of time. The expansion of reflexive moderniza-tion places individuals in quite a different 'decision matrix' and, bound up with this, creates a series of directly interrelated tensions at the heart of the institutions of modern societies. Such tensions fall along the lines of connection of four institutional areas experiencing detraditionalization – these form something of a structural diamond.

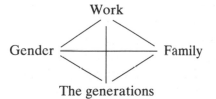

In exploring these, let me concentrate on one of the social categories mentioned by Latouche: old age, a phenomenon closely linked, of course, to the passing of the generations. One of the problems of the welfare state, so it is widely said, is the ageing of its population (the societies of the South have the opposite 'problem', the large majority of their populations being composed of individuals under twenty-five). By three decades from now, if current trends are maintained, people over sixty-five in the US, for example, will outnumber those under twenty-one by a factor of more than two to one.

What is old age? For many purposes, and not just statistical ones, old age in Western society begins at age sixty-five – the age at which, in most countries for some while past, men become 'pensioners'. Old age at sixty-five is a creation, pure and simple, of the welfare state. It is a form of *welfare dependency* much more widespread than any of the dependencies noted by the rightist interpreters of the underclass. Bismarck established the first official age of retirement in 1889, when setting up the world's earliest state system of social security. The age picked was the biblical 'three score and ten'; this was later reduced by his state officials to sixty-five.

Pensioner – the very term sounds incapacitating and in fact designates a dependent person. Welfare systems here define old age, not as a status worthy of respect, but as a disqualification from full membership of the society. Ageing is treated as 'external', as something that happens to one, not as a phenomenon actively constructed and negotiated; against such a backdrop it isn't surprising that the population over age sixty-five is widely regarded as a medical and financial burden on the rest of the national community.

Yet why shouldn't older people be regarded as a rich resource rather than a financial dilemma – almost as prefiguring an 'alternative society' in the manner of Latouche? Older people need not be seen as either physically or economically dependent on the rest of society. It is a myth to suppose that to be an older person is to be ill or incapacitated. Moreover, many illnesses or infirmities at the moment statistically more common among older people are open to generative interventions. Research by the National Institution on Ageing in the US, for example, suggests that many of the physical difficulties of old age are not to do with ageing at all, but rather with lifestyle practices. There are close parallels and overlaps here with models of 'positive health' as a lifestyle endeavour discussed earlier. As in the case of illnesses and disabilities suffered by people in younger age groups, the likelihood of disease at relatively advanced ages is strongly affected by environmental factors, exposure to extended psychological or physical stress, eating habits and propensity to take exercise. One calculation has it that 80 per cent of the health problems of people over sixty-five are in principle preventable through lifestyle changes.[17]

Demographic changes associated with increasing longevity and lowered birth rates have shifted the balance of young and old in the developed societies since Bismarck's time. Instead of a small group of older people receiving benefits from a wide category of younger people in paid work, a large mass of longlived retirees are supported by a diminishing group of younger employees. A man who retired at age sixty-five in 1935 in the US had more than forty workers contributing to his pension. By 1950, this proportion had shrunk to seventeen. For those retiring in 1990, it was 3.4 to 1. By 2000, it may have diminished to less than 2 to 1.[18]

A 'problem' of large proportions, certainly, when seen as something the state must 'cope' with; but looked at from the standpoint of generative politics a major opportunity for positive restructuring also. In most of the industrialized countries today the young are on average poorer and have bleaker immediate life prospects than older groups. The more becoming older is regarded as providing life opportunities rather than as inherently a source of deprivation, the more the idea that welfare provision should be directly linked to old age must be placed in question.

Generative political programmes relevant to older people will not necessarily increase longevity further, but they will certainly see such people as contributing to the solution of current welfare dilemmas rather than just as helping create them. Even measured only in material terms, older people are becoming less poor in relation to other groups. In the UK the proportion of the poorest tenth of the population who were over sixty-five was 36 per cent in 1979; by 1990, it had declined to 22 per cent. Among children (aged under sixteen) the trend is in the opposite direction. In 1979 the proportion of children living in households having an income below the median for the whole population was 10 per cent; by 1990 the proportion had grown to more than 30 per cent.

When old age was 'invented' as being over sixty-five, the stages of life were still set out as sequence – as a 'linear life plan' to be accepted as fate:

stated simply: first you learned, then you worked (at family and career), and then you died . . . By your late teens, you were supposed to know 'what you wanted to be' for the rest of your life. If you were an unmarried woman over thirty, you were on your way to spinsterhood. When you chose a mate, it was 'till death do you part'. The thirties and forties were the years for child-rearing; the fifties and sixties, if you lived that long, were for grandparenthood . . . the path from childhood to old age was linear: it moved in one direction, with little room for hesitations, detours, experimentation, or second chances. This linear life plan was kept in place by the forces of tradition . . .[19]

'Second chances': this phrase sums up a great deal, not only about the new opportunities – and anxieties and deprivations – involved with ageing, but also those affecting the family, gender and work. A *politics of second chances*, where 'second' is understood, as it were, in a plural way, has to form a key aspect of a life-political rethinking of welfare in each of these institutional domains.

A more extended life has important and direct implications for each of the other three areas of the structural diamond. New relationships, and possible schisms, between the generations are affecting the family as much as the changes influencing marriage and sexuality, fundamental though these undoubtedly are. With the advance of detraditionalization in the area of family life, recombinant families come into being not only through divorce and remarriage, but as a result of novel connections formed across the generations. Here again what might seem only like a process of disintegration, creating welfare problems, is – from the point of view of generative politics – resonant with possibilities for recapturing family solidarities. As many as four, sometimes even five generations are now alive simultaneously; there is much evidence of new forms of intergenerational ties emerging from this historically unprecedented situation.[20]

All such ties, as with those within nuclear families, are coming to be negotiated rather than given by blood, in the manner analysed in a previous chapter. The nuclear family in any case does not mean the same thing as it used to when understood in the context of the spread of the generations. Relationships that cut across or miss out generations have already become much

more common than they were. Parent–child relationships frequently change their character when extended across time as
adult–adult relationships. It becomes quite common, for
example, for daughters and mothers to survive together for forty
years or more; perhaps for less than two decades are their
relationships like those of traditional parents and children.

Masculinity, detraditionalized, and – for the first time – placed
on the defensive, plays a key role in all this. The basic question
here is not so much whether men will be able to hold on
indefinitely to their economic privileges, as whether they will be
able to break with ideals of masculinity pinned on performance
in the public sphere, in the domain of work or in other activities.
For at the moment the 'emotional revolution' in which women
are the prime movers is running headlong into a recalcitrant male
sexuality – a prime source, as I shall try to show in a subsequent
chapter, of violence. Seen in a negative way, one of the consequences is that the family degenerates into a diversity of unstable
or short-term social arrangements, which jeopardize the 'normal'
development of children and produce an increasing number of
'broken homes'. The state is then forced to pick up the pieces –
or, perhaps, has helped to create the problem in the first place.
At the same time, women's questioning of their traditional
gender roles causes them to enter an already cluttered marketplace in large numbers. They become dependent, not on a
breadwinner, but on a labour market which simply cannot create
enough jobs to go round, for them or for men.

Get rid of minimum wages and allow the labour market its
necessary flexibility, says the right – perhaps coupling this attitude with a demand for a reversion to traditional 'family values';
shore up the welfare state and increase taxes so that everyone
can be cared for, replies the left – or did so until such an outlook
became electorally problematic. Each approach, however, is out
of kilter with the changes that have transformed the social order
over the past few decades, and which offer new opportunities if
the usual debates about welfare are recast.

7

Positive Welfare, Poverty and Life Values

The welfare state cannot survive in its existing form; or, if it does, it is likely to be progressively corroded or cut back, even by governments which strongly support the principles underlying it. The alternative, a feasible one within the framework of utopian realism, is the fostering of tendencies promoting the emergence of a post-scarcity order. Philosophic conservatism can contribute a great deal to exploring the parameters of such an order, especially when integrated with the concerns of life politics understood in a generative mode. A post-scarcity society, which is not a nation-state but an inherently globalizing society, is one that accommodates to manufactured risk and, more broadly, to the limits of modernity as an orientation to control and to 'solutions' provided by productivism and by technology to life problems.

It is possible to see close and potentially fruitful connections between the structural changes now happening in the industrialized societies and the demand for a reexamination of values which we have seen coming from critics of quite different political persuasions. Living a happy and satisfying life is one thing, wealth creation is another. Can the two be brought closer together? And if they can indeed be reconciled, can this be achieved in a manner which promotes greater equality, whether within particular societies or on a more global level?

Contrary to what Latouche says, there isn't any alternative *to* development, at least in the poorer regions of the world, if 'development' is understood as economic growth. But there are certainly different modes of development, with differing strategies and objectives; and in this respect there are some important connections between immanent trends of change in the rich countries and in the poorer countries.

Work, productivism, productivity

These connections can be brought out by comparing some of the traits of the informal sector with the characteristics of an emergent post-scarcity order. Such a comparison suggests several main areas of similarity concerning the nature and role of *work* in relation to *social solidarity* and *local tradition*. The 'other society' which Latouche finds prefigured in the life of the very poor finds its echo, and perhaps starts to take concrete form, in a post-scarcity world. We couldn't say that one comes 'before' modernity and the other 'after'; each constitutes a sort of partial repair and recovery of modes of life which modern institutions essentially destroy or repress.

Productivism is an ethos where work has a very distinctive and central role – work expresses the primacy of 'industry', in the active sense of that word, in the life of modern society. Max Weber, of course, long ago showed how historically unusual is the attitude towards work characteristic of the modern order, and disclosed some of the main cultural origins of productivism. Following Weber, productivism can be seen as an ethos in which 'work', as paid employment, has been separated out in a clear-cut way from other domains of life. Work becomes a standard-bearer of moral meaning – it defines whether or not individuals feel worthwhile or socially valued; and the motivation to work is autonomous. Why one wishes, or feels compelled, to work is defined in terms of what work itself is – the need to work has its own inner dynamic.

In a detraditionalizing society, one can say, the chief enemy of happiness is compulsiveness. It is a society which tends to stimulate *addictions* – addiction being understood as a driving emotional or motivational force which is unmastered by the individual. The notion of addiction really only makes sense in a post-traditional order. In a traditional culture, it is entirely reasonable to suppose that what one did yesterday offers a guide to how one should act today and tomorrow, however fast traditions might change; tradition provides a moral and interpretative framework gearing the emotions into a set of life practices. Addiction, by contrast, marks the influence of a past whose impelling power has no rationale other than itself.[1]

Weber showed that work was one of the earliest arenas of social life to become detraditionalized and also diagnosed its compulsive character. Most premodern societies seem to have had no word for 'work', presumably because working wasn't readily distinguishable from other activities. Moreover, in so far as it was recognized as a distinctive type of activity, work was not something which defined a specifically male role.

Much has been made of Weber's discussion of Puritanism, and such 'ascetic Protestantism' may very well have been the original impetus that helped to shape the formation of early modern economic institutions. Modern civilization, according to Weber, was based on self-denial and the repression of need – everyone is a secular Puritan. Anyone who follows this thesis in a strict way, however, has difficulty explaining the spread of consumerism, which seems almost the very opposite of self-discipline and frugality.

One might reconstruct Weber's thesis in a rather different fashion. The attitude displayed by the early entrepreneurs towards accumulation, one can say, which spread throughout the whole society, is obsessional. Once Puritanism drops away, it is driven by its own inner logic. This logic is actually an expression, not of self-denial, but of the orientation of modernity to control. Productivism, where work has become autonomous, squeezes to the margins of social life most of those forms of moral experience which once linked human existence to tradition and to independent nature.

Since work is defined mainly in terms of a male role, a concern with the emotions, care and responsibility tends to become devolved on women.[2] Women become the keepers, so to speak, of much of the moral fabric of social life once woven more closely into wider traditional forms. The autonomizing of work in simple modernization was hence closely related to a recasting of gender divisions and a reshaping of the family. Women became 'specialists in love' as men lost touch with the emotional origins of a society in which work was the icon. Seemingly of little importance, because relegated to the private sphere, women's 'labour of love' became as important to productivism as the autonomy of work itself. Productivism, that 'industry' which created the wealth of nations, presumed a 'shadow economy' where sheerly economic values were in fact effectively discounted and disclaimed.

In the informal sector of societies of the South, this shadow economy usually remains entangled with patriarchal family relations. Work and familial interaction tend to mingle. In other respects, however, the informal sector and the post-scarcity order start to resemble one another. In a post-scarcity society, productivism begins to dissolve – and is also actively struggled against. The reasons for this are several. A society of intensive reflexivity is not one where a compulsive attitude towards work can go unremarked, because of the demand to subject motives to open interrogation. Women's mass entry into the paid labour market, coupled to the impact of feminism, break down the infrastructural conditions which alone made a compulsive orientation to work tolerable. Women fight for equality in the public domain, and strive to forge a 'public self', and as women come to refuse to undertake the emotional tasks on which the autonomy of work depended, men are compelled increasingly to confront their own 'undisclosed selves'.

The autonomy of work still survives as the dominant ethos and defines what the experience of unemployment means. At the same time, there are very clear counter-trends. More likely than the whole-scale incorporation of women into male-style employment is the breaking down of the typical male pattern of work itself. The overall numbers of hours worked by men in paid employment has dropped by half over the past fifty years. As yet, most men still face or expect to face a fulltime working life. But even if they should actively desire it, for many this expectation will prove unrealistic. The objective of full employment, so closely tied to the welfare state, makes little sense any more. The questions now are different. Employment under what conditions? And, what relation should work have to other life values?

These are exactly the questions which the informal sector in the industrializing countries – and to a lesser extent in the industrialized ones too – has in a certain sense 'answered'. The distinction between work which achieves a direct economic reward and work undertaken with other aims in mind is blurred. People are in touch with wider moral dilemmas of their lives – which now reemerge into open view in modern societies too.

A society which moves away from productivism does not necessarily move away from wealth creation. I take it that this is true of both the informal sector and the post-scarcity order. Here we should differentiate clearly between *productivism* and *productivity*. Reductions in time spent at paid work and shifting family patterns are emancipatory if they diverge from productivism and towards productivity. Productivism today inhibits productivity; distinguishing the two helps us see why a post-scarcity economy is not necessarily a no-growth economy.

It is improved productivity that has led to the shortening of the working day. Productivity in this sense means the return generated by the investment of *time*, whether this be in the form of wage labour or capital. The productivity of labour has always been of prime concern to employers, by the nature of the contract between worker and capitalist. Taylorism, the application of 'scientific management' to the workplace, was a fruit of this concern and at one time looked set to maximize productivity by 'mechanizing the worker'. Productivity heightened in this fashion proved to be as historically limited as was the centrally planned economy. If Taylorism has by no means disappeared, it has become plain that productivity now is closely involved with autonomy and flexibility in production systems.

Productivity of capital and of material resources, however, are just as important as the productivity of labour, and long neglected. Most economists, orthodox and more radical, long took it for granted that money capital was productive once invested. However, as the experience of the centrally planned economies showed above all, the return on invested capital varies widely, whether this be looked at in the longer or shorter term. The very same experience shows that the productivity of resources (like land or mineral wealth) is not by any means given in those resources themselves.

Like the productivity of labour, the productivity of capital does not depend solely on economic conditions. And in neither case can productivity be defined in purely economic terms. The basic flaw of neoliberalism is to see both only in relation to market conditions and market competitiveness. Each is organizational and each, in current conditions, responds to autonomy and bottom-up decision-making. 'Productivity' in turn can only be measured in a solely economic way where work is autonomous and no thought is given to the reproduction of material resources. In a post-scarcity economy, social indicators of productivity necessarily gain a fundamental importance alongside economic ones.

It isn't clear whether lean production, the production system first introduced in Japan, can be more or less universally implemented.[3] But lean production does have some very interesting features in relation to my discussion at this point. There is no doubt about its influence on productivity, at least in certain key industrial sectors; there is a big differential in productivity between Japanese and European firms in the car industry, for example.[4]

Lean production is about the effective use of time, but does not regard time as something that mustn't be wasted, a calculus of commodified labour. Rather, the value of time is understood in relation to cooperative work and established partnerships between assemblers and suppliers. Lean production uses less of everything, including immediate labour time, than other production systems; but it does so within a rich social context and as part of long-term processes of investment. Many have said that lean production methods can be effectively introduced outside the East only if the West adopts more generalized Eastern values. These concern, to anticipate the following chapter somewhat, a view of nature as in harmony with human beings, rather than as something to be treated instrumentally; an attitude of confidence in the self; and a holistic outlook on self and body. As I shall seek to show below, however, what is at issue in a world oriented to productivity rather than productivism is not an Eastern value transplant, to go along with transplanted industries, but a recovery of a range of ethical concerns crushed by a productivist system.

Where productivity means productivism it has unfortunate associations. Freed from this connection, there is no reason why it should not be extended to non-economic areas in a post-scarcity order. Productivity stands opposed to compulsiveness and to dependency, not only in work but in other areas, including personal life. There is a close tie between autonomy and productivity. A productive life is one well lived, but it is also one where an individual is able to relate to others as an independent being, having a developed sense of self-esteem.

From the welfare state to positive welfare

Let me repeat at this point the thesis stated earlier: the current problems of the welfare state should not be seen as a fiscal crisis (nor are they the result of the need of the Western societies to compete more fiercely than before on world markets), but one of the management of risk. What follows, in the light of the social changes and structural tensions just analysed?

Suppose we take seriously the proposition that the aim of good government should be to promote the pursuit of happiness, and that both individual and social 'welfare' should be defined in such a way. Let us also accept that happiness is promoted by security (of mind and body), self-respect and the opportunity for self-actualization plus the ability to love. The idea that human beings strive for happiness above everything else goes back at least as far as Aristotle. Yet one could also see the pursuit of happiness, as a universalizable value, as a distinctive quality of modernity. Aristotle's 'virtuous activity of the soul' linked happiness to the attractions of sedimented tradition; happiness as both the means and object of emancipation is a much later development. It is one which is both called into existence by modernity, and yet repressed by the very forces of development which modern institutions have released on the world.

Happiness is not a threatening condition to others if universalized and it is not one refractory to social solidarity. It is also, in modern conditions of life at least, necessarily an active pursuit, at least if defined in the way mentioned above. 'Happiness', it has been said by one of the most prominent contemporary students of the subject, 'is not something that happens.' It is not 'the result of good fortune or random chance'. Happiness 'does not depend on outside events, but rather on how we interpret them'; it is 'a condition that must be prepared for, cultivated'. It depends less on controlling the outer world than controlling the inner one. 'People who learn to control inner experience will be able to determine the quality of their lives, which is as close as any of us can come to being happy.'[5]

Place these thoughts alongside the following statements:

we don't have to stay victims. The present is the point of power. We can always choose, in the present, to change our negative beliefs . . . My body, my health, my relationships, my work, my financial situation – everything in my life – mirror my own inner dialogue . . . Our experiences all arise from our inner dialogue. Therefore, if we change our thoughts, we will have different feelings and different experiences.[6]

Could anything sound more distant from debates about the welfare state, which conjure up a different ethos altogether? Such observations are likely to be anathema in particular to those on the left. For ever since Marx spoke of religion as the heart of a heartless world, leftists have tended strongly to emphasize material conditions as the dominant influence on the quality of life open to individuals. Power, they would say, is objective, structured into the real circumstances of social life; how could it make any sense, therefore, to speak of 'the present as a point of power' for a person living in poverty, whose life is drudgery? Inner experience, inner dialogue: what possible relevance could these have to such a person, except as a weak substitute for proper, material emancipation? Anyone who takes this sort of route when talking of social reform, they would argue, is likely to end up simply acquiescing in the inequalities and deprivations of the status quo.

Yet the point bears reemphasizing that happiness and its opposite bear no particular relation to either wealth or the possession of power. A research group in Italy carried out in-depth interviews with those people who are the greatest source of concern to the left at the moment, and the most anxiety provoking for the right – homeless vagrants or 'street people'. The researchers found much evidence of Latouche's 'horrors': people who have given up hope, or turned to a life of violence, drugs and crime. But they were also astonished to see how many had been able to transform bleak conditions of life into a satisfying, even enriching set of experiences. One respondent, an Egyptian who spends his nights in the parks of Milan, gets his food from charity kitchens and does odd jobs when he can, describes his life as an odyssey:

> After the war of 1967 I decided to leave Egypt and start hitch-hiking toward Europe . . . I had to struggle against many things. I passed through Lebanon and its war, through Syria, Jordan, Turkey, Yugoslavia, before getting here . . . it has been an adventure that so far has lasted twenty years, but it will keep going for the rest of my life . . . The lion, when he runs after a pack of gazelles, can only catch them one at a time. I try to be like that, and not like Westerners who go crazy working even though they cannot eat more than their daily bread.[7]

Welfare in a post-scarcity society

How might systems of welfare – supposing one wants still to retain the name – be reorganized in a post-scarcity order? The following considerations can provide the framework of an answer. Such systems would have to escape from reliance on 'precautionary aftercare' as the main means of coping with risk; be integrated with a wider set of life concerns than those of productivism; develop a politics of second chances; create a range of social pacts or settlements, not only between classes but between other groups or categories in the population; and focus on what I have earlier called a generative conception of equality. The list is a formidable one, but that very fact helps drive home the tenuous position of those who make the defence of the welfare state the core of their political outlook.

Precautionary aftercare not only means dealing with situations and events after they have happened, but is closely involved with the actuarial outlook which supposes that the future is in principle predictable. Social reflexivity combined with manufactured uncertainty destroys both of these assumptions, but at the same time opens up other opportunities.

Consider again as an example the position of older people. From a generative point of view, it is important to create conditions under which the talents and skills of older people are made use of, and where 'retirement' is not an all or nothing thing. Mandatory retirement at a fixed retirement age seems functional from a productivist point of view, because it takes people out of the labour market and thus contributes to reducing unemployment. In a post-scarcity system, the situation looks different. While older people may generally continue to work, voluntary exits and reentries to labour markets are likely to become more common at all ages. Sabbaticals, phased retirement and 'retirement rehearsals' are all possible where retirement in the traditional sense has effectively ceased to exist.

Older people are already pioneering some of those very ways of life which Latouche commends in his appraisal of the informal sector. The majority of people over sixty-five, men and women, want to do some sort of paid work, given that it is not too onerous or mechanical. They don't want to work for the sake of it, but for the satisfactions work can bring; and they assess the value of work in relation to other life concerns. As with all other sectors of the population, modes of social life are much less 'given' for older people than they used to be; they are active 'social experimenters' in the domains of family relations and sexuality just as in the world of work.

Older people who seem to want to stay young: one could see in this a denial of death. Yet it could be argued that the placing of older people into their own 'welfare ghetto' has been a social mechanism perpetuating that very denial – part of a wider set of social repressions whereby sickness and death are sequestered away from general view.[8] A life politics of old age recovers finitude as a horizon of existence, but sees its acceptance as a means of intensifying life's pleasures and rewards.

From abstract philosophy to the mundane business of funding: how would a life-political orientation to old age be paid for? And who would pay? These are very difficult questions if posed in the context of the assumption that the problems of the welfare state are primarily fiscal – where old age is an 'external problem' that requires a distributive solution. There simply isn't enough money to go round to continue to finance universal pension schemes providing for significant benefits, given the other commitments welfare states must meet. Looked at generatively, basic problems of costs and economic efficiency would still have to be resolved, but these wouldn't be examined only in terms of distribution, or only in terms of what the state could provide. The restructuring of work is a prime requirement for a society moving from productivism towards productivity; and this is likely increasingly to cross-cut divisions of age. Older people can and should, in other words, be regarded as part of the wealth-creating sectors of society, and as able to contribute to taxation revenue.

Breaking away from an emphasis on precautionary aftercare means confronting risk in a direct and engaged way, not expecting to create wholly controlled contexts of action. Where, as has now become the case, lifestyle decisions are highly consequential for others (in principle, even on a planetary-wide basis), and also for one's own quite remote future, new ethics of individual and collective responsibility need to be formed. For the most part, these can only be confronted generatively; the state can only seek to provide circumstances which favour their emergence, including enforcing negative sanctions relevant to them. Moreover, in many respects they escape the scope of the state in terms of their extent – as is true, for instance, of the impact of some forms of environmental pollution on health.

In some situations, moving beyond productivism may mean protecting local traditions or solidarities, even if this conflicts with the objective of raising material living standards. Defending tradition in the traditional way, as I have asserted throughout the book, is potentially dangerous. The same point applies when the autonomy of the local community is treated as an overriding value. The fate of 'community control' in the US in the 1960s is illustrative in this respect. Originally, the idea was a slogan coming from the left. Yet, as critics at the time pointed out, community control was what those who fought to preserve segregated schooling demanded; and it is what those in well-to-do suburbs, removed from the inner city poor, have.[9]

These things having been said, welfare projects which don't

respect local ties and modes of life can be almost as destructive as the market forces they seek to counteract. When Glazer remarks that 'the creation and building of new traditions, or new versions of old traditions, must be taken seriously as a requirement of social policy itself,'[10] he is surely correct. Yet such traditions should be understood in a post-traditional manner, as forms of conventional or ritual practice open to dialogic contact with others. One might note what Claude Lévi-Strauss wrote about these issues. Freedom which 'is planned on a rational basis', he argues, can undermine itself; for such a strategy often ignores 'that indefinite number of everyday allegiances, the web of private solidarities which save the individual being crushed by society as a whole'.[11] These may surely sometimes be, in Lévi-Strauss's words, 'traditions and customs whose roots are obscure'; but they may equally well be the sorts of innovative activities noted by Latouche.

Fostering an 'indefinite number of everyday allegiances' has to be one element of a politics of second chances. 'Starting again' is an inevitable component of social life no longer lived as fate, whether this be in the domain of personal relationships and marriage, work, or in other spheres. Welfare measures may create exclusionary ghettos, as in the case of old age: what seem to be economic benefits serve actually to fix an individual in a social position or status from which it is difficult to escape.

A politics of second chances, like other aspects of life politics, cannot be only a matter of material provision, but has to focus on personal experience and self-identity. Take as an example the issue of unemployment. Like 'retirement', 'unemployment' was the creation of a society in which patriarchy was the norm and where work was equated with involvement in the labour market. If work isn't defined in the terms of productivism, the question of what unemployment actually is becomes very complex. 'Inner dialogue' and 'personal experience' would seem to be miles away from unemployment, but of course they are not. Unemployment can't even exist without a basic element of subjective experience: to be unemployed one has to want to have a paid job. And not just a job; virtually no one who is unemployed would take *any* job that was available.

It is not usually noticed that many older people, probably the majority, are in fact unemployed by orthodox definitions of the term. Surveys indicate that about 40 per cent of people over sixty-five who don't have jobs – and 60 per cent of men – would like to work if suitable employment could be found. Here, by force of circumstances, the 'desire to work' has become substantially disentangled from productivism; this is also true of a high proportion of housewives bringing up children, who say they would like to work if there were any way it were possible. Productivism sees paid work (for men) as central to life; the subtle motivations and experiences surrounding what it is to be 'in work' and 'out of work' get short shrift. The 'natural' condition of men between school-leaving age and the age of retirement is to be in paid employment. Unemployment is simply defined as a situation in which this is not the case.

From this point of view, the concept of second chances is so easy to define as to be uninteresting. Welfare policy consists either in expanding the labour market to meet demand or in paying for those out of work; second chances consist of placing the unemployed in jobs. In a society more concerned with productivity than productivism, the notion becomes very much richer and more openly psychological or experimental. A politics of second chances would concentrate on how paid unemployment relates to other aspects of individuals' experiences and life values, in respect of various different transitions in, or changes of, their social circumstances.

Involuntary unemployment, like unwanted divorce, is often traumatic because of the damage it does to an individual's sense of security and self-respect as much as because of the economic deprivation it causes. 'The present is the point of power': this thesis makes a great deal of sense in the context of the apparently wholly material circumstances of unemployment. Everyone who studies the experience of unemployment, whether from a narrow perspective of productivism or not, comes more or less immediately to the question of self-identity. Just as what unemployment actually is depends substantially on subjective attitudes, so too do reactions to it; these flow from narratives of self-identity, as well as acting to disrupt or alter them. In their study of people living on the margins of the labour market in Britain, for example, Bill Jordan and his co-authors make clear how closely incapacity and empowerment mesh with images of the self. The management of identity is the centre-point of how far a person's relation to the world – whether he or she is 'unemployed' or not – is experienced as incapacitating or generates opportunities for self-enhancement or self-renewal.[12]

A politics of second chances would not, of course, neglect the material conditions which might allow individuals to negotiate changes in their life circumstances. It is at least equally important, however, to seek to develop means whereby damaged identities can be healed and a strong sense of self-respect developed. Objections at this juncture are likely to abound. Can people change their psychological outlook in the face of material deprivations they are powerless to control? And are individuals' psychic states something which governments can or should influence?

The answer to these questions is: yes, they can – and do. How far such change is possible is dependent less on sheer material circumstances than on factors such as the 'everyday allegiances' on which they can draw. Thus one woman in the study above speaks of her struggle to break away from confinement to household chores and reenter the wider world. She was able to do so partly because her responsibilities for childcare lessened and partly because she was able to gain support from a network of friends: 'So it was a while ago that I . . . sort of breaking away from it all [laughs]. Not breaking away from it all anyway. Spreading my wings . . . it's nice to know that once the kids are off to the school in the morning the day is my own . . . Forgot what it [indistinct] well I'd completely forgotten what it was like.'[13]

If good government, among other objectives, is about facilitating the pursuit of happiness, it certainly has to be concerned with the psychic states of its citizenry, and not only with its level of material prosperity. Many factors can come into play here. Policies which sustain or create networks of social interaction can provide conditions for the mobilizing of psychic development; the support of self-help groups of a diversity of kinds can play an important role; situations which corrode self-respect can be actively attacked – and much more besides.

Class divisions and social conflicts

The postwar welfare state 'settlement' has usually been interpreted mainly in class terms. Today such a 'settlement' has been
brought about more by the globalization of capitalist enterprise
than by the institutions of the state. The quiescence of the labour
movement is not the result of the 'institutionalization of class
conflict', but of the new conditions of global economic competition. Class relations simultaneously become more centred on
the labour market and refracted through new exclusionary
mechanisms.

Class in the sense of collective action is partly taken out of the
play, but its influence is felt strongly in other social divisions
which become the focus of actual and potential social tensions.
Such tensions concentrate on the four diagonals of the structural
diamond analysed earlier. These have the capacity to tear the
social order apart just as threateningly as the old class conflicts
ever did, albeit in quite a different fashion. Could divisions
between younger and older age groups become a threat to the
social fabric? Most assuredly they could, however strange the
prospect may seem. In the US the American Association of
Retired Persons has no fewer than thirty million members – if it
were an independent country, it would be the thirtieth largest
society in the world. It is an extremely active group, which has
achieved notable success in Congress, including securing the
abolition of enforced retirement based on age.

The power and influence of older people, however, as they
break out of their 'dependency ghetto', is likely to stretch far
beyond the influence of pressure groups. Their needs are likely
to come to dominate some aspects of the political agenda, inside
and outside the formal electoral process. The proportion of older
people turning out to vote in national and local elections is
growing in most Western countries, in specific contrast to that of
younger age groups. 'The giant', it has been said, 'has just begun
to waken' – 'a battle is brewing that threatens to divide the nation
and set generation against generation.'[14]

A battle between parents and children, a second side of the
structural diamond, might reflect these divisions, but also has

other sources. The gap between the generations at this level is created by the pace of social and technological change, which detaches the experience of children from that of their parents; and by the resentments which children, who have more formal rights than they used to, may come to feel about inadequate parental care.

The advance in children's rights is certainly to be welcomed and is a significant contribution to the potential for emotional democracy. In spite of the furore it has caused in several countries, the right of children to divorce their parents is perfectly consistent with post-traditional family relations. As in the case of divorce between spouses, its implications depend not on its statistical spread but on surrounding social conditions; rights can create new solidarities and also destroy old ones. A generalized battle of children against parents could place major sources of strain on welfare institutions. Not only has the proportion of children in the care of welfare agencies increased over the past two decades in most industrialized countries, but a high proportion of the homeless are children or young people.

Young people also make up a large number of the unemployed. Some such people are among today's social pioneers, sensitive to the multiple meanings of work and deliberately steering clear of the labour market to pursue other possibilities. The large majority, however, are simply blocked from employment opportunities. Will they, and others among the unemployed, become alienated from the majority in work, who in turn will conduct a class struggle against them, mediated by the fiscal structure of the state? Possibly, if the welfare state remains oriented to the goal of full employment in the orthodox sense – a dying ideal the more a post-scarcity society is approached.

Of all the political and real battles described here, the conflict of the sexes is the most profound in its implications, for personal and social emancipation but also for tension and division. The neoliberal agenda for a revival of 'family values' is usually coupled with an attack on the welfare state, but in fact a defence of such values, were it in any way feasible, would be a main support keeping the welfare state intact. Current systems of welfare depend for their functioning in a quite fundamental manner on established family forms and gender differentials.

Women's claim to autonomy and equality is irreversible. Yet women continue to carry out most tasks associated with the care of others in modern societies and for the most part these are not remunerated. A reassertion of 'family values', it has been remarked, drawing on the caring role of women, is conceptually no different from a tax levied on them – 'a hidden tax without representation'.[15]

Not just economic equality is at issue here but a battle, as it were, between two very generalized forms of life politics. With all due allowance for a multiplicity of individual variations, women on the whole speak 'in a different voice' from men.[16] Who will speak for us all? Will modes of life generally associated with Western forms of masculinity – that driving, compulsive masculinity which Max Weber identified – become increasingly generalized, perhaps associated with the supremacy of market relations in all corners of life? Or will femininity, with its greater emphasis on interdependence, emotional understanding and care, increasingly be transferred to the public sphere? These questions, the answers to which remain open, relate to almost all the other issues raised in this work.

A *pact between the sexes*, were it to be achieved, within the industrialized societies and on a more global level, is in many ways the key to the retrieval of other forms of solidarity. What happens to family life, for obvious reasons, serves either to connect or disconnect the generations; and what happens to gender divisions is deeply consequential for, although of course also strongly affected by, transformations in the world of work, paid and unpaid. Welfare systems which continue to depend, implicitly or otherwise, on a model of patriarchy are likely in the end to come apart at the seams in a comprehensive way.

The affluent against the poor? A generative model of equality

The welfare state, by and large, hasn't succeeded in transferring resources from the more affluent groups to the poor.[17] The wealth creation/trickle down model of the neoliberals hasn't worked either; in those countries where this approach has been tried in a serious way, the result has been an expanding differential between rich and poor.[18] What to do? Must we become resigned to a social order in which all hope of further equality has gone by the board? We need not, but we do have to think of equalization in a somewhat new way, in the manner suggested in the previous chapter. The context for such an assumption is a post-scarcity society, moving beyond productivism; and a society which increasingly forms part of a globalized order, rather than being concentrated within the nation-state. What would such equalization involve? In what sense, if any, would socialist ideals of equality still be held to?

The goal of equality, as I have emphasized earlier, was never fully integrated with the core suppositions of socialist thought – it corresponds more to the residue of Durkheim's 'communism'. The 'intelligent control' of social life – subjecting market forces to central direction – stands in no particular relation to an ethos of equality, save perhaps as creating the authoritative power that might take from the rich to give to the poor.

The generative model of equality, combined with a conception of post-scarcity, does not face this problem. Equalization here is understood in two linked senses – in terms of mutual collaboration to overcome collective 'bads' and in terms of a generalized movement away from productivism. It is based less on a rigorous sharing of material things than an indifference to them, coupled to a 'defensive' understanding of the limits of unending economic growth.

Go back to the goods relevant to the pursuit of happiness: security, self-respect and self-actualization. The possession of wealth does not necessarily allow individuals to achieve these qualities, just as material poverty does not necessarily eradicate them. Wealth is certainly not irrelevant to them, but how relevant it is depends on the conditions in which it is both produced and actualized. Moreover, there are many more existential circumstances which cut across the possession of wealth (individual or social) more or less completely. In a society moving away from modernity's orientation to control, neither accidents nor the basic phenomena of birth, sickness and death can be fully neutralized. They cannot simply be 'accepted' (the new medievalism), or the result is certainly incapacity or demoralization; they can, however, be actively confronted in a way which conforms to the notion of positive welfare. As elsewhere, risk has to be confronted as risk, including the 'riskiness of risk'.

Placing happiness as a prime and universalizable value might seem to raise the possibility of a society of happy robots, deadened to initiative and content to meander aimlessly through the day. Quite the opposite is the case. The pursuit of happiness demands an active engagement with life tasks, involving pleasure in the deployment of capacities and skills. On a psychological level, the chances of living happily seem to presume facing up to challenges, whether these be self-induced or come from the outside.[19] Poverty, like other potentially debilitating life circumstances, can be oppressive because it can lead to the undermining of such capacities and skills and because it can induce an atmosphere of hopelessness. The two enemies of happiness are demoralization – a lapse into apathy or despair – and compulsiveness, that driven dependency on an unmastered emotional past.

Schemes of positive welfare, oriented to manufactured rather than external risk, would be directed to fostering the *autotelic self*.[20] The autotelic self is one with an inner confidence which comes from self-respect, and one where a sense of ontological security, originating in basic trust, allows for the positive appreciation of social difference.[21] It refers to a person able to translate potential threats into rewarding challenges, someone who is able to turn entropy into a consistent flow of experience. The autotelic self does not seek to neutralize risk or to suppose that 'someone else will take care of the problem'; risk is confronted as the active challenge which generates self-actualization.

In a post-traditional order, the management of choice in relation to reflexively ordered information has to be geared to the creation of commitments. Commitment, whether to people or to life goals, is one of the main forces of 'override' – that which allows individuals to handle stress and cope with otherwise disturbing patterns of events. Commitment focuses the development of the self, but is almost the contrary of egoism; it is the capacity to sustain involvement in a series of tasks maintained over an extended period of time.

A person who pays attention to an interaction instead of worrying about the self obtains a paradoxical result. She no longer feels like a separate individual, yet her self becomes stronger. The autotelic individual grows beyond the limits of individuality by investing psychic energy in a system in which she is included. Because of this union of the person and the system, the self emerges at a higher level of complexity . . . [this, however,] requires determination and discipline. Optimal experience is not the result of a hedonistic, lotus-eating approach to life . . . one must develop skills that stretch capacities, that make one become more than one is.[22]

As a result of the way in which the welfare state developed, from a concern to assist (as well as to regulate) the poor, 'welfare' has generally come to be equated with improving the lot of the underprivileged. But why not suppose that welfare programmes should be directed at the affluent as well as those in more deprived circumstances? Such a conclusion follows from the concept of positive welfare; and, as I shall try to show, rather than accentuating pre-existing inequalities, such programmes could be a major means of overcoming them.

Security, self-respect, self-actualization – these are scarce goods for the affluent as well as the poor, and they are compromised by the ethos of productivism, not just by distributive inequalities. Moreover, the effects of distributive inequalities have to be set alongside the collective damage to which affluence gives rise – its effects cannot by any means be wholly offloaded on to the poor.

The pursuit of happiness can be undermined by compulsiveness just as thoroughly as by hopelessness. At one time such an observation might have seemed a pious appeal to communism in Durkheim's sense – the wealthy should renounce their riches or pass them on to the poor, since the possession of wealth is psychologically as well as materially corrupting. Piety or altruism have nothing much to do with it, however, in a society where productivism, and the psychological orientations underlying it, have run up against their limits; and where 'more of the same' has become self-contradictory and destructive.

The relief of dependency becomes a *generalized* aim in a post-scarcity society. Overcoming welfare dependency means overcoming the dependencies of productivism, and both can be combated in the same way. As elsewhere, we stand today at a crossroads. Existing inequalities might become further entrenched. Yet such a situation isn't likely to enhance the sum of happiness either of the privileged or of the deprived. For the latter, poverty will become more and more a source of degradation, social disintegration and dependencies of all sorts, as underclasses become more firmly rooted. For the more affluent, the price is likely to be a fortress existence, where increasing prosperity carries a heavy price and where all groups suffer from the effects of environmental decay and hazards associated with it.

A generative model of equality, or equalization, could provide the basis of a new pact between the affluent and the poor. Such a pact would be an 'effort bargain' founded on lifestyle change. Its motivating forces would be the acceptance of *mutual* responsibility for tackling the 'bads' which development has brought in its train; the desirability of lifestyle change on the part of *both* the privileged and the less privileged; and a *wide notion* of welfare, taking the concept away from economic provision for the deprived towards the fostering of the autotelic self.

Mutual responsibility for coping with 'collective bads' tends to derive directly from the increasing significance of manufactured risk. The pollution of the air, death of forests or the aesthetic despoilation of the environment do not conform to class divisions. Seen as external risk, these would be treated as environmental 'insurance costs', to be picked up by business firms or the taxpayer; treated as manufactured risk, they suggest lifestyle change instead. Anyone who wishes to live more healthily shares a common interest with others in confronting a life gone sour – where the advantages of affluence simultaneously produce damaging effects which affluence itself cannot repair. Thus neither paying to repair such damage nor buying one's way out are what are at issue here. They are in effect dead-end solutions.

The common interests the affluent and the poor have in lifestyle change concern a move away from productivism and towards productivity. This move in turn connects with other changes noted previously as bound up with an emerging post-scarcity order. The autonomy of work, and its opposite, the unequivocally negative connotation of unemployment, tend to be defined in relation to the compulsiveness noted by Weber. That compulsiveness is gendered and anchored in a division of sex roles which has now either dissolved or has come under intense strain. A questioning of the autonomy of work and of the gender divisions associated with it is rich in implications for generative equality. For an orientation to productivism has long been primarily a phenomenon of the masculinized public domain. No one can say with any confidence at the moment whether or not masculine ideals will become hegemonic for both sexes. However, a world in which men no longer value economic success in the way they once did and where they live more for love and emotional communication – the least one can say is that this would look very different from the present one.

In placing in question the autonomy of work, the privileged could learn more from the poor than the other way around. For those who are more or less constantly 'out of work', whatever the hardships they have suffered, have perforce come to have knowledge about a life that doesn't have paid work as its centre or as its main motivating influence. The effort bargain with the poor would not be the direct transfer of wealth but a transfer of employment opportunities coming from changed attitudes towards work on the part of the more affluent. To speak of the poor making a reciprocal lifestyle contribution might sound strange; how might such a contribution be envisaged? It would draw on exactly the same traits disclosed by alternative development models for the impoverished of the Third World. Self-reliance, integrity and social responsibility, including local environmental care, would be the 'levy' that the rest of society would ask for – and seek to promote.

What role would the state have – would there still be a welfare state in a post-scarcity society? There would not. The state would certainly have to continue to provide a wide range of goods and services, oriented to the prevention of dependencies rather than to their persistence. However, it would have to act in cooperation with a diversity of groups, particularly self-help groups, of a local but also of a transnational kind.

All this is said from the point of view of utopian realism. But just how realistic is it? What would be the social means of forging lifestyle pacts, particularly one between the affluent and the poor? The considerations potentially motivating such a pact are plain enough, but are there either the will or the available social mechanisms to bring it about? So far as the industrialized societies are concerned, we might seem to be back with the problem of a fiscal and ethical shortfall.

Such is not necessarily the case, however – although it is not my purpose here to propose specific reform packages or to consider how electoral support might be created for them. The means of generating an affluent/poor lifestyle pact could be several:

1 A common interest in environmental protection and in reducing toxicities can be used to establish policies which are in effect redistributive in favour of the poor. This is because, as mentioned earlier, underprivileged groups tend quite often to be driven to follow environmentally harmful practices or ways of life, and these act to reinforce their deprivation. Moreover, a reduction in general hazards will improve the life of the less privileged to a relatively greater degree than that of the more affluent.
2 The same considerations apply to the protection of traditions and local solidarities.
3 Greater job flexibility for the more affluent need not lead to dual labour markets if combined with moves towards other social 'settlements' (particularly that between the sexes). Equality promoted through transfers of employment opportunities can be furthered by a variety of short-term measures. These might include, for example, 'third sector' employment provided by the state and devoted to tasks of social and community care.
4 Existing welfare systems can be reconstructed so as to disentangle 'life-cycle' provision from the objective of reducing structural inequalities -- in particular, the objective of preventing the formation of excluded underclasses.
5 In enhancing the sum of human happiness, just as important as economic measures and provisions are those affecting democratic rights and the avoidance of violence. While these are plainly influenced strongly by economic inequalities they are

by no means wholly determined by them. Moreover, many 'reverse effects' are possible, acting to help reduce economic deprivation.

The question remains whether a lifestyle pact such as suggested here for the wealthy countries could also work when applied to the divisions between North and South. Empirically, one certainly could not answer this question positively with any degree of assurance. Analytically speaking, however, one could ask, what other possibility is there? Direct transfers of wealth on a large scale are unlikely to be forthcoming and in any case might be counterproductive. A positive move towards a post-scarcity system on the part of the global consumer class, coupled to an 'alternative development' for the world's poor, are the only plausible means of creating a more equal world.

The question of isolating the life values relevant to a post-scarcity order turns in a direct way on ecological issues – appropriately defined. Since ecological movements have been seen by many as so important today, it is appropriate to discuss them at this juncture at some length; it is to this task that I turn in the chapter that follows.

8

Modernity under a Negative Sign: Ecological Issues and Life Politics

Could one see in the extraordinary upsurge of green ideas over the past few decades the springs of a renewed political radicalism? Certainly the advocates of ecological theories believe so. Carolyn Merchant, for example, says that 'radical ecology' proposes a 'new consciousness of our responsibilities to the rest of nature and to other humans. It seeks a new ethic of the nature and the nurture of people. It empowers people to make changes in the world consistent with a new social vision and a new ethic.'[1]

Murray Bookchin is only one of many who hold that ecological thinking can, as he puts it, 'recover the very idea of a radical critique of social life'. Radical thought today, he argues, has lost its identity. What we now call 'radical' – the radicalism of the left – has become 'an odious mockery of three centuries of revolutionary opposition', composed of 'the mere shadows of direct action, embattled commitment, insurgent conflicts, and social idealism that marked every revolutionary project in history'. Marxism, and socialism more generally, are complicit with the social order they claim to attack. In describing Marxism as 'nothing but state capitalist monopoly made to benefit the whole people', Bookchin says, Lenin did not so much vulgarize Marx's ideas as reveal the basic character of the socialist project. Enlightenment thought had an ethical vision of the good life; but rather than being developed by it, this vision was betrayed by socialism. In socialist theories (and in some otherwise quite opposing views as well) 'nature becomes for the first time simply an object for mankind, purely a matter of utility; it ceases to be recognized as a power in its own right; and the theoretical knowledge of its independent laws appears only as a stratagem designed to subdue it to human requirements, whether as the object of consumption or as the means of production.'

Radicalism can be rescued, and even deepened, Bookchin continues, by the ecological movement. Most of the gains produced by several centuries of economic 'development' have been negated by the separation of human beings from nature and the ecological degradation that has followed. A new harmony between nature and human social life must be established, on the basis of profound revisions in our current ways of life. We have to foster 'a new sensitivity towards the biosphere' and 'restore humanity's contact with soil, plant and animal life, sun and wind.'

An ecological society, in Bookchin's view, would be one in which the balance and integrity of the biosphere would be preserved, or restored, as an end in itself. Such a society would promote diversity among human groups and in nature. It would presume a dramatic decentralization of power to local, self-governing communities, based on 'small' technologies, and would be guided by 'an ethical holism rooted in the objective values that emerge from ecology and anarchism'.[2]

The 'deep ecology' of Arne Naess, much debated in the literature of green politics, develops comparable ideas. Expressed in brief, deep ecology proposes that a new political and moral philosophy is needed which sees human beings as in, and of, nature, rather than superior to it: 'biospheric equality' places humans on an equal level with all other living things. Deep ecology also stresses the interconnected character of nature and the social community – something understood, so it is said, in 'primitive' cultures but abandoned in modern civilizations. Horticulturalists and hunter-gatherers provide models to which humanity should return, the virtual eradication of such groups by the 'advance' of modernity notwithstanding. Human carrying capacity should be the guideline for all ecological regions; people will be able to live as 'future primitives', recovering ecological diversity as 'dwellers in' the land.[3] As Edward Goldsmith puts it, 'it is to the traditional societies of the past that we must turn for inspiration.'[4]

In spite of the hostility of writers such as Bookchin, many authors on the left have seized on ecological thinking. The move from red to green, after all, provides a useful refuge for a foreclosed radicalism. If a socialist revolution is no longer feasible, why not think instead of green utopias? For if capitalism is not after all going to fall into an economic crisis that will generate a transition to socialism, perhaps it will succumb instead to the ecological crisis? Thus Alain Lipietz echoes the *Communist Manifesto* in speaking of a 'spectre that stalks the world' near the turn of the new millennium – a spectre that is no longer Communism but ecological radicalism.

'Crimes against nature', he says, 'are on the increase, and every crime against nature is a crime against humanity.' The logic of capitalist accumulation depends on maximizing economic returns at the expense of all else, leading to the despoiling of nature, something which today has reached desperate straits. The whole-scale expansion of capitalist forms of production has 'saturated our ecosystem and reduced significantly the time available to adapt to the disruption which we ourselves cause'. There can be no partial solutions, only more thoroughgoing ones: 'ecology, previously on the "periphery" of the economy, is today right at the heart of the problem . . . the challenge we have given ourselves is to take responsibility for the fate of the whole planet . . .'[5]

Yet although green movements often tend to situate themselves on the left, there is no obvious affinity between radical ecology and leftist thinking. Early forms of ecology and conservationism were associated particularly with the critique of modernization coming from Old Conservatism. It was Burke who wrote that the French Revolution had made everything 'stray from nature's path into this strange chaos of foolhardiness and infamy'. Nature was to be defended against the inroads of economic expansionism, which threatened its inner harmonies as well as its beauties. Such ideas became important in fascism; the National Socialists envisaged major conservation and reforestation programmes.[6]

No need to mention these historic connections to see the

affinities between green philosophies and conservatism. The 'conservation of nature', however that be interpreted, has clear ties to conservatism as the protection of an inheritance from the past. Some of the key concepts of green theory, as I mentioned early on in this book, such as sustainable development, the fostering of local variety, or respect for the interdependence of things, resonate with basic strands of philosophic conservatism. The pronouncements of ecological theorists sometimes closely match those of conservatives. Here is Goldsmith, for example, talking about the decline of the community and the family. 'The greatest damage done by state welfare . . .', he says, 'is to bring about the disintegration of the family unit.' This 'basic unit of human behaviour, without which there can be no stable society, cannot survive a situation in which the functions which it should normally fulfil have been usurped by the state'. Going on to the issue of gender, he asserts that the natural differences between men and women should form the basis of the division of labour:

> Men and women look different for the very good reason that they are different . . . [in current times] women tend to be subjected to precisely the same education as men and are encouraged by every means to compete with them. This can only mean the further breakdown of the family unit which depends for its survival on a clear division of labour among its members . . .[7]

Gray notes that green writers and green parties have been widely attacked by conservative critics during the recent period. Greens have been accused, among other shortcomings, of propagating socialist ideas in another guise, being hostile to science, making apocalyptic judgements that are quite unwarranted, and corroding social solidarity. Yet green concerns share with conservatism a range of ideas:

> of the social contract, not as an agreement among anonymous, ephemeral individuals, but as a compact between the generations of the living, the dead and those as yet unborn; Tory scepticism about progress, and awareness of its ironies and illusions; conservative resistance to untried novelty and large-scale social experiments; and, perhaps most especially, the traditional conservative

tenet that individual flourishing can only occur in the context of forms of common life.[8]

Gray, in fact, wants to appropriate green thought for conservatism, toning down along the way more far-reaching green proposals for social reform.

However, ecological ideas do not have a privileged connection with conservatism any more than they do with the left or with liberalism. It would be more accurate to see green philosophies as reflecting the shifts in political orientation I have sought to document throughout this study. They are neither distinctively of the right nor distinctively of the left. They resist that progressivism which holds that everything can be changed for the better; but at the same time they stand for forms of radicalism having implications well beyond anything that could be developed within the usual frameworks of socialism. It does not follow from this observation that we should accept green political theory at its face value; such theory is as much an expression of the social and political problems which confront us today as a solution to them. And of course there are many versions of green political philosophy, not all of them consistent with one another.

Thinking about nature

Worry that an industrializing world would outgrow its resources dates back to the nineteenth century, but it only became widespread from some thirty or forty years ago. Disquiet concentrated first on population growth. Thus in 1948 Fairfield Osborn wrote that 'the tide of the earth's population is rising, the reservoir of the earth's living resources is falling.'[9] This Malthusian theme was elaborated to include ways in which economic development was producing environmental destruction. As late as the 1970s, most discussions still concentrated on environmental issues in the context of national boundaries and national interests. The publication of the report of the Club of Rome, *The Limits to Growth*, described by a reviewer as 'Malthus with a computer', did much to focus debates on a more global level. The computer model used in the study projected something like a global collapse at a certain point in the next century. The report met with its fair share of criticism. One author, for example, called it a 'fascinating example of how scientific work can be outrageously bad and yet be very influential'.[10]

Since the date of its initial publication, concern about the depletion of non-renewable resources has remained strong, but has been joined by other worries. What has been called the 'second environmental wave' has focused on threats to the biosphere. None of these (like global warming) are indisputed processes. For ecological writers, they signal a situation of great danger to humanity and to the earth's ecosystems. To their critics, such threats are exaggerated, and perhaps don't result from human intervention into nature at all. Thus, according to Lal, the evidence about global warming is ambiguous and scientists disagree about its interpretation. Depending on which scientist is consulted, 'we could frizzle or we could freeze or there may be no change.'[11] The thinning of the ozone layer, he says, might be linked to variations in the solar cycle rather than to human activities. Other authors, even those very sympathetic to ecological concerns, have questioned the universal applicability of ideas such as overgrazing and desertification.[12]

No one, however, doubts that in a few short decades human actions have had a much larger impact on the natural world than ever before, and environmentalism, from being a fringe concern, has come to be something which almost all observers take seriously. Defending the environment, rescuing nature, advocating green values – these notions have become commonplace. Yet how should we understand the notion of 'environment' and more particularly that of 'nature'? For in any interpretation of ecological thinking an enormous amount hangs on these terms.

Many green writers distinguish between 'environmentalism' and 'ecology' – essentially regarding the former as reformist and the latter as revolutionary. The distinction is similar to that which Naess draws between shallow and deep ecology. Environmentalism, or shallow ecology, does not focus on the 'retrieval of nature' but on the more modest aim of controlling the damage that humans have wreaked on the physical world. The 'environment' is basically a cluster of resources; humanity must be careful not to squander them if its own future is to be safeguarded. The attitude of environmentalism is one of promoting 'the thrifty use of non-renewable resources and the use of renewable resources without diminishing their quality or endangering their supply'.[13] Nature is regarded as perhaps an object of beauty, separate from human beings, but not as intrinsic to the definition of an acceptable form of human social life itself. Compare Naess on deep ecology: 'To distance oneself from nature and the "natural" is to distance oneself from a part of that which the "I" is built up of. Its "identity", "what the individual I is", and thereby sense of self and self-respect, are broken down.'[14]

While environmentalism can largely do without it, 'nature' is as important to ecological thought as 'tradition' is to conservatism. In each case, however, these tend to be received ideas, and can be deployed to support various different interpretations or positions. Some versions of ecology have a theological cast: it is not for us to tamper with what is a divine creation. Others take seriously the metaphor of nature as mother nature. Thus, in opposition to the 'mechanistic approach' to nature, associated with science, in which 'nature' is conceived of as the inanimate source of natural resources', Rupert Sheldrake asserts a view which sees nature as alive. This perspective allows us to 'begin to develop a richer understanding of human nature, shaped by tradition and collective memory; linked to the Earth and the heavens, related to all forms of life; and consciously open to the creative power expressed in all evolution'. Such an outlook, he says, is 'implicitly feminine': for the words 'nature' and 'natural' have their origins in the mothering process.[15] The theme has been developed in more detail by numerous 'ecofeminists'.

Most such versions of green theory lack precision exactly because 'nature' remains undefined or is understood in a catch-all way. Some philosophers sympathetic to green politics have tried to inject more hard-edged arguments into ecological theory. Goodin's work is a prominent example. There is a coherent 'green theory of value', Goodin claims, on which the more developed forms of ecological ideas rest, and which allows us to put to one side 'some of the crazier views' – to do with transformations of consciousness, New Age cosmologies and so forth – which greens 'happen sometimes to espouse'.

Goodin distinguishes three approaches to the theory of value.

The neoliberal view analyses value in terms of consumer satisfaction; it is based on an interpretation of preferences. Socialist and particularly Marxist conceptions, on the other hand, discern value in production. The green theory of value differs from each of these because it traces value to natural resources – or, since the word 'resource' suggests environmentalism, to natural attributes which make them valuable. They are valuable, Goodin argues, exactly because they result from natural processes rather than from human activities.

How can this be? Goodin proceeds by means of an example. Suppose a development company is going to mine an area of natural beauty. The company guarantees that once it has finished it will recreate the area exactly as it was. Would the spot have the same value for us as if it had been left untouched? In Goodin's view it would not. Although the landscape in each instance looks identical, the recreated version would not have the same history as the pristine one. An object which is faked, no matter how meticulously, does not have the value of the authentic article.

It is not its history as such, Goodin says, that leads us to value the natural landscape, it is the fact that such a landscape, as part of a wider natural world, provides a context in which people are able to see 'some sense and pattern to their lives'. 'What is especially valuable about the products of natural processes is that they are the products of something larger than ourselves.'

For this to be so, nature cannot be tyrannized by human beings. Compare a traditional English village, with its church, houses and hedgerows (which adapt to nature) with a city like Los Angeles (which superimposes its own, artificial order on nature). One cannot say, Goodin accepts, that the English village is any more 'natural' than Los Angeles. Both are human productions; conversely, humans are part of nature. 'What is at issue is not the naturalness of its creation . . . it is rather that, in the one case, humanity does not ride roughshod over other parts of nature. And that allows humanity to derive satisfaction from reflection upon its larger setting, in a way that it cannot where that larger setting is more exclusively of its own creation.'[16]

The difficulty with Goodin's defence of green values is that nature cannot any longer be defended in the natural way. To say that we need something 'larger' or more enduring than ourselves to give our lives purpose and meaning may be true, but this is plainly not equivalent to a definition of the 'natural'. It fits 'tradition', in fact, better than it does 'nature'; this is why the idea of tradition crops up quite a lot in green theory.

The paradox is that nature has been embraced only at the point of its disappearance. We live today in a remoulded nature devoid of nature and this has to be our starting point for a consideration of green political theory. As Ulrich Beck has written:

> Nature is not nature, but rather a concept, norm, memory, utopia, counter-image. Today more than ever, now that it no longer exists, nature is being rediscovered, pampered. The ecology movement has fallen prey to a naturalistic misapprehension of itself . . . 'Nature' is a kind of anchor by whose means the ship of civilisation, sailing over the open seas, conjures up, cultivates, its contrary: dry land, the harbour, the approaching reef.[17]

This doesn't mean that we can have *no* coherent idea of nature any more, even if A. D. Lovejoy was able to count over sixty different senses in which it has been used. But any attempt to derive values *from* nature is surely doomed. The ecological crisis is a crisis brought about by the dissolution of nature – where 'nature' is defined in its most obvious sense, as any objects or processes given independently of human intervention.

Ecological questions, I want to propose in what follows, should be understood as part of coming to terms with reflexive modernization, in the context of globalization. Problems of ecology cannot be separated from the impact of detraditionalization. Each raises the age-old question, 'how shall we live?' in a new guise – in a situation where the advance of science and technology, coupled to economic growth mechanisms, force us to confront moral problems which were once hidden in the naturalness of nature and tradition. The hazards associated with manufactured uncertainty bring home the need to deal with these problems – but if they are seen simply *as* 'natural dangers' their real character is misinterpreted.

The theme I wish to develop follows on from ideas introduced in previous chapters. Modern civilization proceeds through the attempted imposition of human control on environments of action, including the natural environment, which were once largely external to such action. This orientation to control, strongly bound up with a stress on continuous economic development but not reducible to it, comes up against its limits as it is generalized and globalized. One such limit concerns the prevalence of manufactured uncertainty, which compromises the very control orientation itself; another concerns the effects that such a control orientation has on basic moral questions and dilemmas of our existence.

Environmentalism, by and large, understands risk only in terms of external risk; ecology, by contrast, tries to seize hold of the practical and ethical issues that face us in terms of natural criteria or the recovery of lost natural harmonies. Since they are first of all experienced as failures, these questions return first of all 'under a negative sign'; yet each, when viewed positively, discloses moral considerations relevant to the question 'how shall we live?' in a world of lost traditions and socialized nature.

Several main domains or contexts in which 'nature' (often also interwoven with tradition) has disappeared, or is disappearing, can be distinguished.[18] Nature here means what is 'natural' or pregiven in our lives; if this is not too paradoxical, a subcategory is nature understood as the non-humanized physical environment.

Nature:	− pollution, environmental degradation
	+ renewed protection of the non-human world
Reproduction:	− random genetic engineering, eugenics
	+ positive appropriation of life, sexuality
Global systems:	− large-scale disasters, accidents stemming from manufactured risk
	+ global cooperation and sustainable development
Personhood:	− environmental health threats, personal meaninglessness, addictions
	+ holistic approach to body and self

Let me in what remains in this chapter discuss these various domains in relation to risk and to moral renewal.

Nature: living in and with it

Protests against pollution and other forms of environmental damage began as localized reactions to accidents in Ewald's sense – oil spills, contaminated land, spoiled trees. Understood as external risks, environmental degradation is seen by scientists and laypeople alike in terms of 'side-effects'.[19] Industrial development, in other words, has unlooked-for secondary consequences; but the risks involved can be assessed and danger levels controlled. Thus air quality in a given city can be monitored and kept to 'acceptable' levels, even if this means that factories sometimes have to be closed down for several days when pollution levels mount.

'Acceptable levels', however, are possible to determine with any accuracy only at a given time or place. How can anyone know what effects a particular process or set of chemicals might have on the earth or human bodies thirty years – or several generations – from now? The measures taken to limit risks, if they involve technological innovations, might themselves have side-effects not discovered until later, perhaps much later.

When risk is still seen as external risk, science may continue to offer a sense of security, even of certainty, to lay individuals (and political officials). Manufactured uncertainty, however, has quite different connotations – for science, technology and industry are at the very origins of it. Some may start to mistrust science and retreat from modern industry. Yet science and technology are the only means of bringing their own damage into view. Ecological thinkers develop their critiques only by presuming an apparatus of science and the whole social infrastructure which goes with it. Many look to the very forms of science and technology which in other contexts they attack to define for them what 'nature' is.

A number of incoherences or lapses appear in green political theories which advocate a return to an independent nature:

1 It has become commonplace in the literature of deep ecology

to call for 'a non-violent revolution to overthrow our whole polluting, plundering and materialistic industrial society and, in its place, to create a new economic and social order which will allow human beings to live in harmony with the planet'.[20] Yet were such a strategy even remotely feasible, it would undermine the emphasis on the interdependence of things, continuity and so on supposed to be central to green values. Such an agenda is as internally contradictory as it is implausible.

2 Protection of the biosphere and the cultivation of local biotic idiosyncrasy are routinely confused with the preservation – or reinvention – of social or cultural traditions. From the maintenance of village life and customs through to the revival of religion and the spiritual, a 'return to nature' is assumed to provide a justification for preserving tradition. Sheldrake, for example, moves directly from an analysis of the natural world to talking of how 'members of different religious traditions have been engaged in a rediscovery of their spiritual relationship with the living world.'[21] Yet there is no intrinsic relation between one and the other.

3 It is assumed that those who live 'close to nature' are intrinsically more in harmony with it than are moderns – hence the admiration often expressed for hunting and gathering or small horticultural societies. However, as anthropological critics have observed, nature often only becomes a beneficent force once it has been largely subjected to human control; for many who live close to it, nature may be hostile and feared. Moreover, even societies with a low level of technological development sometimes have a record of environmental destructiveness.

4 Mastery over nature means destroying it in the sense that socialized nature is by definition no longer natural; but this is not *ipso facto* the same as harming the environment. The socializing of nature, as follows from the previous point, may render it benign and thus actually permit a 'harmony' with it unavailable before. Moreover, mastery can quite often mean caring for nature as much as treating it in a purely instrumental or indifferent fashion.

5 The call of radical ecology for a profound decentralization of social life – and even for the disappearance of cities – rests on the idea that biotic diversity produces cooperative interdependence.

Yet such an aim stands in tension with the claim that strong measures must be introduced to control environmental damage. Such measures could often only be taken if there were in fact more centralized global authorities than exist at the moment.

6 Small, local communities are assumed to maximize solidarity and democracy, as well, of course, as adapting more gracefully to nature. Bookchin expresses the views of many when he remarks that 'Small . . . is not merely "beautiful"; it is also ecological, humanistic, and, above all, emancipatory . . . we must begin to decentralise our cities and establish entirely new ecocommunities that are artistically moulded to the ecosystems in which they are located.'[22] Small communities, however, don't typically produce the diversity ecologists are looking for, they discourage it. In small communities, as I have emphasized previously, the individual tends to become subject to the 'tyranny of the group'; mechanical solidarity is the enemy of independence of mind. The hostility of some greens to city life seems, if not thoroughly misplaced, naive as well as unrealistic. Cities have long been centres of diversity and cultural sophistication. A wide variety of interests and outlooks flourishes much more readily in cities than in the more homogeneous milieu of the isolated local community. Nor are cities, as Claude Fischer has shown, necessarily settings in which anonymous, impersonal interactions dominate over more personalized ones.[23]

Ecology privileges naturally occurring systems above others, but this is a mistake. There is no doubt a range of situations in which humanity should attempt to draw back from interventions that affect the environment, or should try to eliminate side-effects. Most of the modes of life we have to deal with, however, are *ecosocial* systems: they concern the socially organized environment. No appeal to nature can help us decide whether or not such withdrawal is appropriate in any particular case. In most environmental areas we couldn't begin to disentangle what is natural from what is social – more importantly it is usually irrelevant to policy-making endeavours to seek to do so. This rescues us from the impossible task of having to say that Los Angeles is in some way less natural than an English village; and it commits us to making judgements about *all* landscapes or ecological arenas. 'The environment' shouldn't be used as a surreptitious way of smuggling in 'nature'. Los Angeles is as much part of the environment as a country meadow.

All ecological debates today, therefore, are about managed nature. This doesn't mean to say, of course, that nature has passed wholly into human control; the boundaries of such control are exposed by the very failures of attempts to extend it indefinitely. The question of how far we should 'defer' to natural processes doesn't depend, however, on the fact that there are some such processes much too large for us to encompass. It depends on how far we agree that some natural phenomena which we have influenced or could influence are best reinstated. Any such reinstatement is itself, at least obliquely, a form of management – the creation of parameters of 'protection'.

The management of nature today clearly has to be in some substantial part defensive – too many new threats and high-consequence risks have been generated for such not to be the case. The criteria for assessing managed nature in a positive vein concern not nature itself, but values which guide that management, no matter whether we speak of heavily urbanized areas or of wildernesses.

Where conservation is involved, the protection of tradition has to be separated from the protection of nature. Or, to put it another way, we shouldn't suppose that we are defending nature – much less so defending it in a natural way – when in fact we are protecting a particular social setting or way of life. Goodin has argued that the two are in fact linked. Conservationists often want to preserve, not just land, but the buildings on it: for example, old houses, churches or farmhouses. No one could claim that these are part of nature, no matter how liberally that term be interpreted. They would thus appear to stand outside Goodin's 'green theory of value'; for seemingly one couldn't say that such items are 'larger than human beings', since they are human constructions. In fact, Goodin says, they can qualify. For it is not just that objects or phenomena are spatially larger than ourselves that can make them a focus of green values; the fact that they are situated in a wider history than one's own personal history can have just the same effect. 'There is, then, a case to be made for the conservation of things in general on account of their history, whether human or natural. That provides an argument which is both intellectually important and politically powerful for the preservation of ancient monuments and historical landmarks.'[24]

Such an argument, however, is no more than a version of philosophic conservatism, and subject to the objections which can be made against such conservatism where it seeks to defend tradition in the traditional way. We might very well want to preserve old buildings, but we wouldn't want to, and mostly couldn't in any case, sustain the ways of life with which they were associated. Yet without those ways of life, the old buildings are scarcely 'larger than ourselves' – they are symbols of the past, relics or monuments. If we *do* want to preserve at least some of the old modes of life, we can't do so just on the basis that they are larger than ourselves, for they may include forms of activity that are noxious. We might wish to preserve the local gibbet, for instance, but not the practice of publicly hanging petty criminals on it.

Every bit as important to ecological questions as the management of the environment is the management of science and technology, seen in the context of modern industry. We cannot escape from scientific-technological civilization, no matter what 'green nostalgias' it tends to provoke. Living in an era of manufactured risk means confronting the fact that the 'side-effects' of technical innovations are side-effects no longer. More needs to be said on this issue in the light of other considerations to be developed below.

The question 'how shall we live?' is raised by any attempt to decide what to preserve – of nature or of the past – short of problems that bear in a brute way on global survival. Ecological problems disclose just how far modern civilization has come to rely on the expansion of control, and on economic progress as a means of repressing basic existential dilemmas of life.

Questions of reproduction

One of the most signal developments in science of the past few years has been the convergence of biology and genetics. In the wake of new forms of reproductive technology, such as *in vitro* fertilization, comes the project of deciphering and possibly controlling the mechanisms of human inheritance. The aim of the Human Genome Project is to chart every gene in human DNA. A variety of inherited defects, or illnesses with a genetic component, can be identified and in principle corrected. It has been said that if the researchers proceed with the success which some predict, the Genome Project 'will make the twenty-first century the age of the gene. Although the Human Genome Project can be compared to the Apollo programme, it will transform human life and human history more profoundly than all the high-tech inventions of the space age [and may even] . . . bring us to understand, at the most fundamental level, what it is to be human.'[25]

The implications spin out in all directions. Modern genetics is big business, not just attracting large-scale funding from governments, but carrying the lure of enormous profits for those who are able to patent and market the discoveries made. Genetic engineering is already a large-scale industry in its own right. The Human Genome project is likely to isolate many thousands of human genes from which corresponding proteins can be mass-produced. No matter how far that particular project may or may not proceed, geneticists have already managed to identify the functions of, and make widely available, proteins vital to the human organism.

The human growth hormone is an instructive case in point, symptomatic of an indefinite variety of current and future possibilities.[26] A certain proportion of children do not reach normal height because they lack sufficient quantities of the protein which makes 'natural' growth take place. From the early 1960s it was possible to treat a few such children using hormone derived from the pituitary glands of people after death. However, it seems that one person from whom the material was extracted was suffering from a rare form of infectious brain disease. As a result, in several of the countries where the procedure was used, some of those treated died of the illness.

Later it was discovered how to make the growth hormone artificially, without any danger of such contamination. As a result, however, the hormone is now being employed to 'treat' children who have no pituitary deficiencies, but whose parents simply wish them to be taller. Most are people who are short themselves, but the hormone has been used simply by parents who believe that greater height is likely to confer advantages in life. This is in spite of the fact that it is not at all clear whether in fact the hormone does make normal children grow any taller than otherwise they would do. In addition, there is some (rather insubstantial) evidence that older people injected with the hormone are less prone to the muscle shrinkage that tends to occur with advancing age. Human growth hormone has also been used to try to improve the strength and endurance of athletes, although again whether it actually does so is contentious. In spite of this, the demand is so strong that counterfeit hormone is being widely sold. Yet there are indications that the growth hormone can do active harm to people who take it to improve their athletic prowess; some deaths have been attributed to it.

The story (and of course this is only the story so far) is entirely typical of such scientific innovations and of the opportunities and perils of manufactured uncertainty in general. The dilemmas posed by the Human Genotype Project and kindred research seem to some extent obvious. How far should scientists be allowed to go on with work which opens up possibilities that are as frightening as they are potentially beneficial? Anatomy is no longer destiny: but is it morally acceptable for us to design not just the environments we live in, but our physical, and perhaps even our psychological, makeup? Some have imagined the creation of a new super-race of humans, immune to a variety of now common illnesses and disablements.[27]

Such responses and questions are certainly important, but they imply that research of this type can and should be dealt with in its own terms – within the domains of action to which it directly pertains. However, there is no difference of principle between such scientific innovation and the dissolution of nature as found in other domains of human activity. All the connotations of manufactured uncertainty are there in the example of the growth hormone. Tracing through the history of its implementation thus far, we begin with the 'routine' discovery of side-effects: the initial extraction of the hormone discloses certain risks to health. Producing the protein through genetic engineering seems to minimize the risks involved in the earlier procedure, and at the same time considerably extends the potential range of application of the hormone. Yet new risks are thereby created, of a more imponderable character than those perceived before. And who knows whether there will be any longer-term effects on those exposed to the growth hormone, or even their descendants – or what those effects might be?

What starts off as a form of treatment for a specifiable malady comes actively to undermine and change the definition of what is 'normal'. For the normal in respect of height, as with regard to so many other things affecting the body now, was once given by nature. How tall is tall? The question had some meaning when one accepted the luck of the draw, as it were, as to one's height; it becomes more difficult to respond to if height is no longer a given in this way.

It isn't science itself which is on trial here; it is the involvement of science and technology with modernity's orientation to control. The close integration of science with modern institutions depended on scientific authority having the force of the traditions which it supposedly set out to discard. Pure science proceeded within its own demarcated sphere: 'truths' emerged from this sphere once observations and theories had been tested out in a satisfactory way within the scientific community. This arrangement worked well enough so long as 'nature' remained relatively intact and the risks facing the technological applications of science were external rather than manufactured. Once this relation shifts and the disputes 'internal' to science start reflexively to enter non-scientific arenas of discourse and activity, such a situation can no longer be sustained. Or, rather, it *is* sustained commonly enough, even when the problematic character of the circumstances we are now routinely called on to deal with is only deepened by treating manufactured uncertainty as external risk.

In the new circumstances of today, the progress of science participates in, yet also reveals, the limits of modernity. Science and the orientation of control can no longer do the job of legitimation which for so long was basic to modern social development. The 'protected' sphere which made disinterested scientific activity possible has been broken through as reflexivity develops and as manufactured risk appears. Modernity itself has become experimental – a grand experiment with all our lives caught up in it; but this is not in any sense an experiment carried on under controlled conditions.

The findings of science are interrogated, criticized, made use of in common with other reflexively available sources of knowledge. In a detraditionalizing order, few can afford to ignore claimed findings in relation to, for example, the benefits and risks of eating various kinds of foods, health hazards of various sorts, ecological dangers and so forth. On local, collective and more global levels, we all in some sense and in some contexts actively engage with the findings of science – as well as with the technologies which may stem from or be involved with them.

As a result science changes its role, in our individual lives and in the wider social order.[28] Many scientific claims enter public discussion well before – according to the pre-established formulae of science – they could be said to be 'proven'. Where the 'bads' of scientific innovations are concerned, individuals or groups are often disinclined to wait until claims have been 'properly established', for the dangers they may face if these claims are valid may be pressing. Hence it is not surprising that, for instance, food scares become common. A particular food item that one is used to consuming in a regular way suddenly becomes suspect, no matter what the scientists – or some of them, given that scientific opinion is frequently divided – say on the issue.

Although the reactions may be less intense, something similar applies in respect of positive benefits claimed for scientific discoveries. The growth hormone was seized on by athletes interested in improving their bodily strength, in spite of the fact that this effect was only poorly documented and even the short-term consequences for health of taking the hormone are unknown. One might say that scientific testing will eventually 'catch up' as more testing is done; but, quite apart from the impossibility of testing for long-term consequences, the point is that each context of use of a scientific innovation is likely to create new circumstances under which the old tests no longer apply.[29]

Core components of science as 'traditionally' understood thus come under strain and sometimes dissolve altogether. Science depends on the disinterested assessment of validity claims. Disinterestedness in turn presumes that scientists are free from having to account for the social consequences of their findings; for science, dedicated to the pursuit of truth, follows its own path.

Yet where so many practical reflexive implications attach to scientific enquiry, even the validity of findings cannot be judged only from within science itself. Those who established the Human Genome Project in the US proposed that 3 per cent of the funding for the enterprise should be spent on studying the social and ethical implications of the researches – the largest bioethics research programme in the world. Yet the real interrogation of the project will come from the diversity of reflexive involvements it will produce, and has already produced.

The moral or ethical dilemmas raised by research such as the Human Genotype Project might seem to come solely from the new fields it has opened up. It might appear, in other words, that ethics comes in only where nature dissolves in the face of human intervention. For, after all, we (with all the ambiguities that small word entails) have to make decisions, make choices, where previously things were fixed by a natural order; and these decisions continually escape a 'technical' framework.

I want to propose a different view, however. The ethical issues which confront us today with the dissolution of nature have their origins in modernity's repression of existential questions. Such questions now return with full force and it is *these* we have to decide about in the context of a world of manufactured uncertainty. The longing for a return to 'nature' from this point of view is a 'healthy nostalgia' in so far as it forces us to face up to concerns of aesthetics, the value of the past, and a respect for human and non-human sources of life alike. We can no longer answer these questions through tradition – understood in the traditional way – but can draw on tradition to do so. In the case of reproduction, what is at issue is the possibility of a positive appropriation of the moral character of life. As the chronicler of the Human Genome Project quite rightly comments:

By the time it is complete, the Human Genome Project will have cost more than $3 billion and occupied the energies and intellects of thousands of the world's most creative scientists over a period of nearly two decades . . . It will have set out a complete genetic blueprint for humanity, uncovering not only the differences between one human and another but also deep underlying similarities between humans and the rest of the living world. Yet at the end, after all that effort, [the challenge it poses] . . . is to redefine our sense of our own moral worth . . . that human beings retain a moral value which is irreducible.[30]

The Genome Project may be technologically more avant-garde than other areas of reproductive technology, but returns us to the same issues as they do.

Consider, for example, the controversies about abortion. The reaction one might have to the controversies surrounding abortion is one of despair: how can the warring parties ever come to agreement? Yet the whole debate could be seen as one that fruitfully explores problems of the value of human life. The abortion issue stimulates certain sorts of fundamentalisms; but at the same time, perhaps, it undermines others. If Ronald Dworkin is right in his analysis of the question, both the main parties to the debate share, and have been in fact forced to make explicit, a commitment to the sanctity or inviolability of human life.[31] It is also possible, he tries to show, that such a principle spreads to other non-human activities that have an investment of creativity in their reproduction. Every abortion is a matter for regret, because it denies the fulfilment of the potential for creativity of the foetus. Although always a bad thing, early abortion can be justifiable in cases where not aborting would cause greater harm to the realization of human potential. It is not being alive as such which is credited with value, but what kind of life an individual is capable of.

Dworkin's arguments, of course, will not do away with the clashes over abortion. His discussion, however, suggests that the reason why the question has become so important today is precisely that the sanctity of human life has emerged as a universal value claim, the very contrary of an arbitrary value pluralism. Those who believe that abortion is wrong in all circumstances by definition cannot agree with opponents who hold that abortion should be quite freely available. Yet what this debate really signals is a global situation in which the moral claims of life and the fulfilment of human potential are more or less taken for granted premises. And this circumstance is certainly quite new.

The order of high-consequence risks

Consciousness of the sanctity of life, consciousness of the importance of global communication: these are the connected poles of life politics today. Global awareness – or as one should perhaps say, awareness of the common interests of humanity as a whole – figures as the other side of the most threatening of the 'bads' on the human horizon. The metaphors and imagery abound, of course, from 'spaceship earth' to 'progress for a small planet' among many others. In more sophisticated vein there is the idea of Gaia, the world 'as a living entity with the equivalents of senses, intelligence, memory and the capacity to act'.[32] What seems on the face of things to drive us away from human beings, as despoilers of the biotic unity of nature, really propels us towards them. High-consequence risks are the negative side of rapidly burgeoning human interdependence.

High-consequence risks are in a category of their own, as I have stressed before, only in terms of their sheer scale. Scale undeniably gives such dangers a peculiar phenomenology. Remote from everyone and apparently wholly unaffected by anything individuals may do, such risks none the less impinge on people's consciousness more universally than other threats simply because there is no escape from them. More than any other dangers, such risks are refractory to being tested out according to the usual procedures of science. Their diagnosis has a strong counterfactual element and so do whatever remedies are instituted to try to counter them. For there is a sense in which, if those remedies work, we will never know whether the original diagnostic claims were right.

Global warming exemplifies this point perfectly. Whether or not global warming is occurring is a contentious matter. The most prudent course of action – always given that the necessary steps could feasibly be taken on a global level – would be to take preventative measures on the presumption that global warming is indeed taking place, and that it will have harmful consequences. Yet if such measures are in fact implemented, it would be easy to argue in retrospect that this was just another scare and a great deal of effort was deployed for nothing.

The same can apply in reverse, where modes of minimizing high-consequence risks are said to have 'worked'. Thus many have argued that nuclear weapons kept the peace between the US and USSR during the Cold War. Yet obviously a critic could claim that the peace was kept in spite of the existence of the nuclear armaments. The theory of deterrence could have been proved wrong only in circumstances when no one would have been around to tell the tale anyway.

Awareness of high-consequence risks is no doubt one of the factors prompting a desire to return to the security of nature. As collective humanity, many feel, we have seriously interfered with the regenerative properties of the natural environment, which should be allowed to recover their original form. As elsewhere, however, there are few natural solutions and a pronounced tendency to naturalize social problems. Short of some sort of cataclysmic happening, our new-found global interdependence won't go away, no matter how far an orderly withdrawal – which is not really feasible in any case – from the socialization of nature is undertaken.

High-consequence risks, more than any other form of danger, make plain the contrast between external threats and manufactured uncertainty. Natural calamities, of course, have always been more or less commonplace. Many natural catastrophes still occur, but in the developed sectors of the world in particular they have mostly been displaced by *disasters* – and by the looming threat of 'worse to come'. Disasters open the veil that separates external risk from manufactured uncertainty. Disasters of a relatively minor kind can be predicted in the aggregate with reasonable accuracy and their likely consequences assessed. Their consequences are mostly short-term and manageable. Hence they can be fitted within the parameters of external risk.

Large-scale disasters are a different matter. The bigger a potential disaster, the more likely governing authorities and technical specialists are to say that it 'cannot occur'. Much of the time, moreover, we don't even know what it is that 'cannot occur' – the unforeseen consequences are legion. Or, alternatively, they are counterfactual possibilities to which the past offers little guide, as is the case with all the largest threats hanging over us.

Disasters such as the meltdown at the nuclear power plant at Chernobyl have consequences which ramify indefinitely into the future. So far as the reactions of security experts elsewhere go, 'it cannot happen' becomes 'it cannot happen here' (until, perhaps, it does). But for many people Chernobyl has already 'happened here' – even if it may be many years before it is known, if it ever is, what the real, long-term consequences of the disaster are. Although the escape of radiation has already led to many deaths, and although the ways of life of whole peoples such as the Lapps have been affected, although animals have been slaughtered and crops destroyed, Chernobyl was quite rapidly normalized. Levels of radiation have been declared 'safe' in most parts of Europe for some while since. Yet who knows what safety is when dealing with events that have no historical precedent?

Unlike small-scale disasters and all but a few naturally occurring hazards, the effects of large-scale disasters cannot normally be easily delimited in terms of time and space. On the other hand, the environmental effects of such disasters can also be exaggerated; thus in retrospect some can appear as just another scare. Some major oil spills, for example, have been cleared up quite quickly and the side-effects (at least seemingly) controlled. When alarms turn out to be only scares, those who point to the continuing existence of major hazards are likely to find themselves branded as doomsday merchants. Yet scares are just as intrinsic to conditions of manufactured uncertainty as are 'genuine threats'. The point is that threats in such circumstances are just that – how far they are 'real' cannot be known in advance in the manner of external risks, for they are situations which are always liable to involve factors that have not been encountered before.

In July 1993 the Mississippi burst its banks and flooded wide areas of the US from St Louis to further south. The flood laid waste to an area the size of England; fifty thousand people were forced to evacuate their houses, more than thirty people were killed and the costs of repairing the damage were estimated at $10 billion. An observer commented that the event was a 'humbling of the richest and most powerful nation on earth, rendered impotent and reduced to the status of a Third World country by a caprice of nature . . . images of a Third World disaster abound: bridges down, refugees fleeing with whatever possessions they could carry, the stench of drains and raw sewage everywhere.'[33] A natural catastrophe, like many others before it in history? Perhaps – but then again, perhaps not. Some claim that the very system of levées, storm walls, dykes and irrigation channels constructed to control the river's propensity to overflow its banks led to the flood, or at least worsened it. Moreover, the heavy rains themselves were unseasonal: July is normally a time of extreme heat and even drought. Were the rains perhaps a product of humanly produced climatic changes? No one can be sure.

The level of flooding that occurred was quite unanticipated; but if someone had claimed a disaster was imminent, and the flood prevention system had in fact held, that person might very well have been accused of scaremongering. Suppose, however, that a warning given in this way was listened to and the now reinforced system had held very easily. Creating anxiety in the minds of the powers that be may have been the condition of getting something done. Yet the very success of the measures taken might have made them seem unnecessary in the first place.

There is a general principle here affecting manufactured uncertainty. Consider, for example, education programmes instituted to combat the spread of AIDS. No one knows (as yet, anyway) whether AIDS is an illness that has cropped up 'naturally', or whether it has its origins in as yet unidentified aspects of technology or humanly induced environmental change. We have no direct historical precedents to call on in seeking to limit its spread or search for a cure. Programmes of education are important in this context because the main way in which the diffusion of AIDS can be limited is through persuading people to alter their sexual habits.

To make such programmes successful, it may be necessary to emphasize in the strongest possible terms that AIDS will spread rapidly if the appropriate behavioural changes are not made. Two possibilities exist whereby what is a justified warning can become widely seen as an irresponsible scare. Scientific knowledge about AIDS is still insubstantial, in spite of the enormous sums of money being spent on research worldwide. It may turn out that certain influences inhibit the spread of AIDS beyond a certain point, or that current interpretations of the mode of its causation or transmission are erroneous. But a justified warning may also retrospectively become a scare simply because it works. The incidence of AIDS might turn out to be much lower than suggested – but as a result of changes in behaviour that those prophecies and the programmes they inspired brought about.

Like the other 'bads' of modernity, high-consequence risks disclose a utopia – and one certainly with some aspects of realism to it. It is not a utopia of a world returned to its 'natural order', humanity having withdrawn, or having confined its aspirations in such a way as to defer to an organic system much greater than itself. It is a utopia of global cooperation, which recognizes the unity-in-diversity of human beings. The 'bads' show us what we should try to avoid – they are negative utopias. However, they also carry an important positive sign. The reflexive complications of high-consequence risks just noted don't mean that we can't solve the problems that confront us. They do confirm and amplify the conclusion that the difficulties of a scientific-technological civilization cannot be solved just through the introduction of even more science and technology.

Environment, personhood

To switch from globalized risks to the situation of the individual may seem an odd transition, but it is appropriate enough in a world where global developments and individual actions have become so closely tied together. Not the least important field where 'nature' dwindles away is that of the self and the body. Here again, however, as so often elsewhere, what was nature was intermingled with tradition.

The self, of course, has never been fixed, a given, in the manner of external nature. To have a self is to have self-consciousness and this fact means that individuals in all cultures actively shape their own identities. The body has never been purely a given either. People have always adorned and cosseted (sometimes also mutilated) their bodies. Mystics have subjected their bodies to all sorts of regimes in the pursuit of sacred values.

In a detraditionalizing society, however, the requirement to construct a self as a continuing process becomes more acutely necessary than ever before. Regimes of the body are no longer the preserve of religious idealists, but spread to include everyone who seeks to organize a personal future in the context of reflexively available dietary and medical knowledge.

The self was once developed in local contexts of activity and in relation to relatively clear-cut criteria of group membership. To 'have a self' was to 'be' someone of a particular sort; now, however, to 'have a self' is to 'discover who one is' through what one does. Simultaneously an emancipation and a source of major anxieties, the reflexive project of self operates within, yet also compromises, the orientation to control characteristic of modernity. One cannot 'become someone' without rediscovering the moral life, no matter how oblique or fragmentary that re-encounter might be. Or perhaps this should be put the other way around. Without such a contact with an ethics of personal life, a brittle compulsiveness tends to take over – and this certainly becomes common.

The body has had to be reflexively made ever since the combined influence of globalization and reflexivity did away with its acceptance as part of the given 'landscape' of one's life. Today, in the Western countries at least, we are all on a diet, not in the sense that everyone tries to get slim, but in the sense that we have to choose how and what to eat. The production of foodstuffs is no longer determined by natural processes; and local diets are less and less given by what is locally grown and produced, or by local customs. The availability of foodstuffs does not depend on the seasons or the vagaries of the climate, as food production and distribution becomes globalized. Nor does all this apply only to the more affluent; few are exempt as most food becomes industrially produced.

The fact that self and body are no longer 'nature' means that individuals have to negotiate the conditions of their lives in the context of many incoming forms of information which somehow must be dealt with. The complex relation between warnings and scares applies here as in more global areas. Health warnings often proceed in advance of the 'full testing' of scientific hypotheses, and against the better wisdom of the scientists themselves. Some warnings, of course, turn out after the event to have been scares – although later research may cause that judgement to be reversed too. In the longer term, the dangers held to be inherent in the consumption of foodstuffs and the following of certain lifestyles must be faced up to. Individuals might ignore them – all the more so because what is proclaimed as healthy at one point might be questioned by subsequent research. Yet it is virtually impossible not to have some sense of the changes in scientific theories and findings relevant to the risks and advantages of foods and lifestyles. Anyone who persists with a customary local diet does so knowing that some items on it might contain particular health dangers. Moreover, sticking with a pre-established diet, as with other aspects of tradition and custom, might often become a very deliberate endeavour, rather than one flowing from 'naturally given' aspects of the local context. For perhaps it has to be maintained against other trends; or the foodstuffs concerned, having become 'esoteric', can only be obtained with some effort.

In health care as in so many other areas, a return to the 'natural' is a demand heard on all sides. From the revival of traditional medicine, the substitution of herbs for industrially produced drugs, through to the practice of homoeopathy, a turn away from modern medical methods occurs. This happening is not mainly produced by social movements, although those associated with ecological groups frequently favour 'natural' therapies over scientific medicine. It is found wherever individuals start to develop a scepticism about science, scepticism bred by the increasingly public and controversial character of scientific findings noted earlier.

The scientific model of health care is certainly under siege. In some part again this is because of an accumulation of negatives, including the fact that the costs of public health services outstrip the capabilities of governments to pay for them. Behind these factors, however, one can trace a new appreciation of the connection of positive health with the transformation of both local and global lifestyles. Possible and increasingly well documented threats to health from environmental changes abound.

Pollution of the air ranks as high as any known disease syndrome in terms of the numbers of people throughout the world who die from pathologies it induces.[34] Environmental factors may strongly influence the main killer diseases both in terms of their causation and the extent of their spread.

Ecotoxicity is a hazard which potentially affects everyone, no matter how or where people live. It results from chemicals which are either deliberately applied in farming and other contexts, or which enter the environment indirectly from waste disposal sites, sewers and by other channels. Since contamination is so general, direct programmes of purification are of only marginal value: the chemicals circulate through the soil, water and air. Ecotoxicity is said to be 'like being eaten by a thousand ants. It takes a while, but eventually the bites wear you down. It is poisoning in slow motion.' Once again, orthodox modes of risk assessment and safety levels don't have much bearing on the phenomenon, and knowledge of its long-term effects is very scanty. Each potentially toxic chemical is normally examined separately, and under laboratory conditions rather than in the field. Such tests could only be carried out with any real precision (and then only for short-term effects) if we could find people living in an untouched environment and expose them to the particular chemical for which a safety standard was to be set. Yet there is no such environment left anywhere in the world. The usual approach to ecotoxicity, it has been noted, 'is like that of an entomologist who assesses the thousand ants eating you by issuing standards on the bites of three of them, saying be careful of these three.'[35]

Ecotoxicity, like other 'bads' disclosed by reflexive modernization, has its own positives, its own utopias. Considered under a positive sign, it suggests that the care of body and self could be integrated, and perhaps must be integrated, with programmes of environmental renewal. 'How shall we live?': that question can no longer be answered in terms of the control of external risk, or left to the remaining elements of tradition. Facing up to it means deliberating, in an open and public way, how social and environmental repair might be connected to the pursuit of positive life values. Life politics here unavoidably focuses on very basic ethical concerns – concerns that have featured in an important way in the history of conservatism, but which other political perspectives have left almost completely untouched. Philosophic conservatism has been unafraid to broach questions of life, finitude and death; and it places 'existence', as carried in traditional symbols and practices, as prior to 'knowledge' or control. We can see now how valid this view is, while recognizing that conservatism, in and of itself, cannot cope with its implications when confronted with a post-traditional world in which 'nature' is no more.

Conclusion

Ecological politics is a politics of loss – the loss of nature and the loss of tradition – but also a politics of recovery. We can't return to nature or to tradition, but, individually and as collective humanity, we can seek to remoralize our lives in the context of a positive acceptance of manufactured uncertainty. Put in this way, it isn't difficult to see why the ecological crisis is so basic to the forms of political renewal discussed in this book. It is a material expression of the limits of modernity; repairing the damaged environment can no more be understood as an end in itself than can the redress of poverty.

Living without nature or without tradition or, more accurately, living in a situation where nature and tradition can be reconstructed only in an active fashion, need not lead to the moral despair expressed by some on the right, who see the old verities disappearing forever, or to the 'cultivated indifference' favoured by some of the proponents of postmodernism. Nor is there an inevitable incompatibility between a positive ecological politics and egalitarianism – where equality is understood in a generative mode. Seen under a positive sign, the various opportunities and dilemmas posed by the dissolution of nature, as I shall propose in the concluding chapter, disclose universal values for us in a world where human interdependence is far-reaching and integral. These are exactly the values which provide an overall framework for conceptions of positive welfare. For moving away from productivism, as I have tried to show, implies a recovery of positive life values, guided by the themes of autonomy, solidarity and the pursuit of happiness.

From nature, or what used to be nature, to violence: among the high-consequence risks we face today none is more menacing than the threat of large-scale war. The Cold War is receding into the past; does this mean that the world is less dangerous than it was before? How should we seek to limit violence in a world of manufactured uncertainty? These are questions I shall try to answer in the chapter which follows.

9
Political Theory and the Problem of Violence

The problem of managing or limiting violence ranks as one of the most difficult and demanding in human affairs, but left and liberal political theory have only rarely touched on it. A great deal has been written about the origins of war and the possibility of peace. Yet for the most part this literature has remained unconnected with theories of the internal constitution of societies and governments – it has been preoccupied with the behaviour of nation-states in the international arena.

Left political thought has often taken up the question of revolutionary violence, and has discussed this in tandem with the repressive violence of the state. Leftists, however, have mostly assumed that violence would not be a problem in a socialist society and hence have given little thought to how social relations might become free from it. Most varieties of liberal thinking are not in the end too different; for liberal political thought has been built around the idea of the contract, and a contract is essentially a pacific negotiation of exchange.

Conservatives of various persuasions have given more attention to the role of violence, particularly of war, in social life. Some versions of conservative thought, indeed, have glorified war and martial values. What conservative philosophers by and large have not done, however, is to consider how war and violence might be transcended. For conservatives have tended to assume that these are generic to the human condition.

There are of course numerous contexts in which violence

figures in human social life, almost always in relation to structures of power. Violence, as Clausewitz says, is normally at the other end of persuasion; it is one among other means whereby individuals, groups or states seek to impose their will on others. I shall not try to discuss the origins or nature of violence in general, nor shall I consider the issue of violence and crime as such. I shall limit myself to the following issues (large though each of them still is). From the point of view of utopian realism, is it feasible to suppose that the role of warfare might diminish and how might such a process be furthered? What can be done to limit the spread of sexual violence? How can we counter violence which develops on the basis of ethnic or cultural differences? These may seem like disconnected issues, but in the light of the social transformations discussed earlier in the book some clear connections, as I shall try to show, exist between them.

I take it that each of these questions raises problems of pacification and I take pacification to be as important a part of an agenda of radical politics as any of the issues I have discussed earlier. For even if the Cold War has been relegated to the past, the threat of nuclear conflict and other sorts of military violence will remain for the indefinite future; and violence and the threat of violence in social life can destroy or cripple the lives of millions.

Several provisos are in order here. There are respects, and some very important respects, in which the use of violence is necessary to achieve widely desired social ends. Thus pacification itself presumes a control of the means of violence on the part of legitimate authorities. I think one can take it for granted, though, that *all* forms of violence are to be minimized as far as possible, whether legitimate or illegitimate. In other words, the tendency of governing authorities to secure a monopoly over the means of violence should not be equated with an increasing *resort* to violence.

'Violence' has sometimes been defined in a very broad way. Johan Galtung, for example, argues for an 'extended concept of violence' which would refer to a wide set of conditions that inhibit the development of individuals' life chances. Violence is any barrier which impedes the realization of potential, where such a barrier is social rather than natural: 'if people are starving when this is objectively avoidable, then violence is committed . . .'[1] As with Pierre Bourdieu's idea of 'symbolic violence', the point is to apply the concept of violence to a wide variety of forms of oppression which people might suffer, and thereby to relate it to general criteria of social justice. The problem with such notions is that they make an already very widespread phenomenon ever-present. What is specific to violence as ordinarily understood – the use of force to cause physical harm to another – becomes lost from view. I shall therefore understand violence in this straight-forward and conventional sense.

The state and pacification

The issue of pacification has to be understood in relation to the long-term development of modern institutions and the modern state. Violence and the state, as rightist thinkers have always tended to emphasize, are closely connected; the state is the prime vehicle of war. In respect of their deployment of violence, however, premodern states differed in a basic way from nation-states. In the premodern state, the political centre was never able to sustain a full monopoly over the means of violence. Brigand-age, banditry, piracy and blood-feuds were always common, and in most states local warlords retained a good deal of independent military power. Moreover, the power of the political centre depended in a fairly immediate way on the threat of violence. Premodern states were segmental in character: the centre nor-mally had no way of enforcing obedience from subjects in more peripheral areas save by a show of force. In spite of the despotic and bloodthirsty character which many premodern political regimes displayed, their level of substantive power in day-to-day social relations was relatively low.

As a result of a number of factors, including particularly improved communications and an intensifying of surveillance mechanisms, nation-states became 'sovereign powers': the agency of government was able to achieve much greater admin-istrative control over its subject populations than ever before. To cut a long story very short, and to use a good deal of oversimpli-fication, the result was a pervasive process of internal pacification, achieved in most 'classical nation-states' – those developing from the eighteenth century onwards in Europe and the United States.[2]

Pacification doesn't mean, of course, the disappearance of violence from the interior of states; and it is quite consistent with the waging of wars in the international arena. It refers, in this context at any rate, to the more or less successful monopoly of the means of violence on the part of the political authorities within the state. Internal pacification went along with the formation of professionalized armed services, 'pointing outwards' towards other states in the state system, rather than being preoccupied with the maintenance of internal social order. The convergent development of capitalism and parliamentary democracy, together with systems of centralized law, played a major role in 'extruding' violence from the immediate mechanisms of government.

Although processes of internal pacification have proved much harder to achieve in 'state-nations' and ex-colonial societies than in the classical nation-state, they have almost everywhere proceeded far compared with the premodern state. Civil war is by now a specifically abnormal situation in most states throughout the world, particularly in the economically advanced regions. In earlier forms of state, by contrast, it was almost the norm; contestation of the power of the ruling authorities by rival military groups was frequent and often protracted.

The era of the internal pacification of states was also the time of the industrialization of war: war changed its character as weaponry became mechanized and mass-produced. The industrialization of war destroyed militarism in one guise, although it sustained it in another. The 'warrior values' long promoted by aristocratic strata went into prolonged decline. War could no longer be seen as an occasion for display and ritual. The highly coloured clothing that had so often been favoured by warrior groups and traditional armies gave way to sober uniforms of camouflage. In the shape of admiration for valour, esprit de corps and military discipline, militarism survived in an altered form. Indeed, if 'militarism' be defined as the widespread support for military principles and ideas in the larger society – and the preparedness of civilian populations to support war *en masse* if need be – militarism became more rather than less common.

It can be argued, however, that with the further development of industrialization of war, and above all with the invention of nuclear weaponry, these processes started to go dramatically into reverse. During the Cold War, the existence of large-scale nuclear arsenals formed part of the (remote) experience of everyone – the most threatening of all high-consequence risks. Yet at the same time, Clausewitz's theorem became turned around. Although smaller wars were fought out 'by proxy' in many places, a nuclear confrontation was 'unthinkable' because of its devastating consequences. War could no longer be turned to when diplomacy failed; diplomacy had to have as its goal the avoidance of large-scale war altogether. From this point onwards, one could say, militarism started to go into decline.

The emergence of what Martin Shaw calls a 'post-military society' would certainly be of interest to any programme of radical politics in the present day.[3] A post-military society responds to the changing global situation following the Cold War, but also builds on longer-term trends within the developed societies. Militarism, Shaw argues, has been diminishing in many countries across the world since the end of the Second World War. It was a consequence of a state system which mixed internal pacification with external preparation for war. Its institutional backdrop was the sovereign state, the nation-in-arms and mass (male) conscription. Militarism, in the terminology used in this book, was a characteristic of simple modernization. Current social, economic and political transformations undermine it.

Militarism in this sense was characterized by large-scale, hierarchical systems of command which paralleled the industrial and state bureaucracies. There was in fact a direct connection, often remarked on, between militarism and the early development of both democracy and the welfare state; citizenship rights were forged in the context of mass mobilization for war. Militarism has declined as a result of several trends: the shifting, and in some ways diminishing, autonomy of classical nation-states; the disappearance of clear-cut external enemies; the reduced influence of classical nationalism and the rise of substate nationalisms; and the functional obsolescence of large-scale war.

Can we see these processes, in so far as they are sustained or accelerate, as leading to a reduction of the role of military violence in settling disputes? Is there now an extension of internal pacification into external areas?

We might give a cautious assent to both of these questions. A post-military society is not one where the threat of large-scale military violence is removed, especially given the massive economic differences within the global system. Geopolitical rivalries are likely to remain strong, and destructive war remains a possibility in many parts of the world. A post-military order is none the less likely to be more resistant to mass mobilization for military purposes than used to be the case. Smaller, more 'civilized' armed forces may still wield large destructive power. Yet it seems likely that the military will become functionally more separate from other groups than before. The expectation that has affected the lives of young men for generations – their possible, even probable, involvement in war – could end.

I don't want to pursue here the difficult question of how the world might police itself if the post-military society, in combination with other trends, helps reduce tendencies to large-scale war. Pacification on a global scale is unlikely to reproduce the processes involved in the internal pacification of states. I shall consider only the implications for features of cosmopolitanism discussed earlier. Consolidating a post-military society would mean generalizing the attitude that violence should play less and less part in settling international tensions and problems. The active side of citizenship responsibilities would imply recognition of an obligation to nourish pacific rather than warlike values, this to be as basic a part of a democratized polity as any other.

Peace movements played an important role in producing the shifts in social consciousness – West and East – which contributed to the ending of the Cold War. Like ecological movements, peace movements were driven in the first instance above all by awareness of high-consequence risk: consequently, they were largely single-issue movements. They were oriented to the Cold War, and with its collapse have either disappeared or changed their form. The mass mobilizations such movements were periodically able to generate have more or less ceased, and don't look likely to be revived in the near future. How does one mobilize for peace in a society with no enemies – but many real military dangers? Peace movements have become peace organizations and they still have plenty of concrete tasks. They can seek to raise the consciousness of citizenries and governments concerning the dangers of nuclear proliferation and they can keep alive the debate over nuclear power, especially its connection with the political production of weaponry.

The single most important factor here, however, is the altered relation between peace movements and the interests of governments in an emergent post-military order. States without enemies, and marked by a concomitant decline in militarism, are in quite a different situation from either the Cold War or pre-existing systems of military alliance and national antagonism. Although border disputes may remain, and invasions sometimes occur, most states no longer have any incentive to wage offensive war. 'Peace' takes on quite different connotations in such circumstances than it did when it meant absence of war in a nation-state system permanently geared up for it. Hence the interests of governments and peace organizations are much more convergent than they used to be; and there is no reason why they shouldn't often work in tandem rather than in opposition.

Masculinity and war

So far as civic values and responsibilities are concerned, what should we make of the fact that the propagation of military violence has always been a resolutely male affair? Feminist authors have quite often drawn direct connections between masculinity and war: warfare is a concrete expression of male aggressiveness. The civic virtues that would promote peace rather than war, it is said, are those characteristically associated with the activities and values of women. Expressed in such a way, however, this thesis is somewhat implausible. War is not an expansion of a generalized aggressiveness, but associated with the rise of the state. Although there might be some men who actively relish war, the large majority do not.[4]

One couldn't deny, of course, that there is a relation between war, military power and masculinity. Men may have to be indoctrinated in order to wage war, but war and the military have formed part of the ethos of masculinity – or masculinities – in a deeprooted way. This was true most especially of warrior aristo-cracies: war-making was glorified as the highest of all values. With the decline of the warrior ethic, military violence was no longer widely seen as the chief testing ground for heroism, honour and adventure – although some strands of Old Conserv-ative thought long continued to regard this situation as reversible. Valour remained a dominant value in military circles, particularly in officer corps, but the professionalizing of the armed forces separated military ideals from the concrete experience of the rest of the male population. To 'serve' in the military became instead part of a shifting male ethos of instrumentality and protection. Masculinity came to be associated with a commitment to work and with 'providing' for dependants; assuming the role of soldier when called on to do so was part of the intrinsic maleness of the public domain.

In the post-military society there is a push and pull between the decay of ideals of masculinity in these various senses and the entry of women into the public arena. Women have gone into the armed forces in increasing numbers. They have mostly accepted existing military norms and have agitated for complete inclusion: that is, they expect to achieve full combat rights alongside men. In the meantime, the masculine values which went along with militarism are corroding or becoming ambiguous as a result of the advance of gender equality and the growth of social reflexivity. It is in this context that we should examine the idea of a war against women, most boldly developed by Marilyn French. French interprets such a war as a long-term phenom-enon, dating back even to the first origins of civilization. Up to some six thousand years ago, she says, humans lived in small, cooperative groups in which the status and power of women was either equivalent, or superior, to that of men. With the formation of the first states, women became enslaved and subject to male domination – a situation which the advent of modernity only served to worsen:

In personal and public life, in kitchen, bedroom and halls of parliament, men wage unremitting war against women . . . Men start repressing females at birth: only the means vary by society. They direct female babies to be selectively aborted, little girls to be neglected, underfed, genitally mutilated, raped, or molested . . . The climate of violence against women harms all women. To be female is to walk the world in fear . . . Women are afraid in a world in which almost half the population bears the guise of the predator, in which no factor – age, dress or colour – distinguishes a man who will harm a woman from one who will not.[5]

As French describes it, the war against women is widespread indeed. It embraces all systems of patriarchal discrimination against women and is an expression of them. Male violence, 'the physical war against women', follows on from broader structures of inequality. The battering of women, rape and sexual murder form a material expression of the larger system of domination. Even much male on male violence, she suggests, is a sublimated form of violence that would otherwise have women as its object. 'When women are not available, men turn other males into "women". So male prisoners regularly rape other male prisoners, and many ministers and priests betray the trust of little boys or male teenagers by molesting them.'[6]

I think one can in fact agree that there is a war of men, or some men, against women today, but not in the manner in which French represents it. A war is an exceptional rather than a permanent state of affairs, and it doesn't make much sense, except in a metaphorical way, to speak of such a thing as enduring for thousands of years. Moreover, such an analysis misses what is new about the situation of the present day. Patriarchy has indeed existed for millennia; however, the circumstances in which it has become contested, and has to some extent broken down, are of much more recent provenance. Over most of the course of human history, patriarchy was accepted by both sexes; collective women's protests against the male rule may have been staged sometimes, but the historical record is not littered with them in the way in which it is with other forms of rebellions, such as peasant rebellions.

As with other systems of power, patriarchy has never been sustained mainly through the use of violence. The power of men over women has endured because it has been legitimated on the basis of differentiated gender roles, values associated with these, and a sexual separation between private and public spheres. In terms of legitimacy, particularly important has been the schismatic view of women which contrasts 'virtue' with the corrupt or fallen woman. The fallen woman in premodern systems of patriarchy referred not only to a category of persons – prostitutes, mistresses, courtesans – who stood outside the pale of normal family life. To become 'fallen' was a disgrace that could happen to anyone if she did not abide by codes of virtue and proper behaviour.

Patriarchy in premodern cultures was maintained by women as well as by men: women wielded their own sanctions against those who transgressed. So far as control of the means of violence was concerned, however, this lay in the hands of men. As a means of last resort, violence was as significant a sanctioning mechanism of power in patriarchy as elsewhere. Kate Millett has summed up all this very well: 'We are not accustomed to associate patriarchy with force. So perfect is its systems of socialisation, so complete the general assent to its values, so long and so universally has it prevailed in human society, that it scarcely seems to require violent implementation.' Yet, she goes on to add, it still had 'the rule of force to rely on . . . in emergencies and as an ever-present instrument of intimidation.'[7]

At this point, however, a major qualification needs to be added to Millett's view. The violence by means of which men policed patriarchy was not mainly directed at women. In many societies, including those of premodern Europe, women have been chattels of men and have no doubt often been treated with the casual violence that the status of a mere possession might provoke. But respect, even love, can be much more powerful forms of domination than the sheer use of force. Probably more often than not, men have treated ('virtuous') women with moral approval and esteem. The violence by means of which patriarchy was sustained was mainly from men towards *other men*. This was particularly true in respect of organized or semi-organized violence.

Hostile images of women, and physical maltreatment – such as the punishments meted out to witches – were important sanctioning mechanisms against female misbehaviour. Male on male violence, however, integrated the defence of patriarchy with the upholding of other forms of order. In many premodern societies a man's honour was directly dependent on the honour of his family, which he had a duty to uphold no matter where the threat was coming from. The reputation of a family could be tainted in various ways, but certainly this always included the virtue of its female members. Feuds conducted between kin groups commonly sprung from the defence of honour, or from an attempt to compromise it; but even where women were directly involved it was usually other men who were the targets of hostile response.[8]

What has happened today is that this system of violence has collapsed, or is collapsing, on a worldwide basis. Processes of internal pacification in most developed countries long ago displaced the feud, but remnants of the moral foundations of patriarchy were reshaped in the eighteenth and nineteenth centuries. Briefly put, the legitimation of patriarchy came to depend on a reiteration of the schism between the virtuous woman and the harlot – the second of these subjected to the sanctions of the state, the first bolstered by specific legal and moral structurings of the 'normal family'. Male sexuality was retraditionalized and was something that could be 'taken for granted', while female sexuality was in large part controlled through being subjected to an interrogatory gaze: it became understood as the 'dark continent', problematized by the first stirrings of the assertion of independent women's rights.

The large-scale entry of women into the labour force, together with universal democratization and the continued transformation of family forms, has radically altered the 'tradition in modernity' compromise which characterized simple modernization. Patriarchy can no longer be defended by violence directed by some men against others. Men (or, as one must say, some men) turn directly to violence against women as a means of shoring up disintegrating systems of patriarchal power – and it is in this sense that one might speak of a war against women today. It is not an expression of traditional patriarchal systems but, instead, a reaction to their partial dissolution.

Much of such violence, then, results from a system which is decaying; it results from the fact that women's challenge to patriarchy has in some part been successful. Its successes have provoked violent reactions; but they have also brought a great deal into the open that was previously hidden, and enforced an interrogation of much that was carried in tradition.[9]

From the point of view of utopian realism, overcoming male violence aginst women is contingent on the structural changes now affecting work, the family and the state, and the possibilities these yield – combined with an expansion of dialogic democracy. Masculinity and feminity are today identities and complexes of behaviour in the process of reconstruction. Increasing gender equality is paradoxical for the overall social community unless it goes along with structural changes which promote democratization and new forms of social solidarity – and unless there is a mutual emotional realignment of the sexes. Men's movements that have developed thus far are of various types, some seeking to reassert patriarchal forms of masculinity. In so far, however, as such movements contemplate and act on the detraditionalizing of masculinity in its diverse forms, they can be an important influence in promoting an emotional realignment. Although their influence thus far is tiny compared with that of the feminist movement, it makes sense to see them as the functional equivalents of peace movements – trying to help put an end to the undeclared war of men against women.

The transformation of masculinity and femininity, or rather their multiple forms, as inherited from the past, will depend in a basic way on how far a post-military society comes into being, and what consequences flow from the changing character of work, the family and sexual relationships. Male identity has undoubtedly been bound up with the centrality of work – as fulltime permanent employment – in modern societies. Or rather, it has been bound up with the intersections between work, the family and sexuality. For commitment to fulltime work in the paid labour force was not just an economic phenomenon – it was an emotional one. The engagements of men in the public sphere enforced a schism in men's lives of a different nature from that characteristic of women's experience. Men, or many men, across different class categories, became cut off from the emotional sources of their own lives – the origins of the by now celebrated phenomenon of 'male emotional inexpressiveness'. They left women for the most part to manage these areas in their role as 'specialists in love'.

The fact that the higher echelons in most occupational domains are still dominated by men, while men continue to play a much smaller part in childcare than women, is quite often regarded as cause for despair. Yet is it surprising that things have not yet changed to the degree that most feminist thinkers would hope? For those same thinkers have demonstrated that patriarchy has been deeply entrenched for thousands of years; it would be surprising if they could be overcome over a number of decades.

Women have won a variety of legal rights they did not hold before, and are more strongly represented in most occupational domains than they used to be, including the higher levels. Rates of unemployment of men have risen more than those of women, and the 'feminizing' of some male careers is placing in question the old models of work associated with productivism. Equal parenting – with the socioeconomic arrangements which might permit it – may still be utopian, but now carries more than a dash of reality.[10]

Male violence against women could be lessened if these developments progress and at the same time new forms of sexual identity were pioneered. As Lynne Segal has observed,

> The conscious subversion of men's power . . . is partly the work of those who travel the slow and grinding route taken by mainstream reformist political parties and organisations committed to sexual equality. It is also the work of those engaged in the more erratic, more radical, spurts and retreats along the volatile route of interpersonal sexual politics, as feminists, lesbians, gay and anti-sexist men refashion and live out their new versions of what it is to be 'woman' or 'man'. It is finally, as feminists have always preached and often practised, also a matter of cultural subversion – the creative work of remoulding the lives and experiences of women and de-centring the androcentric positioning of men in all existing discourses. Though it might be difficult to perceive, these routes do intersect. Interpersonal struggles to change men, attempts by men themselves to refashion their conceptions of what it is to be a man, always encounter and frequently collide with other power relations . . . It is not so hard to imagine a world free from the fear of too little work for men, and all too much work for women . . . It is just as easy to envisage a world free from fears of the interpersonal violence, rape, and child sexual

abuse which, in their most dangerous and prevalent forms, are the violent acts of men . . .[11]

Easy to envisage, a critic might say, hard actually to bring about: how might the combating of male violence against women relate to other forms of pacification? There is a clear connection, as has been mentioned, with the decline of militarism. Male violence is certainly not all of a piece with the waging of wars, but there are common elements that spill over from one to the other. Mass rapes are quite often perpetrated in times of war; conversely, attitudes of adventurism found among some who enlist in the armed forces seem empirically linked to a tendency to violent behaviour towards women.[12]

More important, probably, are potential connections the other way around. The creation of a democracy of the emotions, as I have sought to show earlier, has implications for social solidarity and citizenship. Men's violence against women, or a great deal of it, can be understood as a generalized refusal of dialogue. Couldn't one see this as a Clausewitzean theory of interpersonal relations? Where dialogue stops, violence begins. Yet such violence is (in principle) as archaic in the personal domain as Clausewitz's theorem is in the wider public arena.

Violence, ethnic and cultural difference

As I write these lines, a tenuous dialogue has been established between warring parties in Israel and in Bosnia; the armed conflicts in Somalia, Angola, Afghanistan and elsewhere look set to continue. To move from violence against women back towards such military confrontations might appear as heterodox as the link developed with overall processes of pacification. Yet the connections are there. The war in Bosnia, for example, witnessed the systematic rape of Muslim women as a deliberate way of humiliating them – and as statements from those involved made clear, of humiliating their menfolk also.

Confrontations such as those in the former Yugoslavia and other regions might perhaps be a residue of the past – a clearing-up of lines of division and hostility. Alternatively, and more disturbingly, they may be the shape of things to come. For the very changes that act to reduce the possibility of wars between states might increase the chances of regional military confrontations – the more so since fundamentalisms of various kinds can act to sharpen pre-existing ethnic or cultural differences.

Under what conditions are the members of different ethnic groups or cultural communities able to live alongside one another and in what circumstances are the relations between them likely to collapse into violence? The question is again a large one, and I shall discuss only a few aspects of it. There are virtually no societies in the world where different ethnic groups are wholly equal to one another. Ethnic division, and some other kinds of differences, such as religious ones, are normally also differences of stratification. The inequalities associated with ethnicity are often sources of tension or mutual hostility, and thus play their part in stimulating conflicts which may lead to a collapse of civil order.

Yet such inequalities are too commonplace to provide sufficient explanations of outbreaks of major violence. Without seeking to analyse how common or otherwise such conflicts are likely to be, or what their main origins are, I want to discuss three sets of circumstances relevant to how they might be inhibited or contained. The first is the potential influence of dialogic democracy; the second, the countering of fundamentalism; the third, controlling what I shall call degenerate spirals of emotional communication. All relate to, or draw on, ideas discussed in other parts of this volume.

There are only a limited number of ways, analytically speaking, in which different cultures or ethnicities can coexist. One is through segmentation – through geographical separation or cultural closure. Few groups or nations, however, can sustain a clear-cut separation from others today. Small communities which try to cut themselves off from the outside world, or limit contact with it, nearly all become reabsorbed to a greater or lesser degree – as has happened, for example, with the vast majority of the communes of the 1960s. States which seek isolation, such as in a sense the whole Soviet bloc did, or China or Iran, have not been able to preserve it in the longer term.

As a 'solution' to problems of living along with clashes of

values, then, segmentation is much less significant than it used to be, with the emergence of a global cosmopolitan order. Although complete withdrawal from the wider social universe has become problematic, various kinds of group separation and national differentiation can of course be maintained. Groups can keep to themselves and physical segregation has not lost all its meaning. In cities, for example, different ethnic groups often occupy distinct neighbourhoods which have only limited contacts with one another. Geophysical separation is one means by which the stratification of ethnic groups and underclasses is organized. Those in the poorer areas may lack the capacity to travel, while the members of more affluent groups rarely if ever visit the deprived neighbourhoods.

Given the diasporic character of many ethnic and cultural differentiations, however, and the penetrative influence of mass media, segmental cultures now only function with some degree of harmony in a cosmopolitan climate. Where segmentation has become broken down, and exit difficult, only two options remain: communication, or coercion and violence.

There is a tension between communication and violence, then, of a more acute kind than existed in earlier phases of modern social development – and this is true not only in the industrialized societies but on a global scale. In such a situation, whether combined with more orthodox democratic institutions or not, dialogic democracy becomes a prime means for the containment or dissolution of violence. It isn't far-fetched to see a direct line of connection here between male violence against women in everyday life and violence between subnational groups.

Difference – whether difference between the sexes, difference in behaviour or personality, cultural or ethnic difference – can become a medium of hostility; but it can also be a medium of creating mutual understanding and sympathy. This is Gadamer's 'fusion of horizons', which can be expressed as a virtuous circle. Understanding the point of view of the other allows for greater self-understanding, which in turn enhances communication with the other. In the case of male violence against women it is well established that dialogue can dispel the 'Clausewitzean theorem'. That is to say, violent individuals become less so – in other spheres of their lives also – if they manage to develop a virtuous circle of communication with a significant other or others.

Dialogue has great substitutive power in respect of violence, even if the relation between the two in empirical contexts is plainly complex. Talk can in many circumstances lead to hostility, and to the possibility of violence, rather than serving to undermine them. In a diversity of situations, a refusal to engage with the other is tied to systems of coercive power, as is its opposite, the absence of voice. The advance of dialogic democracy almost always depends on correlate processes of socioeconomic transformation. These things having been said, dialogic democratization is likely to be central to civil cosmopolitanism in a world of routine cultural diversity. Difference can be a means of a fusion of horizons; what is a potentially virtuous circle, however, can in some circumstances become degenerate. I would define a degenerate spiral of communication as one where antipathy feeds on antipathy, hate upon hate.

And this observation brings us full circle. For how else could one explain the events in Bosnia, and parallel happenings elsewhere? Fundamentalisms, as I have said earlier, are edged with potential violence. Wherever fundamentalism takes hold, whether it be religious, ethnic, nationalist or gender fundamentalism, degenerate spirals of communication threaten. What is originally merely an isolationism, or perhaps only an insistence on the purity of a local tradition, can, if circumstances so conspire, turn into a vicious circle of animosity and venom. Bosnia sits on a historic fault-line dividing Christian Europe from Islamic civilization. Yet one cannot produce a sufficient explanation of the Yugoslavian conflict only by reference to old hostilities. Those hostilities, when refocused in the present, provide a context; once conflict begins, and hate starts to feed on hate, those who were good neighbours can end as the bitterest of enemies.

10
Questions of Agency and Values

Let me in conclusion draw together some of the themes of the study as a whole. Radical political programmes today, I have argued, must be based on a conjunction of life politics and generative politics. Life political issues come to prominence as a result of the combined influence of globalization and detraditionalization – processes that have a strong Western connotation, but which are affecting societies throughout the world. Political policies need to be generative in character in so far as social reflexivity comes to be the connecting link between the two other sets of influences. Life politics centres on the problem: how shall we live after the end of nature and the end of tradition? Such a question is 'political' in the broad sense that it means adjudicating between different lifestyle claims, but also in the narrower sense that it intrudes deeply into orthodox areas of political activity.

Seen in a comprehensive way, a framework of radical politics is developed in terms of an outlook of utopian realism and in relation to the four overarching dimensions of modernity. Combating poverty, absolute or relative; redressing the degradation of the environment; contesting arbitrary power; reducing the role of force and violence in social life – these are the orienting contexts of utopian realism.

Whether seen in the context of the industrialized societies or not, seeking to overcome poverty, I have suggested, means adopting a generative model of equality. The idea of generative equality also connects closely with the diagnosis I have offered of the ecological crisis. I don't mean to say that policies designed to reduce inequalities are always compatible with ecological objectives. They are certainly not always so; and the same applies to the relations between the other dimensions. The ecological crisis, however, as I interpret it here, is essentially a crisis of moral meaning in a world turned cosmopolitan. 'Saving the environment' seems a fairly easy objective to formulate, but in fact it is a gloss for the problem of how we should cope with the double dissolution of tradition and nature. For 'the environment' is no longer nature; and traditions have to be decided about, rather than taken for granted.

The notion of a post-scarcity order, as an orienting ideal, and the critique of productivism, flow from these concerns. A post-scarcity system is not one in which economic development comes to a halt. It is, simply put, a system in which productivism no longer rules. I define productivism as an ethos where work is autonomous and where mechanisms of economic development substitute for personal growth, for the goal of living a happy life in harmony with others. This is the context in which a critical assessment of welfare institutions within Western societies can learn from the solidarities and life ethics of the informal sector. Such an approach does not in any way deny the hardships of the very poor, or the demoralization which poverty can cause. Yet in overcoming productivism, the rich have much to learn from the poor and this situation is one factor raising the possibility of a lifestyle pact promoting generative equality.

Productivism stands close to capitalism, and it is important to ask how far the framework of radical politics portrayed here continues the long-established animosity of the left towards capitalistic enterprise. What should be salvaged from socialist critiques of capitalism and what discarded?

Some of the basic ideals associated with socialism, I believe, remain as persuasive as ever, but a critical encounter with productivism has to take quite a different tack from socialist thought. Its prime object is the overcoming of compulsiveness, whether in respect of the autonomy of work or of other areas of social life; and its guiding positive aim is the expansion of human happiness. As integrated with the concept of generative equality, the critique of productivism draws on philosophical conservatism to suggest a retrieval of suppressed moral concerns. More concretely, it presupposes the creation of a range of social pacts, including that between affluent and poor but also especially between the sexes.

The main question to be asked and answered here isn't 'how much regulation and how much market?' It is: 'how can productivity be disentangled from productivism?' Capitalism is not all of a piece, and the conditions of productivity, especially where the term is used in a wide sense, cut across pre-existing divisions between 'socialized production' and market forces. A post-scarcity order would look to markets as signalling devices, but wouldn't accept the theorem that everything has its price. Its guiding impetus isn't the restricting of market forces by central-ized agencies, but the generative encouragement of lifestyle change.

In all this, utopianism might appear to outweigh realism, but I don't think such is the case. A post-scarcity order seems remote, even a fantasy, in the context of an ever-expanding capitalist world economy. However, in some respects, in the industrialized societies in particular, we already live in such an order and there are powerful influences pushing things further. It isn't likely that there will be a general revolt against consumerism, or that a halt will be called to economic growth processes. But of post-scarcity phenomena, examples abound. Far more food can be produced by two or three per cent of the population in Western countries than can ever be consumed within them. Jobs today have become as important in distributing as in producing goods. The destruc-tive aspects of untrammelled economic growth have become so pervasive and obvious that no state, or even industrial corpor-ation, can ignore them. Women are everywhere pressing men for a different division of labour between paid work and the home – the list is very large.

A rampant industrialism might seem to be crushing everything in its path, especially as Third World countries embark on successful economic development. On the other hand, through-out the world there is a consciousness of the futility of modes of development which undercut themselves, destroying the very means of their own reproduction. Moves away from productivism such as those noted above are expressions of the ecological crisis and at the same time a direct response to it. Similarly, democratizing processes are stimulated, if in complicated and paradoxical ways, by the burgeoning of social reflexivity; and, as I have tried to show, these connect closely with the struggle against violence.

Thus far I have left aside the issue of agency. How is theory to be connected to practice? Where radicalism generally meant socialism, there was a clear-cut tie between the two. Socialist thought, particularly in Marx's version, diagnosed the irrationalities of history, but showed that history provided its own means of overcoming them. If Marx's idea of the coming classless society was never particularly coherent, his account of the role of the revolutionary proletariat was compelling; the 'riddle of history' was resolved by the actions of the oppressed class. Particularly in its Marxist form, socialism invoked a providentialism having deep roots in European culture. History poses problems for us, expressed as social contradictions; but those very contradictions promise a higher synthesis, driving us onwards.

Today we must break with providentialism, in whatever guise it might present itself. Not for us the idea that capitalism is pregnant with socialism. Not for us the idea that there is a historical agent – whether the proletariat or any other – that will more or less automatically come to our rescue. Not for us the idea that 'history' has any necessary direction at all. We must accept risk as risk, up to and including the most potentially cataclysmic of high-consequence risks; we must accept that there can be no way back to external risk from manufactured risk.

Marx was right to criticize utopian thought separated from any substantive account of immanent historical possibilities. Yet he could only reject utopianism *in toto* on the basis of a teleological, and providential, view of human social development. In his view, it was utopian not to relate theory directly to practice. Some have suggested that the decline of socialism means an end to utopianism, but I hold that the opposite is the case. A recovery of the contingency of history, and the centrality of risk, opens up space for utopian counterfactual thought.

Utopian realism, such as I advocate it, is the characteristic outlook of a critical theory without guarantees. 'Realism' because such a critical theory, such a radical politics, has to grasp actual social processes to suggest ideas and strategies which have some purchase; 'utopianism' because in a social universe more and more pervaded by social reflexivity, in which possible futures are constantly not just balanced against the present but actively help constitute it, models of what could be the case can directly affect what comes to be the case. An outlook of utopian realism recognizes that 'history' cannot simply be 'reflexively grasped'; yet this very recognition adds weight to the logic of utopian thought, since we no longer hold fast to the theorem that greater understanding of history means greater transparency of action and thus greater control over its course.

But does radicalism still have any connection with orthodox divisions between left and right? And what values should guide a critical theory of late modernity? How can such values be justified in a cosmopolitan world that seems almost by definition to be alien to any universal value claims?

Difficult questions – or so it would appear. But they perhaps aren't as puzzling or enigmatic as many claim. Dropping providentialism has its advantages. If there is no necessary direction to history, there is no need to look for privileged agents who would be able to 'realize' its inner potentialities. Thinking radically is not necessarily thinking 'progressively' and is not necessarily associated with being in the 'vanguard' of change. Social movements play a significant role in radical politics, not just because of what they try to achieve, but because they dramatize what might otherwise go largely unnoticed. Yet it would be wrong to give social movements, or self-help groups for that matter, too much prominence as the carriers of radical programmes. The truth is that no group has a monopoly over radical thought or action in a post-traditional social universe. The thesis that history is made above all by the deprived – socialism's version of the master-slave dialectic – is seductive, but false.

Many of the ideas discussed in this volume, for example, are relevant to the activities of parties operating within the normal domains of national politics. There are terrains to be colonized here, from the democratizing of democracy and the fostering of social solidarities right through to the management of violence. Different parties are likely to camp in these territories, but there are many opportunities for parties of the left to refurbish their doctrines – particularly where they face neoliberal rather than more centrist conservative and liberal parties.

How can the divisions between left and right be transcended, even in part, it might be asked, at a time when people who explicitly call themselves neofascists are back on the streets? Aren't we now in fact going back to something of an earlier age, where atavistic emotions have again come to the surface, and where a renewed progressivism must once more fight against racism and reactionary sentiment?

I think not. The struggles in question are very real, and likely to be of decisive importance for the future. But they shouldn't be interpreted as just marking a regression. Rather, they can be analysed in terms of the notions I have elaborated in the foregoing chapters. Neofascism isn't fascism in its original version, however much those who pursue it look back nostalgically to the past. It is a species of fundamentalism, steeped with the potential for violence.

No doubt the differentiation of left and right – which from the beginning has been a contested distinction in any case – will continue to exist in the practical contexts of party politics. Here its prime meaning, in many societies at least, differs from what it used to be, given that the neoliberal right has come to advocate the rule of markets, while the left favours more public provision and public welfare: straddling the ground of right and left, as we know, is a diversity of other parties, sometimes linked to social movements.

But does the distinction between left and right retain any core meaning when taken out of the mundane environment of orthodox politics? It does, but only on a very general plane. On the whole, the right is more happy to tolerate the existence of inequalities than the left, and more prone to support the powerful than the powerless. This contrast is real and remains important. But it would be difficult to push it too far, or make it one of overriding principle. Virtually no conservatives now defend inequality and hierarchy in the manner of Old Conservatism. The neoliberals accept the importance of inequality and up to a point view it as a motivating principle of economic efficiency. But this position is based primarily on a theory of the necessary flexibility of labour markets, not on a justification of inequality *per se*. It is certainly not an in-principle justification of poverty – although perhaps sometimes used as such ideologically.

Moreover, the neoliberals have actively attacked traditional forms of privilege more than latter-day socialists have done; and these forms of privilege have frequently included modes of entrenched power. Conservatives critical of the neoliberals are often so because they see free market models as producing too much of a divided society; they want less inequality rather than more.

Can one say that there are certain more or less universal ethical principles emerging which tend to unite all perspectives outside the domains of the various fundamentalisms? I believe one can, much as such a conclusion flies in the face of the conventional wisdom of the moment. A world dominated by the influences of globalization and social reflexivity might seem one of hopeless fragmentation and contextuality. This is the view of postmodernism; and it isn't difficult to see why some of its advocates have been so attracted by Nietzsche. For aren't there many truths about how the world is, as well as about what the good life should be? And if there are many truths – as many as there are human contexts of action – doesn't all in the end depend on power? Perhaps we should just salute Nietzsche and all go our independent ways, leaving the world as a whole to rot as it may?

Moreover, it might be added, the guiding principle of our age is methodical doubt, having its intellectual origins in Cartesian philosophy. The principle that everything is revisable, that we can't be sure even about our most cherished ideas, has now become revealed as the most central feature of science itself; and science, after all, was supposed to produce certainties for us. Isn't universal scepticism in the end just the same as nihilism? For it would seem to declare that nothing is sacred – and it is this idea that fundamentalism objects to in much of modern social life. Perhaps the fundamentalists have in some way got things right after all.

But this is just the point. A Nietzschean view is sometimes lauded these days as allowing for that recognition of the 'other' – that necessary cosmopolitanism – which makes possible a multinational world. It does nothing of the sort. What it leads to, in fact, is precisely a world of multiple fundamentalisms; and this is a world in danger of disintegration through the clash of rival world-views. Methodical doubt is not the same as empirical scepticism. Rather, it represents the avenue of dialogue, discursive justification and living along with the other. It is not at all the same as nihilism either, because it brings with it the demand to justify arguments (and actions) with reasons, to which others may respond.

The universal values that are emerging today – and which are the gearing mechanisms of the forms of radical politics I have discussed in the preceding pages – express and derive from this global cosmopolitanism. We are now in a world where there are *many others*; but also where there *are* no others. High-consequence risks, the potential 'bads' of modernity, among which must be included the violent clash of fundamentalisms, disclose the negative aspect of such values; but they can be appropriated, as I have argued earlier, under a positive sign.

Unpredictability, manufactured uncertainty, fragmentation: these are only one side of the coin of a globalizing order. On the reverse side are the shared values that come from a situation of global interdependence, organized via the cosmopolitan acceptance of difference. A world with no others is one where – as a matter of principle – we all share common interests, just as we face common risks. Empirically, many disastrous scenarios are possible – the rise of new totalitarianisms, the disintegration of the world's ecosystems, a fortress society of the affluent in permanent struggle with the impoverished majority. But there are counter-trends to these scenarios in reality, just as there are forces counterposed to moral nihilism. An ethics of a globalizing post-traditional society implies recognition of the sanctity of human life and the universal right to happiness and self-actualization – coupled to the obligation to promote cosmopolitan solidarity and an attitude of respect towards non-human agencies and beings, present and future. Far from seeing the disappearance of universal values, this is perhaps the first time in humanity's history when such values have real purchase.

Notes

Introduction

1 Hans Jonas, *The Imperative of Responsibility* (Chicago: University of Chicago Press, 1984), pp. 27, 31.
2 Gilles Lipovetsky, *Le Crépuscule du devoir* (Paris: Gallimard, 1992).

Chapter 1   Conservatism: Radicalism Embraced

1 Roger Scruton, *The Meaning of Conservatism* (London: Macmillan, 1980), p. 11.
2 Louis de Bonald, *Oeuvres*, vol. 12: *Démonstration philosophique du principe constitutif de la société* (Paris: Le Clerc, 1840).
3 Quotations from Edmund Burke drawn from Iain Hampsher-Monk, *The Political Philosophy of Edmund Burke* (London: Longman, 1987), p. 168.
4 Jerry Z. Muller, *The Other God that Failed* (Princeton: Princeton University Press, 1987).
5 Scruton, *The Meaning of Conservatism*, p. 33.
6 Ibid., pp. 33, 36, 40, 55.
7 For instance, Anthony Quinton, *The Politics of Imperfection* (London: Faber, 1978).
8 Paul Franco, *The Political Philosophy of Michael Oakeshott* (New Haven: Yale University Press, 1990), p. 62.
9 Michael Oakeshott, 'Rationalism in politics', in *Rationalism in Politics and Other Essays* (London: Methuen, 1962).

10 Ibid., p. 304.
11 Hans Freyer, *Theorie des gegenwärtigen Zeitalters* (Frankfurt: Fischer, 1954).
12 Irving Kristol, *Reflections of a Neo-Conservative* (New York: Basic, 1983), p. xii.
13 This and previous quotes are taken from ibid., p. 77.
14 Allan Bloom, *The Closing of the American Mind* (New York: Simon and Schuster, 1988), p. 87.
15 Daniel Bell, *The Cultural Contradictions of Capitalism* (London: Heinemann), p. 480.
16 Hannes H. Gisswarson, *Hayek's Conservative Liberalism* (New York: Garland, 1987).
17 Milton Friedman and Rose Friedman, *Free to Choose* (Secker and Warburg, 1980), p. 25.
18 Friedrich A. Hayek, *Rules and Order* (London: Routledge, 1973), p. 47.
19 Arthur Seldon, *Capitalism* (Oxford: Blackwell, 1990), p. 103.
20 George Gilder, *Naked Nomads: Unmarried Men in America* (New York: Quadrangle, 1974), p. 114.
21 Quotations from Shirley Robin Letwin, *The Anatomy of Thatcherism* (London: Fontana, 1992), pp. 104, 342–3, 310.
22 John Gray, *Beyond the New Right* (London: Routledge, 1993), p. vii.
23 Ibid., p. ix.
24 Cf. Ulrich Beck, *The Risk Society* (London: Sage, 1992).
25 Quotations here and above from Gray, *Beyond the New Right*, pp. xi, xiii, 15, 125, 152, 173.
26 For a swingeingly critical discussion of conservative beliefs on this matter, see Ted Honderich, *Conservativism* (London: Penguin, 1991).
27 Scruton, *The Meaning of Conservatism*, p. 42.
28 Torbjörn Tännsjö, *Conservatism for Our Time* (London: Routledge, 1990). Tännsjö also notes the convergence of conservatism with ecological concerns.
29 See Jon Elster, *Logic and Society* (Chichester: Wiley, 1978).
30 Anthony Giddens, 'Living in a post-traditional society', in Ulrich Beck, Anthony Giddens and Scott Lash, *Reflexive Modernization* (Cambridge: Polity, 1994). I believe this definition is more accurate than the more inclusive one offered in Edward Shils's classic work *Tradition* (London: Faber, 1981).

Chapter 2   Socialism: the Retreat from Radicalism

1   Tom Bottomore, *The Socialist Economy* (London: Harvester, 1990), p. 101.
2   R. N. Berki, *Socialism* (London: Dent, 1987), p. 9.
3   J. A. Schumpeter, *Capitalism, Socialism and Democracy* (London: Allen & Unwin, 1987), pp. 170–1.
4   Peter Gay, *The Enlightenment*, vol. 1 (London: Weidenfeld, 1967), p. 26.
5   Quotations from Émile Durkheim, *Socialism* (London: Routledge, 1967), pp. 22, 56, 85.
6   Rudolf Hilferding, *Finance Capital* (London: Routledge, 1981), p. 27.
7   Karl Kautsky, *The Social Revolution* (Chicago: Kerr, 1902), p. 166.
8   Ludwig von Mises, 'Economic calculation in the socialist commonwealth', in F. A. Hayek (ed.), *Collectivist Economic Planning* (London: Routledge, 1935), p. 104.
9   E. F. M. Durbin, *Problems of Economic Planning* (London: Routledge, 1949), p. 41.
10   Sidney Webb, 'The basis of socialism: historic', in G. Bernard Shaw, *Fabian Essays in Socialism* (London: Fabian Society, 1931), pp. 27, 30.
11   Herbert Marcuse, *Soviet Marxism* (London: Routledge, 1958).
12   John Gray, 'Hayek as a conservative', in Gray, *Post-liberalism* (London: Routledge, 1993).
13   Gray, *Beyond the New Right*, p. 95.
14   T. H. Marshall, *Class, Citizenship and Social Development* (Westport: Greenwood, 1973), pp. 84, 96–7.
15   Quotes from C. A. R. Crosland, *The Future of Socialism* (London: Cape, 1967), pp. 3, 69, 342, 355, 361.

Chapter 3   The Social Revolutions of our Time

1   John Sours, *Starving to Death in a Sea of Objects* (New York: Aronson, 1981).
2   Susie Orbach, *Hunger Strike* (London: Faber, 1986).
3   Anthony Giddens, *Modernity and Self-Identity* (Cambridge: Polity, 1991), ch. 3.
4   For the most comprehensive study, see Martin E. Marty and R.

Scott Appelby, *The Fundamentalism Project* (3 vols, Chicago: Chicago University Press, 1993).

5 This and many other examples are described in John Knight, 'Globalisation and new ethnographic localities', *Journal of the Anthropological Society of Oxford*, vol. 3, 1992.

6 Norberto Bobbio, *The Future of Democracy* (Cambridge: Polity, 1987).

7 Paul Ekins, *A New World Order* (London: Routledge, 1992).

8 Marilyn French, *The War Against Women* (London: Penguin, 1992).

9 Ekins, *A New World Order*, p. 1.

Chapter 4   Two Theories of Democratization

1 Quotations here and below from Francis Fukuyama, *The End of History and the Last Man* (London: Hamilton, 1992), pp. xiii, 21, 43, 200, 206, 332, 283.

2 Deirdre Boden, 'Reinventing the global village', in Anthony Giddens, *Human Societies* (Cambridge: Polity, 1992).

3 David Held, 'Democracy: from city-states to a cosmopolitan order?', in Held, *Prospects for Democracy*, Political Studies Special Issue, vol. 40, 1992, p. 17. See also David Held, *Models of Democracy* (Cambridge: Polity, 1987). I'm much indebted to Held's work for what follows here.

4 Quotations from David Miller, 'Deliberative democracy and public choice', in Held, *Prospects for Democracy*, pp. 55, 57.

5 Anthony Giddens, *The Transformation of Intimacy* (Cambridge: Polity, 1992).

6 Anthony Giddens, 'Living in a post-traditional society', in Beck, Giddens and Lash, *Reflexive Modernization*.

7 'The fall of big business', *The Economist*, 17 April 1993, pp. 13–14.

8 Peter F. Drucker, *Post-capitalist Society* (Oxford: Butterworth Heinemann, 1993), ch. 5.

9 Quotations from Alexis de Tocqueville, *Democracy in America* (New York: Vintage, 1945), vol. 2, p. 338.

10 Ulrich Beck, *Ecological Politics in an Age of Risk* (Cambridge: Polity, 1994).

11 Quotations from Michael Oakeshott, *On Human Conduct* (Oxford: Clarendon, 1991).

12 John Dewey, *Democracy and Education* (London: Macmillan, 1916), p. 120.

Chapter 5 Contradictions of the Welfare State

1 Quotations from Mitchell Dean, *The Constitution of Poverty* (London: Routledge, 1991), pp. 25, 27.
2 Claus Offe, *Contradictions of the Welfare State* (London: Hutchinson, 1984).
3 Abraham de Swaan, *In Care of the State* (Cambridge: Polity, 1998), p. 9.
4 Douglas E. Ashford, *The Emergence of the Welfare State* (Oxford: Blackwell, 1986), p. 4.
5 Quotations here and below from Robert E. Goodin and Julian Le Grand, *Not Only the Poor* (London: Allen and Unwin, 1987), pp. 46, 47.
6 W. H. Beveridge, *Social Insurance and Allied Services* (London: HMSO, 1942).
7 Nancy Fraser, 'Women, welfare and the politics of need interpretation', *Thesis Eleven*, vol. 17, 1987, p. 97.
8 Patricia Hewitt, *About Time: The Revolution in Work and Family Life* (London: Rivers Oram, 1993), p. 2.
9 John Kenneth Galbraith, *The Culture of Contentment* (London: Sinclair-Stevenson, 1992), p. 17.
10 Charles Murray, *The Emerging British Underclass* (London: Institute of Economic Affairs, 1990), p. 4.
11 William Julius Wilson, *The Truly Disadvantaged* (Chicago: University of Chicago Press, 1987), p. 10.
12 Ibid., p. 57.
13 Oscar Lewis, 'The culture of poverty', in Daniel Patrick Moynihan, *On Understanding Poverty* (New York: Basic, 1968), p. 188.
14 Gray, *Beyond the New Right*.
15 Cf. Martin Janicke, *State Failure* (Cambridge: Polity, 1990).

Chapter 6 Generative Politics and Positive Welfare

1 François Ewald, *L'état providence* (Paris: Grasset, 1986), pp. 17ff.
2 Ibid., pp. 545–6.
3 Janicke, *State Failure*.
4 Wolfgang Zuckermann, *The End of the Road* (Cambridge: Lutterworth, 1991).
5 The Brandt Commission, *Common Crisis* (London: Pan, 1983).

6   Ekins, *A New World Order*, p. 23. I am indebted to Ekins's analysis for much of what follows at this point.
7   Ibid., p. 29.
8   Ibid., p. 209.
9   David Werner, *Where There Is No Doctor* (Palo Alto: Hesperian Foundation, 1977).
10   Alan Thein During, *How Much Is Enough?* (London: Earthscan, 1992).
11   Ibid., p. 21.
12   Ibid., p. 95.
13   Brigitte Erler, *L'aide qui tue* (Lausanne: Éditions d'en-bas, 1987).
14   Quotations from Charles Murray, 'The prospect for muddling through', *Critical Review*, vol. 4, 1990.
15   Charles Murray, *In Pursuit of Happiness and Good Government* (New York: Simon and Schuster, 1988).
16   Quotations from Serge Latouche, *La planète des naufragés* (Paris: Éditions la Découverte, 1991), pp. 110, 118–19, 194–5.
17   Ken Dychtwald, *Age Wave* (Los Angeles: Tarcher, 1988), p. 35.
18   Ibid., p. 68.
19   Ibid., pp. 90–1.
20   Ulrich Beck and Elisabeth Beck-Gernsheim, *The Normal Chaos of Love* (Cambridge: Polity, 1995).

Chapter 7   Positive Welfare, Poverty and Life Values

1   Giddens, 'Living in a post-traditional society'.
2   Carol Gilligan, *In a Different Voice* (revised edn, Harvard: Harvard University Press, 1993).
3   On these matters I have profited from personal communications with Dr Peter McCullen. I am indebted to him for having clarified for me some key issues to do with the character of lean production methods.
4   W. Womak et al., *The Machine that Changed the World* (New York: Free Press, 1990).
5   Mihaly Csikszentmihalyi, *Flow: The Psychology of Happiness* (London: Rider, 1992), p. 2.
6   Nancy Corbett, *Inner Cleansing: Living Clean in a Polluted World* (Bridport: Prism, 1993), pp. 150, 151.
7   Study quoted in Csikszentmihalyi, *Flow*, pp. 196–7.
8   Giddens, *Modernity and Self-Identity*, ch. 5.

9   Nathan Glazer, *The Limits of Social Policy* (Cambridge: Harvard University Press, 1988), p. 122.
10 Ibid., p. 8.
11 Claude Lévi-Strauss, 'Reflections on Liberty', *New Statesman*, 26 May 1977, p. 387.
12 Bill Jordan et al., *Trapped in Poverty?* (London: Routledge, 1992).
13 Ibid., pp. 314–15.
14 Dychtwald, *Age Wave*, p. 63.
15 Howard Glennester, *Paying for Welfare*, Welfare State Programme, London School of Economics, 1992, p. 21.
16 Gilligan, *In a Different Voice*.
17 R. F. Tomasson, *The Welfare State, 1883–1983* (London: Jai, 1983).
18 Christopher Pierson, *Beyond the Welfare State?* (Cambridge: Polity, 1991).
19 Csikszentmihalyi, *Flow*.
20 Ibid., pp. 208ff.
21 Anthony Giddens, *The Consequences of Modernity* (Cambridge: Polity, 1990).
22 Csikszentmihalyi, *Flow*, pp. 212–13. See also Csikszentmihalyi, *The Evolving Self* (New York: HarperCollins, 1993), especially chapter 8, for an elaboration of these views.

Chapter 8   Modernity under a Negative Sign: Ecological Issues and Life Politics

1   Carolyn Merchant, *Radical Ecology* (London: Routledge, 1992), p. 1.
2   Quotations from Murray Bookchin, *Toward an Ecological Society* (Mantred-Buffalo: Black Rose, 1986), pp. 1, 202.
3   Arne Naess, 'The shallow and the deep, long-range ecology movement: a summary', *Inquiry*, vol. 16, 1972.
4   Edward Goldsmith, *The Great U-turn* (Hartland: Green Books, 1988).
5   Alain Lipietz, *Towards a New Economic Order* (Cambridge: Polity, 1992), pp. 51, 55.
6   David Harvey, 'The nature of environment', in *Socialist Register* (London: Merlin, 1993).
7   Goldsmith, *The Great U-turn*, pp. 17, 45.
8   Gray, *Beyond the New Right*, p. 124.

9   Fairfield Osborn, *Our Plundered Planet* (London: Faber, 1948), p. 68.
10 L. J. Simon, *The Ultimate Resource* (Princeton: Princeton University Press, 1981), p. 286.
11 D. Lal, *The Limits of International Cooperation* (London: Institute of Economic Affairs, 1990), p. 12.
12 W. M. Adams, *Green Development* (London: Routledge, 1990), pp. 91ff.
13 A. MacEwen and M. MacEwen, *National Parks: Conservation or Cosmetics* (London: Allen and Unwin, 1982), p. 10.
14 Arne Naess, *Ecology, Community and Lifestyle* (Cambridge: Cambridge University Press, 1982), p. 164.
15 Rupert Sheldrake, *The Rebirth of Nature* (London: Rider, 1991), pp. 189, xiii.
16 Quotations from Robert E. Goodin, *Green Political Theory* (Cambridge: Polity, 1992), pp. 17, 37, 38, 52.
17 Beck, *Ecological Politics in an Age of Risk*, p. 65.
18 These correspond to what I have written of as four basic existential problem areas in social life, see Giddens, *Modernity and Self-Identity*, chs 2 and 8.
19 Beck, *The Risk Society*, pp. 61ff.
20 Jonathan Porritt and David Winner, cited in A. Dobson, *Green Political Thought* (London: Unwin Hyman, 1990), p. 7.
21 Sheldrake, *The Rebirth of Nature*, p. 153.
22 Bookchin, *Toward an Ecological Society*, p. 68.
23 Claude Fischer, *The Urban Experience* (New York: Harcourt Brace, 1984).
24 Goodin, *Green Political Theory*, p. 50.
25 Tom Wilkie, *Perilous Knowledge* (London: Faber, 1993), p. 3.
26 Ibid., ch. 7.
27 John Harris, *Wonderwoman and Superman* (Oxford: Oxford University Press, 1992).
28 These changes are very well documented in Beck, *Ecological Politics in an Age of Risk*.
29 Ibid., p. 211.
30 Wilkie, *Perilous Knowledge*, pp. 120–1.
31 Ronald Dworkin, *Life's Dominion* (London: HarperCollins, 1993).
32 Kit Pedler, *The Quest for Gaia* (London: Paladin, 1991), p. 94.
33 Russell Miller, 'A hard rain', *Sunday Times*, 25 July 1993.
34 Adrian Atkinson, *Principles of Political Ecology* (London: Bellhaven), 1991, pp. 97ff.

35   Quotations from Ross Hume Hall, *Health and the Global Environment* (Cambridge: Polity, 1990), pp. 104–5.

Chapter 9   Political Theory and the Problem of Violence

1   Johan Galtung, 'Violence and peace', in Paul Smoker et al., *A Reader in Peace Studies* (Oxford: Pergamon, 1990), p. 11.
2   I have discussed these changes at some length in *The Nation-State and Violence* (Cambridge: Polity, 1987). For an important analysis, see Charles Tilly, *Coercion, Capital and European States AD 990–1990* (Oxford: Blackwell, 1990).
3   Martin Shaw, *Post-Military Society* (Cambridge: Polity, 1991).
4   Jean Bethke Elshtain, *Women and War* (New York: Basic, 1988).
5   Marilyn French, *The War Against Women*, p. 200.
6   Ibid., p. 198.
7   Kate Millett, *Sexual Politics* (Garden City: Doubleday, 1970), pp. 44–5.
8   Sylvana Tomaselli and Roy Porter, *Rape* (Oxford: Blackwell, 1986).
9   One of the best discussions of these issues is to be found in Lynne Segal, *Slow Motion* (London: Virago, 1990), ch. 5.
10 Jon Gershuny, 'Change in the domestic division of labour in the UK', in Nick Abercrombie and Alan Warde, *Social Change in Contemporary Britain* (Cambridge: Polity, 1992).
11 Segal, *Slow Motion*, pp. 308, 317.
12 Diana Scully, *Understanding Sexual Violence* (London: Unwin Hyman, 1990).

Index